GENERAL MARK CLARK

General
Mark Clark

*Commander of U.S. Fifth Army
and Liberator of Rome*

JON B. MIKOLASHEK

CASEMATE
Philadelphia & Oxford

Published in the United States of America and Great Britain in 2013 by
CASEMATE PUBLISHERS
908 Darby Road, Havertown, PA 19083
and
10 Hythe Bridge Street, Oxford, OX1 2EW

Copyright 2013 © Jon B. Mikolashek

ISBN 978-1-61200-131-9
Digital Edition: ISBN 978-1-61200-143-2

Cataloging-in-publication data is available from the Library of Congress and
the British Library.

10 9 8 7 6 5 4 3 2 1

Printed and bound in the United States of America.

For a complete list of Casemate titles please contact:

CASEMATE PUBLISHERS (US)
Telephone (610) 853-9131, Fax (610) 853-9146
E-mail: casemate@casematepublishing.com

CASEMATE PUBLISHERS (UK)
Telephone (01865) 241249, Fax (01865) 794449
E-mail: casemate-uk@casematepublishing.co.uk

CONTENTS

INTRODUCTION

G EORGE S. PATTON ONCE REMARKED, "I THINK THAT IF you treat a skunk nicely, he will not piss on you—as often."[1] The skunk Patton was referring to was General Mark Wayne Clark. Often ignored and nearly always forgotten, Mark Clark was a member of what historian Martin Blumenson calls, "the essential quartet of American leaders who achieved victory in Europe."[2] Along with Dwight D. Eisenhower, George S. Patton, and Omar N. Bradley, Mark Clark was a key figure in World War II.

Clark commanded the Fifth United States Army and later the 15th Army Group in Italy. Originally intended to quickly capture Rome, the campaign against the "soft underbelly" of Axis power proved much more difficult than Allied planners anticipated and dragged on until 2 May 1945. The campaign eventually became a sideshow for Operation Overlord, the cross-channel landing at Normandy. Allied success on D-Day and the breakout across France quickly made Italy the forgotten war. To the general public the war in Italy remains little known and is believed to be a campaign that took too long or was unnecessary. The main attraction of invading Italy for the Allies was that it would knock Italy out of the war, eliminate its fleet, establish a base for a possible invasion of the Balkans, and would bring Allied bombers closer to German factories and Romanian oilfields. Lastly, and most importantly, the Allied planners hoped that an invasion of Italy would pin down German divisions that might otherwise be used against the Soviets in the east or against the Western Allies after their landing in Normandy.[3]

Both Prime Minister Winston S. Churchill and President Franklin D. Roosevelt realized that the Western Allies needed to fight somewhere between the 1942 invasion of North Africa and the proposed invasion of

France. Following the invasion of Sicily, the two leaders debated what to do next: would it be better to conserve their forces until Overlord or should they continue on into Italy?[4] With fewer than three hundred landing craft available for an invasion of France in 1943, the Allies decided to invade Italy.[5]

The Italian mainland was the logical choice. Proposed invasions of Sardinia and Corsica posed no direct threat to Germany. Furthermore, Stalin and the Soviets would have been furious with the Americans and British for not more directly engaging the Germans. An invasion of the Balkans was discussed, but in order to invade that region, American and British planners needed bases in Italy.[6] Writing in his memoirs after the war, Clark explained the decision to fight in Italy:

> The Allied campaign in the Mediterranean during World War II was, from the beginning, a gigantic calculated risk. . . . We took a chance—and a grave one—that the French in North Africa would join us instead of fighting us. We risked a German counterattack through Spain that would have severed our supply lines. We risked untried American forces against veteran enemy armies at a time when defeat would have been an almost fatal disaster. But most of all, I suppose, we took a chance on Churchill's persuasive eloquence, his conviction that we could "slit this soft underbelly of the Mediterranean." It turned out to be not so soft.[7]

Clark was right: the invasion of Italy was a calculated risk, but it was a risk worth taking.

*   *   *

By 1940, Clark was a well-respected lieutenant colonel with little troop command experience. Yet, by 1943, he was leading the Fifth Army up the Italian peninsula. By the summer of 1944, Clark and his forces had conquered Rome, but at the height of the Italian campaign his forces were stripped for Operation Anvil, later renamed Dragoon—the invasion of southern France—and he was left to fight the remainder of the war with limited resources against a skilled and determined adversary high in the Italian mountains. For this reason, Clark is little known today. Once a household name, Clark has been forgotten, while the legacies of Eisenhower and Patton continue to grow.

Many believe Clark sought out publicity, and was a prima donna like George Patton. Critics point out that Clark would only let photos be taken from his left side and that every news release had to mention Clark's name three times on the first page and at least one time on the rest, and the Fifth Army was always referred to as Mark Clark's Fifth Army.[8] Clark did have a healthy ego, just like most officers of his rank. It was his ego that had driven him his entire life, from West Point through the interwar years and into high command. Without a strong ego Clark never would have risen in rank or become an experienced high commander. This ego, however, would also cause him to make a terrible decision in switching his attack towards Rome, the Eternal City, when he may have had the opportunity to encircle a substantial portion of the German combat forces in Italy. Clark understood, however that his Fifth Army toiled in what had become militarily a secondary theater—Fifth Army liberated Rome on 5 June 1944—and that he needed to seek out more publicity. Clark did not solely want the press for himself, but also for his troops and their families.

Historians have further tarnished Clark's reputation by viewing him as an inadequate commander. As the esteemed historian Carlo D'Este writes, Clark lacked that "ill-defined but vital ingredient for successful command—the ability to sense instinctively the right course of action on the field of battle."[9] While Clark was not as brilliant as Patton, he was still a very capable officer. Unlike Bradley and Patton, who have received high praise for their leadership, Clark fought in a less glamorous theater of the war, with limited manpower and supplies, against German forces that brilliantly used the Italian terrain to slow the advance of the Allies. As Clark explained, the role of his forces in Italy was "more or less that of football guards and tackles who had the task of blocking and 'taking out' the enemy forces which might have made a tremendous dent in the Red Army's advance from the east or General Eisenhower's drive across France and into Germany. Guards and tackles never receive the [attention] of the quarterback, the flashy running back, and the flamboyant wide receiver, but without them the team would never score."[10]

Neither George Patton nor other commanders would have been able to do anything different in Italy. The slowness of the campaign, the defensive terrain, and the skill of German commander Albert Kesselring would have frustrated a mad-dash commander like Patton. To understand the difficulty of Clark's mission in Italy, all one must do is visit the region. Southern Italy is known for its excellent food and wine, but it is also known for its numerous streams, rivers, hills and mountains. Tracing the steps of Clark and the United States Fifth Army from Salerno northward towards Rome, visitors can see the dangers of the terrain. In Salerno, the Allies had to deal with towering hills overlooking the landing areas. Following the advance out of Salerno, Fifth Army was constantly slowed by marshy terrain that bogged down their tanks and by hills that grew into mile-high mountains. At Anzio, with limited forces available, Clark and his troops landed on rough shores, only to face more marshes backed by the towering Alban Hills. After taking Rome, the terrain grew even more daunting as the Apennine leads into the Po River valley and eventually to the Alps of Northern Italy. Adding well led, skilled German defenders to the terrain made the war in Italy a terrible task for Clark, or any other commander. Yet, the Allies were forced to fight in 1943, and Italy offered them the best opportunity. War is never perfect, and the Italian campaign is a perfect example of this. Like Fifth Army commander Mark W. Clark, the campaign in Italy was flawed, but both were essential to winning World War II in Europe.

*   *   *

Born on 1 May 1896 to Captain Charles and Beckie Clark in Watertown, New York, Mark, or "Boy" as he was called, lived a fairly commonplace early life.[11] His father, Charles, was a respected army officer who had fought valiantly in the Spanish-American War and the Philippine Insurrection. Little has been written about Mark's early years, and the few extant studies on him begin in 1940. What most historians know is that Mark lived a comfortable life and had loving parents. Though tall, Mark was frail and prone to sicknesses that kept him bedridden for weeks. By his teen years, he began to show interest in the military and while living at Fort Sheridan even idolized a young lieutenant by the name of George S. Patton.[12] Mark had adequate schooling, and before entering West Point, attended a preparatory school in Highland Falls, New York, that readied him for the academy's entrance examination. Mark passed the exam and entered West Point in June 1913.

Standing six feet, three inches, and weighing only 140 pounds, Clark entered West Point with 185 other young men, including future generals Joseph L. Collins and Matthew B. Ridgway. Along with these two, Clark's class would see nine others win stars in World War Two.[13] One of the tallest cadets, Clark lived in the same barracks division as Dwight D. Eisenhower. Despite Eisenhower being two years senior to Clark, the two became great friends and this relationship later proved beneficial to both.

Never a great student or a tremendous athlete while at West Point, Clark earned promotion every year, serving as corporal, sergeant, and lieutenant.[14] Known as "Opie" to his fellow cadets or Wayne to his friends, Clark was well liked, and despite recurring health problems graduated on time. With the entrance of the United States into The Great War, Clark's class graduated several months early, and on 6 April 1917, 139 cadets received their diplomas and were commissioned as second lieutenants. Clark graduated 110th in his class, and happily accepted his first assignment with the 11th Infantry at Camp Forrest in Chickamauga Park, Georgia.[15] Clark immediately took command of a platoon in Company E. He quickly fell ill, however and had to take a month of sick leave.[16]

After having his appendix removed, Clark returned to his platoon in December. By March 1918, Clark was promoted to captain and set sail for Europe on his birthday, 1 May 1918. Like most soldiers, the thought of going to war excited Clark, and he believed that both he and his father would garner much fame from the experience. Following his arrival, the 11th Infantry marched to their assigned position in the Vosges Mountains, the southern-most part of the Western Front.[17] On 12 June, Clark got his wish for excitement, the 3d Battalion commander became ill and Clark was put in command of the unit. It seemed that the war would greatly advance his career, but two days later Clark was seriously wounded as fragments from a German shell struck his right shoulder and back, knocking him unconscious.[18] Though listed as seriously wounded, Clark recuperated within six weeks, but instead of leading an infantry battalion in combat he supervised food shipments for the First Army. While a less glamorous position, it put Clark in touch with such future leaders as George C. Marshall and John L. Dewitt. With the war's end in November 1918, Clark had done his duty well, but it seemed the war had passed him by and he wondered if it would hurt his career.

The interwar years for Mark Clark were similar to those of most soldiers, slow promotions, poor pay and awful assignments. Clark's first post-war assignment was worse than he could have imagined. He was assigned to command Chautauqua programs, which were little more than traveling circuses. The programs consisted of young men in uniform, and were filled with lectures, musical events, and other performances.[19] While Clark despised his job, it taught him how to give speeches to large audiences, and more importantly, it taught him public relations.

The interwar years were not completely lackluster for Clark. On 17 May 1924 he wed Maurine Doran, a widow of Clark's former classmate Oliver

Brown Cardwell. For the remainder of her life, Maurine Doran was a loyal military wife who won fame during World War II as one of the top speakers in war bonds drives. Now married and content with his military career, Clark's life was turned upside down in 1926 when he met the tyrannical Frank "Bowser" Bolles.

Colonel Bolles took command of the 30th Infantry Regiment and named Clark his "unofficial aide"—then as now full colonels are not authorized an official aide, so Clark's service as an aide was in addition to his regular, official duties as a regimental staff officer. Stripped of his company command, Clark became Bolles' servant commanded to help clean up the regiment and gain Bolles his first star. Bolles was famous for his mistreatment of insubordinates, but he must have seen something in Clark as he would serve under Bolles until 1933. By 1928 Bolles earned his star and took Clark with him to Fort D.A. Russell, just outside Cheyenne, Wyoming.[20] After arriving, Clark became ill again and for a while was free of Bolles' wrath as he recovered and attended the Command and General Staff College at Fort Leavenworth. Along with classmates Walter Bedell Smith and Matthew Ridgway, Clark performed well at the school. He was shocked one day when Brig. Gen. Herbert Brees, commandant of the college, asked why Clark wanted to forgo his second year at the college. Amazed, Clark asked, "What have I done?" Unknown to the young officer, Bowser Bolles had "volunteered" Clark to serve under him again.[21] Fortunately, Clark was allowed to graduate, and later joined Bolles as 7th Corps Area assistant chief of staff for intelligence, assistant chief of staff for plans and training, and the deputy chief of staff for the Civilian Conservation Corps district based in Omaha, Nebraska.[22] Luckily for Clark his name appeared on the list of officers detailed to the Army's War College for 1936–1937.

Finally free from Bolles, a forty-year-old Clark had established a name for himself as a promising staff officer. While at the War College, Clark, along with Ridgway, Bedell Smith, and Geoffrey Keyes looked at the command structure of an infantry division. Their paper was well received and it made its way to the War Department, which appointed a board of three general officers to read the paper. The committee consisted of Fox Conner, Lesley J. McNair, and George C. Marshall.[23] While the board never actually met, the paper brought attention to Clark, and it laid the groundwork of Marshall's "triangularization" of the US Army that helped prepare it for World War II.

After graduation Clark moved to Fort Lewis, Washington, where he became the 3d Division assistant chief of staff in charge of intelligence and training (G-2 and G-3).[24] While busy with his official duty Clark essentially ran the division as the commander was weak and in ill health. With a free hand to try whatever he wanted Clark also rekindled his friendship with Dwight Eisenhower and found a mentor in Gen. George C. Marshall. By 1939 war was approaching and training increased for Clark. In the fall Clark planned for an amphibious assault to take place in January 1940.[25] The operation would involve both the army and the navy, and at that time the size of the exercise was unprecedented. With Eisenhower as the chief umpire, the exercise went well. Clark performed brilliantly and Marshall's praise for division commander Major General DeWitt was actually meant for Clark.[26] Clark had impressed the most important man in the Army, and the next five years of his life would be like nothing he could have imagined.

By the summer of 1940, fresh off his success with the 3d Division at Fort Lewis, Clark was promoted to lieutenant colonel and assigned to General Headquarters, United States Army, in Washington, D.C. As Gen. Leslie McNair's principal aide, Clark traveled widely to help mobilize the army and increase the speed and realism of training. Traveling across the United States, Puerto Rico, Panama, the Philippines and Hawaii, Clark and McNair standardized training, removed incompetent commanders, and inspected countless units. By the start of the German invasion of Russia in June 1941, McNair rated Clark as one of the top officers in his grade and believed him suitable for promotion.[27] Little did Clark know that he would skip the rank of full colonel all together; in July he was promoted directly to brigadier general.

By late 1941 Clark's hard work had paid off, yet success came at a high price. His sudden and quick rise over older, more experienced officers created resentment in the Army. While inspecting units after his promotion Clark received a cold and formal salute and "yes, sir" from Doc Ryder, a good friend who before the promotion would have greeted Clark with a friendly, "Opie, how are you?"[28] At first Clark tried pleading with his friends, but later in life remarked, "When you catapulted over people who were senior to me, years senior," he tried always to, "avoid making myself obnoxious, particularly with people who had been my senior and who had fine records."[29] While Omar Bradley, Eisenhower, and other World War II commanders also skipped ranks, Clark's rise was perhaps the oddest. As Bradley later noted about Clark, "I had some reservations about him personally. He seemed false somehow, too eager to impress, too hungry for the limelight, promotions and personal publicity."[30] George S. Patton, as mentioned before, thought even less of

Clark and believed that he was just "too damned slick."[31] The same could also be said, however, about Bradley and Patton.

The jealousy of friends and other officers affected Clark, but he managed to do his job. Later in the war he was still sensitive to the feelings and pride of his subordinates who often had been senior to him. Usually this did not hurt the operation, but following the Anzio landings Clark was slow to relieve Maj. Gen. John P. Lucas, who was a few years his senior. While perhaps this jealously did not lead to Clark being forgotten by the public, it did, lead to Clark's name and achievements being criticized. After the war, famous commanders all published memoirs on their lives and actions during the war. Few had anything good to say about Clark, or anyone else for that matter. While this may have not contributed to his name being forgotten, it has greatly tarnished his image.

With his star on the rise with this promotion, Clark participated in a seemingly unimportant conversation that established Dwight Eisenhower on the road to military command and the presidency. Following the disaster at Pearl Harbor, George C. Marshall asked Clark for the names of ten brigadier generals capable of becoming the new chief of war plans. Clark answered, "I'll give you one name and nine dittos: Dwight D. Eisenhower."[32] Later Eisenhower would comment to Clark that he was "more responsible than anybody in this country for giving me my opportunity."[33] He was right.

Following the attack on Pearl Harbor and American entrance into World War II, Clark's duties increased dramatically. On 17 April 1942 Clark was promoted to major general and was about to embark on a great challenge.

Chapter 1

TWO MEN
OF DESTINY
The Arrival of the American
Ground Forces in England

T HE DATE 23 JUNE 1942 HOLDS NO SPECIAL MEANING
for most historians or much of the public. There was no
famous battle, no major bombings. But there was an important beginning:
the beginning of the United States armed forces in Europe. On this day two
relatively unknown officers left the United States to go to London. They carried with them the hopes of their nation and those of the Allies. The two
men would become household names, one rising to the rank of general of
the army (five stars) and eventually president of the United States, while the
other would rise in rank to four-star general and spend the war slugging
through the mountains of Italy. These men were Dwight David Eisenhower
and Mark Wayne Clark.

Their mission was to coordinate with Winston Churchill and the British
military to plan an invasion of the European continent and ready the untested
American troops for battle. As for Clark, now a young major general, his task
was to help plan the invasion and to mold the U.S. II Corps into a strong
fighting force. Clark had a daunting task ahead of him, but he was confident
and would ultimately prove an excellent troop trainer. Still, the Allies needed
a plan and Clark and Eisenhower needed to work closely with their British
counterparts; and that meant they needed a close and cordial relationship
with Prime Minister Churchill.

Arriving on 5 July the two American generals traveled to dine with Churchill. Expecting just dinner, the two Americans would have to learn to accept Churchill's late working hours and often odd behavior. Upon their arrival Churchill, dressed in only slippers and a baggy smock, immediately sized up Clark and Eisenhower, writing in his memoirs that he "was immediately impressed by these remarkable but hitherto unknown men."[1] Eventually, the wily prime minister would come to highly regard both American generals and even developed a nickname for Clark, based on his tall and lengthy features: Churchill called him "the American Eagle."[2]

During their first meeting Churchill made it clear that he was in favor of Operation Gymnast. This plan called for an invasion of French North Africa sometime later in 1942. Both Clark and Eisenhower, like most general officers in the United States Army, believed Gymnast would detract from the quicker, more direct invasion of Europe in 1942, codenamed Operation Sledgehammer.[3] Though Clark and Eisenhower were noncommittal, the three men would lay the groundwork for the Anglo-American relationship and planning of the war. Talking until three in the morning Eisenhower and Clark departed the Prime Minister's residence tired, but confident that they could work with Churchill.

Aside from planning the invasion, Clark set out to train the arriving II Corps. Given command of the corps just a month earlier by General George C. Marshall in June 1942, Clark quickly noticed that "US troops look fat and pudgy while the Britishers are hard and lean. . . . [T]hose already here and those to come—must have grueling training to fit them better for battle."[4] Talking to newly arrived officers, Clark gave a simple, yet direct and forceful speech. In these brief speeches, which become a hallmark of Clark's leadership, told the officers, "You are the advance echelon of the American Ground Forces in England. There is opportunity for all of you. You are in on the ground floor."[5] Clark further added that the II Corps would "be on the offensive—not the defensive!"[6] Though new to command, Clark believed it was imperative that he meet every arriving soldier to his unit and throughout the war was very caring and concerned for his troops.

With the troops arriving, Clark needed a headquarters. Carefully studying the area, he and his staff decided on Longford Castle, an ancient work built in 1588, about three miles southeast of Salisbury, Wilshire.[7] The castle grounds were ideally situated for training and offered the growing II Corps space to plan and train. The castle appealed to Clark because it had been captured by Oliver Cromwell in 1645, and he once commented to his staff on the history of the castle "that every time a door is opened he expects to see an armored knight come clanking toward him."[8]

By the middle of July, Clark was busy training II Corps and in meetings with Eisenhower and the British to finalize plans for 1942. On 25 July, Clark told higher ranking officers of the II Corps that the planned invasion of Europe in 1942 was off; "we studied the globe looking for all possible points of attack and figuring what we could use, we agreed that SLEDGEHAMMER was impossible."[9] Without an operation Clark concentrated on further training his arriving divisions, telling his subordinates he wanted "them to make 25-mile marches repeatedly, at least once a week. This will be followed by amphibious training and finally combined training. . . ."[10] He further added, "These men must learn to fight under realistic conditions—they must learn to dig in. They must dig in, by God, every time they stop. I'm not being hard-hearted. I'm doing the men a favor. On their toughness depends their lives and the winning of the war."[11]

With training progressing nicely and Sledgehammer off, the Allies finally agreed to go ahead with Gymnast, renamed Operation Torch. Though pleased with having a plan, Clark, like Eisenhower and Marshall, was less than enthusiastic about the operation. Commenting in his memoirs of his initial reaction upon receiving the news of Torch, Clark wrote, "It seemed to me then that it would be a great calamity if the African operation acted as a sponge to draw off ships, materiel and men from the United Kingdom and weaken our preparations for the 1943 European invasion."[12]

Torch brought with it many complications, the first being the French. On 6 August Clark, along with Marshall, met with Free French leader Charles de Gaulle. Dispensing with small talk, de Gaulle got right to the point exclaiming to Marshall, "Tell me about the Second Front plans!"[13] Skillfully dodging any specifics, Marshall rattled on about plans for 1943 and Torch while de Gaulle grew more impatient. Realizing he would get nothing out of Marshall, de Gaulle shook hands and immediately left. Clark, looking over to Marshall, commented that de Gaulle was "Absolutely without personality and lacking any personal magnetism. He may be an excellent military expert but it was easy to see why he is the United Nations' problem child."[14]

With Torch set and the II Corps growing every day, the American and British public became more interested in the tall American commander. During the war in Italy and afterwards, historians have charged Clark with being a publicity hound and a glory seeker in the mold of George S. Patton and Douglas Macarthur. While Clark did fight for press in Italy and had a healthy ego, it was not solely for himself, but for his Fifth Army. In early August the London *Times* published a story on Clark, praising him for his service so far: "General Clark, at the age of 46, is a vigorous leader of striking personality. He impresses one as the typical democratic soldier, a man who readily gains the confidence of his men and inspires them to give their best."[15] For Clark, the prestige of his command was gratifying, but he would remain ambivalent about his growing fame. At a press conference around the time of the *Times* article, a stern Clark told the news correspondents, "I haven't commanded troops in battle yet. Until I have proven my fitness, the less said about me the better."[16] In the meantime, a huge development occurred that would pull Clark from his II Corps and force him deeper into political and military intrigue.

On 10 August, Clark gave up command of the II Corps and was appointed deputy commander-in-chief under Eisenhower. Overworked, and burdened in trying to be in two places at once, Eisenhower wanted someone he could trust as his assistant, and Clark felt obliged to help his dear friend. Eisenhower asked Clark about leaving the II Corps: "The question was put to me as to whether I wanted that job or whether I wanted to sit on a dead fish."[17] The dead fish was the II Corps. At the time of Clark's decision it had been planned for II Corps to be used solely for training purposes. What Eisenhower meant by the "dead fish" comment was that the corps would not be a combat command for Clark. In the event, however, Eisenhower was mistaken, and II Corps landed at Oran under the command of Maj. Gen. Lloyd Fredendall as part of Operation Torch.

Torn between his desire to command troops in battle and to help Eisenhower, Clark wrote in his diary that his decision to give up command was based on three factors: first, he felt he wanted to do what General Eisenhower wanted him to do; second, he did not want to run the risk of sitting the war out in a relatively inactive theater; third, he did not want "to back away from fire."[18] Clark's decision would have a major impact on not only his career, but the war itself. As deputy to Eisenhower, Clark would participate in one of the most hazardous missions of the war and, following the successful completion of Torch, would be given command of the American field army that would eventually be the first to fight in Europe.

Though saddened to leave II Corps, which removed him from day-to-day contact with troops, Clark immediately took charge of the planning for Torch. Almost immediately upon taking over the operation's planning, Torch became even more convoluted and confusing as Clark and his staff grew increasingly concerned about Spain. With its strategic geographic position directly across the Mediterranean from the planned North African area of operations, Allied leaders and Torch planners were concerned about what Spain would do. British Ambassador to Spain, Sir Samuel Hoare, revealed his great fear with Torch, telling Clark:

> Its success or failure may indeed principally depend on political developments. The temptation to cut our lines of communication will be very great. We shall appear to have put our neck between two Spanish knives, and Spanish knives are traditionally treacherous. The Germans will be on General Franco's back, dinning into his ears: 'Now is your time. You can cut the Allied throat, destroy the naval and air bases at Gibraltar and win a dazzling reward for your country in North Africa.[19]

Clark and other planners believed that if Spain continued to remain neutral that Torch would have an excellent chance of success. Regardless of Spain, however, Torch planning continued, and now the Allies had to deal with the French.

On 17 August 1942, Clark received an intelligence report on the French forces in North Africa. The report indicated that the French had fourteen divisions, all poorly equipped, but stated, "If the French made a determined and unified stand, and if they strongly resist the initial landing, particularly by concentrating the bulk of their forces against either of the major points, they can seriously interfere with, if not prevent, a landing at the chosen points."[20] Further reports believed that there were over five hundred tanks stationed underground in Spanish Morocco.[21] With fear of Spanish involvement and French willingness to resist, Torch seemed an extremely risky operation, but planning continued. Ultimately, the Allies had nothing to fear from Spain; it remained neutral for the entire war.

With Torch still being planned, D-Day for the operation was set for 15 October 1942. Up to this point the plan called for landings at Oran, Algiers and Bone. The planners hoped that both Oran and Algiers would be captured by D+3.[22] The plan, still much in its infancy, was being debated across the Atlantic. Torch appeared dead or at least weakened when on 25 August a sleeping Clark was forced out of his bed at three in the morning to receive a cable from Marshall that stated the beliefs of the American high command. The U.S. Army chief of staff thought Torch was too ambitious and that it should be contracted.[23] A disheveled Clark wrote in his diary later in the day that the new American plan called for "combat teams from 1st and 34th Divisions to move into the Agidir-Marrakech-Casabalanca-Rabat-Fez area in French Morocco and into Oran-Mostaganein-Mascara area in Algiers."[24] This cable caused two problems for Clark. The planning had to be changed again, and he was to have dinner with Churchill, who had yet to receive Marshall's cable, that evening to discuss the planning.

When Clark and Eisenhower arrived for dinner Churchill was in usual form. Telling the two Americans that "Torch offers the greatest opportunity in the history of England! It is the one thing that is going to win the war. President Roosevelt feels the same way. We're both ready to help in any way we can."[25] Looking to Eisenhower and receiving no indication of what he thought and perhaps thinking of the early morning cable, Clark boldly told Churchill what was on his mind and the mind of his planners:

> We're floundering around in a trough of day-to-day changes. We must have had ten sets of details. There have been so many plans that we are dizzy. We'd like to get one definite plan so we can go to work on it. It's not a military man's job to say whether the French will resist or whether Spain will enter the war. The political factors should be handled by politicians.[26]

Clark's statement was correct; D-Day for Torch was only a few weeks away and the Allies still did not have a definite plan. Finally, on 31 August, President Roosevelt cabled Churchill stating his belief that Torch should be an all-American affair. The main argument was the belief that the French would not fire on the Americans, their old allies, but would fire on the British. This would prevent the achievement of a major goal of Torch, to gain North Africa and an ally. Clark believed, however, that the British and Churchill would not blindly abide by Roosevelt's cable and thought they would request that American forces land at Algiers and Oran, with a smaller force at Casablanca.[27]

Operation Torch now consisted of two possible plans, an all-American attack backed by Roosevelt and Marshall and a combined Allied attack supported by British and Churchill. Clark was caught in the middle. Tired of the constant changes and conflict between the Allies, Clark readied himself for a major planning conference on 1 September. The conference consisted of thirty-seven officers, both American and British. Beginning the meeting, it was clear to Clark that the planning team had become confused by all the changes to Torch. Clark, looking to put the group at ease and to help explain the muddled situation, began the meeting by stating the obvious:

> Some of you men are less confused than others about TORCH. Let's all get equally confused. We'll call the President's plan 'Plan A'— that is, General Patton will attack at Casablanca; United States forces now in the United Kingdom will attack Oran, and the operation will have the use of British naval vessels, transports and air force. The US task force from the United Kingdom will be composed of combat teams of the 1st and 34th Divisions and the 1st Armored Division. . . . The other plan, entailing All-American landings in force at Oran and Algiers and the use of a small force from the United States at Casablanca, will be known as 'Plan B.' The United States forces from the United Kingdom will assault at Algiers, secure the port and airfields and get elbow room so General Anderson's British force can come in, disembark at portside without too great difficulty and then start driving to the east for Tunis. The Oran force will turn to the west and establish contact with the force landing at Casablanca.[28]

After breaking the ice, the conference went smoothly, but it was not clear how Churchill would respond to Roosevelt's plan. Later in the day, the answer came when Churchill agreed to the American plan. Torch was on, but Clark and his planners still had a lot of work to do.

Two days later Roosevelt and Churchill changed the plan again when both agreed on three separate landings in North Africa. The new plan called for 34 thousand Americans to land at Casablanca, followed by 24 thousand additional U.S. soldiers. At Oran, 25 thousand Americans would initially land and be followed by a force of an additional 20 thousand. The last landing at Algiers called for an initial landing force of 10 thousand Americans, followed by British troops.[29] Clark, smirking to his staff upon telling them the news, said, "Well, there she is! We're almost back where we started from."[30] The new joint Roosevelt-Churchill plan was basically the original Torch plan. Clark, though pleased with a definitive plan, was growing increasingly tired with the Allied political situation. When asked about how he was getting through the constant political interference, Clark believed that it was due to his close relationship with Eisenhower. "This would be an almost intolerable situation were it not for my fortunate, close, personal relationship with the Supreme Commander."[31] Clark believed the he was finished with political troubles, but further problems with the French would bring Clark to the forefront of inter-Allied politics.

With Torch set for 8 November, the planners still worried about the French and the Spanish. As D-Day grew closer it seemed Spain would remain neutral, but the role of the French grew more unclear. By the middle of September, Robert Murphy, the American Ambassador to French North Africa, met with Clark and delivered a letter from President Roosevelt that told the French the Americans were going to land in North Africa. Clark, already bothered by political intrigue was shocked by the letter and told Murphy it was "dangerous to let them know ahead of time about the operation unless we are assured the North African French will come along with us. If they are going to do so it should be handled through diplomatic channels and we should move in immediately."[32] While the letter was never delivered, the Allies and Clark, through Ambassador Murphy, began talking with the French in North Africa. With D-Day rapidly approaching Clark traveled to the United States to discuss the final Torch plan with Marshall and Secretary of War Henry Stimson.

Clark arrived in the United States on 24 September. As he landed he was met by his wife and quickly escorted to Washington where high level meetings would begin in the morning. Meeting Stimson, Clark clearly explained Torch, and although Stimson rejected Churchill's "soft belly" approach in invading North Africa, he was pleased with the plan.[33] Next, Clark met Murphy for lunch to discuss fifth column activities inside French North Africa and perhaps buying off French naval officials.[34] Due to time constraints and a scheduling conflict Roosevelt was unable to meet with Clark. Nonetheless, Clark's trip to the United States was successful. The plan met with approval from Stimson and others, and the Allies planted the seeds for possibly buying off the French and preventing resistance during the Torch landings.

By early October, Clark returned to England and continued planning for Torch. During this time Clark began to think about his future role in the war. Growing tired with his role as deputy commander in chief, Clark wanted a combat command. Having officially given up command of II Corps on 11 October, Clark did not want to spend the rest of the war as a staff officer dealing with paperwork and trivial decisions such as choosing what kind of flea powder should be used on ships targeted for Torch.[35] With the arrival of

Major General Walter Bedell Smith as Eisenhower's chief of staff, Clark constantly harassed his boss for a combat command, but was told every time by Eisenhower, "Now just keep your shirt on, Wayne."[36] Though not content with his position, Clark did his job to the best of his abilities and continued to meet with Churchill and other top British officials.

During a break in a high-level conference, Clark, Field Marshal Sir Alan Brooke (chief of the British imperial general staff), and Churchill began to talk about smaller subjects when the name of Eisenhower's dog came up. Knowing that Eisenhower's dog was not yet house broken, Clark told Brooke that the dog's name was Paderewski. When Brooke asked why, Clark laughed, "He's the pianist of the lot."[37] (Jan Paderewski (1860–1941) had been a well-known Polish piano virtuoso and composer of the late 1800s and early 1900s.) All joking aside, by the middle of October Torch was a few weeks away and it appeared that all Clark had left to do was to wait. That changed on 17 October when Clark was awakened by his chief of staff, Alfred Gruenther, who said he had a message that was "red hot."[38]

With D-Day approaching, the Allies decided on a gamble that might give them control of North Africa without firing a shot. Robert Murphy, United States Councilor to Vichy and expert on North Africa, was in touch with five prominent French civilians who had access to important military officers in North Africa. Specifically, Gen. Alphonse Juin, commander of French forces in North Africa, who was known to be sympathetic to the Allied cause, as well as Gen. Henri Giraud, whom the Allies believed could rally the French military to the Allied side. Now in his sixties, General Giraud was a hero of both world wars. Called "Papa Snooks" by the Allies, Giraud believed himself to be a genius of war. He was, however, a genius not of war, but of escape. Captured in World War I, he escaped from prison and returned to France by disguising himself along the way as a butcher, a stable boy, a coal merchant, and finally a magician in a traveling circus.[39] Captured by the Nazis in World War II, Giraud proved his genius again as he escaped from Koenigstein, a German prisoner camp for officers of high rank.[40]

By October, Murphy returned from North Africa where Maj. Gen. Charles Mast, chief of staff of the French XIX Corps in North Africa was willing to talk to military representatives about Torch. That representative would be Mark Clark, who, wrote Robert Murphy, "it would seem, is one of those romantic generals destined to move always in an atmosphere of high drama."[41]

The secret cable from Washington called for a senior general officer to meet secretly with French North African officials. The belief was that if the meeting went well the Allies could, according to French general Mast, "gain entry practically without firing a shot."[42] The trouble with the plan was the uncertainty of who would give the order to the French soldiers to lay down their arms. According to Mast, General Giraud could rally the French in North Africa. However, it was known to Allied intelligence that Adm. François Darlan, commander of the French fleet and Marshal Philippe Petain's deputy, was in Algiers visiting his polio-stricken son. It was possible that Darlan could not only give the order for Vichy forces in North Africa to stand down, but save the French fleet from being taken over by the Germans. Before that decision could be made, however, the meeting had to take place.

As commander in chief, Eisenhower was immediately removed from the list of possible candidates to take part in the mission. As Eisenhower's deputy, Clark was both available and very familiar with Torch and its particulars. After discussing the trip with Eisenhower and Churchill it was decided that Clark would go, along with Brig. Gen. Lyman Lemnitzer, head of Allied Forces Plans section, Col. A.L. Hamblen, shipping and supply expert, Capt. Jerauld Wright, U.S. Navy liaison for Torch, and Col. Julius Holmes, a former state department officer who headed the civil-political branch of Torch. Before leaving, Churchill took Clark aside and told him, "You can always keep in mind, Clark, that we'll back you up in whatever you do."[43] With these final words of encouragement, Clark traveled to his apartment to pack, talking to himself, "This is fantastic—really fantastic!"[44] With his packing complete, Clark took a moment to write a hand-written note to his wife that was to be delivered if he did not return:

Darling Sweetheart—

I am leaving in twenty minutes on a mission which I volunteered to do when it was suggested that a general officer do it.

If I succeed and return I will have done a fine deed for my country and the Allied cause. Of course you will know my life is dedicated to military service and now that my opportunity has come for that service I go forward proud of the opportunity which has been given me.

If I do not return know that I loved you and our Bill and Ann. Only one request I make. You have been an angel on earth to me—

continue being that and do everything you possibly can for our Allied cause. Only in doing will you find solace, and only by all so doing, will Victory be won.

God bless and keep you.

Wayne[45]

With everything ready Clark set out on what would become one of the most fascinating secret missions in American history. The mission would greatly aid in the success of Torch and bring Clark his first taste of criticism, as he would be dealing with Nazi collaborators.

Chapter 2

ADVENTURE BELOW, POLITICS ABOVE

Clark's Secret Mission to Africa and the Darlan Deal

O N 19 OCTOBER, DRESSED IN A LIEUTENANT COLONEL'S uniform, Clark left England aboard the *Red Gremlin*, which happened to be piloted by Paul Tibbits, later of *Enola Gay* fame. The group landed in Gibraltar where the H.M.S. *Seraph*, a British submarine commanded by Lt. Norman Ambury Auchinleck Jewell, awaited.[1] Along with Jewell, three British Commandos, Capt. C. P. Courtney, Capt. R.T. Livingstone, and Lt. J. P. Foot, were assigned to land on the beach with Clark.[2] Following introductions Clark told Jewell they were looking for a house "with white walls and a red tiled roof," twelve miles west of Cherchell, a town located about fifty-six miles (ninety kilometers) west of Algiers in French-ruled Algeria.[3] That evening Clark and his comrades trained on how to use folbots (foldable kayaks). After some delicate balancing most of the men managed to board their folbots without much trouble. The training consisted of getting into the boat without getting wet and then paddling out and attempting to find the sub with an unocular that was designed to see a red-infrared light on the sub.[4] After practice, the men climbed back aboard the sub and went to bed.

The submarine arrived at the rendezvous point on October 21 at four in the morning and, using the periscope, kept the house under observation. Unluckily for the lanky Clark and his nervous crew, two Algerian fishing boats got within two hundred feet of the submarine and began to fish. Jewell had no choice but to dive deeper and attempt to land later.[5] Clark and his fellow Americans spent much of their time ducking the low ceilings of the sub, playing bridge and adapting to air so fetid that it prevented them from lighting a match.[6]

By nightfall on October 22 Clark readied himself for departure. Clark discussed scenarios with Jewell. If Clark did not return the submarine was to creep across the bottom of the ocean floor and wait until October 25, before leaving for safe waters.[7] Before departure Clark grew angry with his frightened force because they wanted to land in civilian clothes. Clark knew this was a terrible idea, not only because they would be executed if they were caught, but that it would send the French the wrong message: "Hell no! We'll go ashore as American officers and nothing else. It will help the people we are dealing with to remember who we are and whom we represent. We mustn't allow them to forget for a moment that we are American and that there are millions more Americans behind us."[8]

With the final decisions made, Clark, armed with two thousand dollars in gold, and his crew paddled to shore aboard his folbot. Clark made it to the beachhead where Robert Murphy and his assistant welcomed Clark to North Africa, to which Clark replied, "I'm damn glad we made it."[9] The first "assault" by Americans in World War II was a success; the Clark Expeditionary Force had made it to North Africa.

Around six in the morning Clark and his crew met with General Mast and his aide, Emile Jousse, and immediately began negotiations. Clark was impressed with Mast and remarked later that he was "a man who can be relied on."[10] Mast wasted no time and asked if the planned invasion could be expanded to southern France. Aware that he was being tested, Clark told Mast that was logistically impossible. Disappointed, Mast wanted more specifics for the invasion of North Africa. This put Clark in a precarious situation. He was trying to gain the trust of the French, but he could not tell them exact details. As he later commented in his diary, he began "lying like hell" and tried to keep his poker face while saying that "half a million Allied troops could come in" with 2,000 planes and "plenty of US Navy ready to go in this thing."[11]

With Mast happy with what he was being told, Clark asked what the French general could do for the Allies. Mast was happy to oblige in any way possible, but requested two thousand rifles, ammunition, and grenades to seize key areas.[12] With this assistance, the French would take control of the communication center, take over the troop barracks, arrest pro-Vichy commanders, seize public buildings, and try to prevent the French navy from firing on the Allied convoys.[13] The last was the most important, and Mast and his followers were taking an extreme gamble. There were few Frenchmen in North Africa who supported Free French leader Charles de Gaulle, and, if found out Mast would most certainly be executed for treason. More importantly, if the French refused to fight the landing Americans, the Wehrmacht would immediately take over the rest of France and seize the French fleet stationed in Toulon. Clark, as ordered by Roosevelt and Churchill, gave Mast an official document that stated that if the French would join the Allied cause, the Allies would restore France to her prewar boundaries, allow the French to lead themselves, and would view France as an equal ally in the war.[14]

The last order of business Clark and Mast dealt with was who would command the French forces. Under an earlier agreement with Roosevelt, General Giraud was to be the overall commander of the French in North Africa. This conversation would come back to haunt both Clark and Eisenhower, when Giraud arrived in North Africa and demanded to be Supreme Allied Commander of the entire operation.

With the initial contact made and key information exchanged, a tired Clark changed into a French officer's uniform and went out to stretch his legs and see the North African coast. During this break, Clark's assistants finalized smaller, but important details with Mast and Jousse. Around six that evening Clark and his crew were startled when the French alarmed them that police were on their way to the house. Alerted by "queer goings on" in the house, the police forced everyone to scatter.[15] Clark later remarked in his diary about the arrival of the police, "When we heard that the French police were on their way it was as though someone had tossed 50 loaded skunks on the conference table."[16] Acting decisively, Clark and his landing force fled to the wine cellar underneath the house. While Clark hid, Robert Murphy and Jousse gave Oscar-winning performances. Murphy boldly told the police who he was, but not to embarrass him, because he and Jousse were having a party and women were upstairs sleeping.[17] In the wine cellar, Clark, armed with a pistol, tried to listen to what was going on and prepared for the worst. During the silence, Captain Courtney fought back a cough and told Clark, "General, I'm afraid I'll choke." Clark quietly responded, "I'm afraid you won't," and handed the struggling commando a stick of gum. Later, Courtney asked why American chewing gum was so tasteless. Clark laughed: he had been chewing on that piece of gum for hours.[18]

After a few tense minutes, the police left and Clark returned to the upper level of the house. It seemed that the police were not looking for American officers, but black-market merchants and illegal trading. Arab servants in the house were ushered out before Clark's arrival and contacted the police after they discovered footprints in the sand near the beach. With the police temporarily gone, Clark and his force decided they had completed their mission and prepared to return to the sub. Unfortunately for Clark the seas were rough, and he was prevented from reaching the *Seraph*. Clark and his force discussed possible alternatives if they could not reach the submarine, but by four in the morning on October 23, decided to try one more time. Tired of trying to reach the vessel, Clark went to bed. However, police again interrupted Clark's sleep, but instead of fleeing to the wine cellar, he leapt out the window of the house and sprinted down to the beach where the rest of his men waited.[19]

Before they reached the submarine, a bizarre exchange took place. Wet and fearful that the gold would weigh him down, Clark took off his trousers and wrapped the gold in his pants, and ordered General Lemnitzer to drop his pants and give them to him. What followed next is a prime example of rank. Lemnitzer, now pantless, ordered a colonel to do the same. Eventually, the epic of the pants reached lowly Lieutenant Foote, who outranked no one and was forced to paddle to the submarine without any pants.[20] Finally, after paddling for what seemed like hours, and losing one folbot containing numerous secret papers and Clark's pants, the group reached Jewell and the *Seraph*. Immediately, Clark deemed the meeting "a great success."[21]

Upon arrival a relieved Clark told Murphy to search the beach for his trousers, which contained the gold and the secret papers. Eventually the papers and the trousers were found, but the gold was never discovered.[22] To help get over the shock of the lost gold and the successful mission, Clark asked Jewell, "Haven't I heard somewhere about the British navy having a rum ration, even in subs?" To which Jewell gladly replied: "Yes Sir, but on subs only in emergencies." Clark responded, "Well, I think this is an emergency. What about a double rum ration?"[23] For the remainder of their stay, Clark and all aboard the *Seraph* enjoyed their victory rum.

On 24 October Clark and the *Seraph* emerged from the depths of the ocean and wired Eisenhower of the success of the mission and the incident involving the police: "When intervention by local police who had become suspicious of increased activity rendezvous area brought conference to abrupt conclusion FROGS flew in all directions and party hid in empty repeat empty wine cellar in house while argument with police ensued."[24] Later, Clark and the others involved created the "Panoe Club," an exclusive group that met periodically to remember their mission.[25](Clark was known for telling off-color jokes; the name of the club is a vague reference to an obscene British colloquialism involving punts—long, narrow, flat-bottomed boats with square ends, usually propelled with a pole—and canoes.)

Arriving back in London on 25 October around eleven in the morning Clark immediately went into a meeting with Eisenhower to discuss the trip (leaving out all the humorous anecdotes.)[26] The next day Marshall cabled Eisenhower to inform Clark that the arrival of the police was mere coincidence: "Please inform Clark that police incident which marred end of visit turned out to be innocuous. It resulted from over zealousness of local police official no embarrassing consequences for us are apparent but our friends ask that Clark be informed they regret exceedingly that he and his party were discommoded."[27]

On 27 October Clark received a telegram from Gibraltar about his missing pants that read, "Inform X (Clark) that he has not lost his pants nor his coat in Z (Africa) But he will find them here clean and pressed on his return."[28] Three days later, General Marshall cabled Eisenhower about Clark's adventure: "We are following with great interest and considerable suspense the negotiations going on with respect to Kingpin [Giraud] and Flagpole [Mast]. If the results we hope for are attained it will make an interesting page in history. I am in complete accord with your [Eisenhower's] views as to decorating for Clark and his party. Give him my thanks for his courageous and able performance of a hazardous task."[29]

With all the excitement of Clark's trip, many in his staff believed that Torch would be achieved without great loss. Clark refused to believe that the French would welcome the Allies and made sure his staff would not fall to victory fever, telling them: "it is very important that we do not let the possibility of French non-resistance weaken our plans for active combat in the theater in case things do not go in the way we hope for."[30]

On 29 October the now-famous Clark met with King George, who told the American: "I know all about you. You're the one who took that fabulous trip. Didn't you get stranded on the beach without your pants?"[31] The incident of Clark's lost pants had by this time become so famous that Louis Hollander, general manager of the New York Joint Board, Amalgamated Clothing Workers of America, wrote to Clark's wife asking for his measurements and telling her, "As he did not need to assure you, he lost his trousers honorably.

He is a living example of the fact that a great hero need not lose his dignity thereby."[32]

After discussing the upcoming operation, the king switched back to Clark's trip and told him that he "thoroughly enjoyed the statement in your cable that you have been forced to hide in an 'empty REPEAT empty wine cellar.'"[33] In regards to future dealings with Admiral Darlan the king recalled Darlan's "shifty eyes" and believed that he could not be trusted.[34] After departing the king's company Clark traveled back to his office to find that Eisenhower had received another cable from Marshall about the possible formation of the Fifth United States Army after the Torch troops had landed.[35] Clark anxiously wanted that command, but his time as deputy to Eisenhower was not yet finished.

On the first of November, with Torch only a few days away, Robert Murphy cabled Eisenhower asking for a delay. Giraud, still in Vichy France, could not leave until 20 November. Without Giraud and a two-week delay, Murphy feared that the French would resist the landings. Seething with anger that a diplomat would request such a delay in a major offensive that he had been planning for months, Clark quickly wrote a very angry letter:

> It is inconceivable that Murphy could possibly recommend such a delay with his intimate knowledge of the operation and the present location of troops and convoys afloat. It is likewise inconceivable to me that our mere failure to concede to such demands as have been made would result in having the French North African Army meet us with serious opposition. Such opposition for the reason stated would amount to a double-cross by Mast. I cannot believe that he would degrade himself to this extent. . . . He should be directed to tell Mast that we are coming as planned; that all hell and the French North African Army can't stop us and if he uses the information already furnished him on the operation as to time of its execution to our disadvantage, either by regrouping of his troops to more effectively stop us; by disseminating the confidential information Murphy has entrusted to him; or otherwise betraying our cause, we'll hang him higher than a kite when we get ashore.[36]

After realizing that delivering the letter might not be the best idea, Clark shelved it and sent a much gentler response stating that Torch could not be delayed.

Apart from gaining celebrity status and a meeting with the king of England, Clark was awarded the Distinguished Service Medal, but more importantly he had greatly aided Torch and the Allied cause; the Clark submarine mission was a success. While no exact agreements were reached, the meeting started discussions with the French to end resistance in North Africa, thereby reducing Allied casualties and perhaps preventing the failure of Torch altogether. While the submarine mission is only a footnote in history, the success of Torch, the first major Allied assault, was a strategic imperative.

On 5 November, three days before its scheduled start, Clark and Eisenhower left the safety of London and departed for Gibraltar to prepare for the invasion. With the Torch convoys at sea and Eisenhower and Clark settling into Gibraltar, the two men discussed who would stay in Gibraltar and who would set up a headquarters following the Torch landings. The two decided that Clark would go, and as Eisenhower told others at Gibraltar, "I must have someone who can act for me without having to confer with me or get my opinions. . . . This shows the extraordinary importance of having a deputy. I've just had to have him."[37] Clark was not only pleased about getting closer to troops, but Eisenhower gave Clark a tremendous compliment.

With Clark's role growing in importance in North Africa, his detailed diary entries, which often record entire conversations seemingly verbatim, become increasingly important to historians and biographers, as reflected in the following cited dialogues during his tense negotiations with military and Vichy government officials. While he was not a diarist like George S. Patton, who personally chronicled events, Clark kept an extremely well chronicled diary throughout the entire war; but he largely confided the task to aides, who wrote down daily events, sometimes while Clark was in the same room. Well aware of his position Clark wanted history recorded, but he wanted the diary "to be written daily without the considerate weighing of what a particular entry might mean in future history."[38] While incredibly accurate and revealing, his diaries also served to relieve stress and allow him to gripe about fellow Americans and their Allies.

On 7 November, with D-Day only a few hours away, Giraud finally met with Clark and Eisenhower. Sent from France to Gibraltar aboard the *Seraph*, Giraud immediately went into discussions with the two Americans around 1600. For three hours, Clark, Eisenhower and Giraud debated when the Frenchman would return to North Africa and announce his arrival. After a brief break the discussions continued at ten in the evening when Giraud flatly refused to travel to North Africa unless he was given Supreme Command. According to Clark, when Giraud demanded command he believed Eisenhower "had probably never been so shocked and showed it so little."[39] Growing equally impatient Clark shouted at Giraud: "We would like the Honorable General to know that the time of his usefulness to the Americans for the restoration of the glory that was once France is now. We do not need you after tonight!"[40] Giraud still would not back down and kept repeating, "What about the prestige of Giraud? What would the French people think of me; what about my family?"[41]

As it became apparent that Giraud was waiting on the outcome of the landings to make his move Clark ended the meeting and told Giraud before he left, "If you don't go along, General Giraud, you're going to be out in the snow on your ass!"[42] With the French situation unclear, the soldiers landing in North Africa now had no choice but to fight.

On 8 November 1942 the torch was lit. The Allied convoys safely crossed the Atlantic and American troops stormed the beaches of North Africa. At the same time as the landings Marshal Henri Philippe Pétain wrote to President Roosevelt condemning the attack and telling him that any attack would be defended. The landings were going remarkably well and Clark and the Allies received better news when by afternoon Giraud had changed his mind. Giraud gave up his claim to Supreme Allied command once he knew the landings were successful. With Algiers surrendering at 1900, Torch was off to a great start and Clark left Gibraltar for Algiers.[43]

Clark's plane landed in Algiers just as German Junker 88s were flying across the sky. Clark made great haste to the St. George Hotel where Admiral Darlan awaited. For the next few days, Clark would become entangled with Darlan and what became known as the "Darlan Deal." As Clark remarked upon arrival at the hotel, "What a mess! Why soldiers have to get in things like this when there are wars to be fought—God it's awful!"[44] The deal Clark struck with Admiral Darlan was destined to become one of the most controversial events of the war. Years later, however Eisenhower wrote about the importance of dealing with Darlan: "The military advantages of an immediate cease fire are so overwhelming that I'll go promptly to join Clark in Algiers and if the proposals of the French are as definite as I understand, I shall immediately recognize Darlan as the highest French authority in the region. He can act as the interim head of such civil government as exists, on condition that he carries out any orders I may issue."[45]

At the St. Georges Hotel in Algiers, upon being introduced to Admiral Darlan and his small staff, which included Robert Murphy as interpreter and

Darlan's aide Marshal Alphonse Juin, Clark immediately demanded Darlan issue a cease-fire order. A tense dialogue ensued in which Clark wasted little time in telling Darlan that both the French and the Allies must work together against the Germans. [For the transcript of this dialogue, see Appendix A.].

Darlan agreed with Clark, but believed he did not have the authority to sign an agreement and constantly told Clark that he did not represent the French government and could only proceed with orders from Marshal Philippe Pétain. Clark interrupted Darlan and told him that there was no point in continuing the dialogue and that he would have to find another French officer to deal with.[46]

Understanding that Darlan's acceptance was the key to the agreement, Clark backtracked and specifically asked the admiral if French forces would resist east of Algiers. Darlan returned to his initial response: "Only if Pétain orders me to do so." But, he did tell Clark that he believed the elderly Marshal would agree. Clark, however, did not accept that answer and stressed that there was little time for debate.[47]

Clark grew more furious with every answer from Darlan, but continued to keep on the French commander and threatened again to begin negotiations with someone else. This time he specifically mentioned Generals Mast and Giraud. Darlan believed that neither officer had the authority to reach an agreement and pressed Clark for permission to send a message to France. Clark rejected the request and threatened Darlan with arrest. The French admiral quickly replied, "the army is still with me," and requested five minutes to discuss Clark's request with his staff.[48]

Following their meeting, Clark rejoined the discussion. Darlan laid a copy of an order on the table, asking Clark if he would accept it. In substance it said that the Americans would not take his refusal to declare an immediate armistice, that further battle would be fruitless and that blood would flow. He wanted to tell Marshal Pétain that as a result of fighting France would probably lose Africa. He wanted to cease hostilities and take an attitude of complete neutrality. Clark responded that he was looking instead for "orders to the troops," and Darlan responded he would pass an order to Juin, Nogues (Vichy high commissioner in North Africa), Barres (commander of French forces in Tunisia), the air force and the navy, which Clark found unacceptable.

Keeping his composure, Clark told Darlan that each individual American commander would decide the terms of the armistice. Darlan seemed to relent, but then asked the status of General Giraud. Clark brushed the question aside and astutely told the admiral that Giraud wanted to help France and that there was plenty of room for everyone. Seemingly growing to accept Clark's demands, Darlan still wanted to punish French officers who had collaborated with the Americans and disobeyed his orders. Clark had little time for this idea, but said he would look into the matter. It was very clear to all at the meeting that Darlan considered French officers like General Mast traitors.[49] However, a deal was struck and Clark got what he wanted: a cease-fire and the hope that the French would join the fight against the Axis.[51]

After leaving the meeting, Clark quickly sent out a cable that summarized the whole ordeal:

> Just concluded lengthy conference with Darlan and his cohorts. He repeatedly refused to accept terms of armistice reason lack of authority from Vichy. I demanded he sign them to include all North Africa and stated he would be taken into custody if he refused and further negotiations would be with Giraud. He finally agreed to issue me an order to all the ground, air and naval forces in North Africa, including Morocco and Tunisia to discontinue hostilities immediately.[50]

Reports flowed in to Clark, and he was relieved to learn that the French troops were obeying the order. Clark had achieved remarkable success; the French had stopped fighting the Americans and promised to attack the Germans in Tunisia. And yet, his day had just begun.

Later that day Pétain dismissed Darlan and replaced him with General Auguste Paul Nogues, resident general of Morocco.[51] Clark immediately rushed over to see Darlan and found the admiral "looking like a dejected little pig." Looking up at Clark, Darlan told him he had no choice but to revoke the recently signed armistice. Shocked, and on the verge of losing his temper, Clark shouted down the smaller Darlan, "Pétain is the mouthpiece of Hitler," further adding that "You're not going to revoke any order!" A gloomy Darlan sighed and told the American general, "Then, I must be taken prisoner." Not taking "no" for an answer, Clark switched tactics and attempted to get Darlan to move the fleet, but he would not budge: "It's not my fleet; I've been relieved."[52] Knowing that nothing more could be done, Clark left, but was content with the fact that Darlan's order was being carried out.

The next morning Clark once again hammered away at Darlan to bring the French fleet to North Africa: "Although you have told us repeatedly that you want to free France, you have given us no visible indication or decision in support of us or the Allied cause. There are two ways you can demonstrate your fidelity to the Allied cause: first, by summoning the French fleet to a North African port, and, second, by ordering the governor of Tunisia to resist invasion by the Germans."[53]

Darlan repeated that he had no authority to do so, but that the fleet would be scuttled before it fell into German hands, and a flustered Clark replied that this would "be an act against the Allies as much as against the Germans." Each grew more upset until Clark finally exploded at the Frenchman. "This just verifies the statement I made when I came here: It shows no visible indication [of] any desire on your part, despite your statements, to assist the Allied cause. Good-day!"[54]

Clark went away to cool off and Darlan went to lunch, after which he informed the tired American general that he had changed his mind. Clark's diary reports Darlan decided to call for the fleet after learning that Pétain and the Germans were at odds over the occupation of unoccupied France. Darlan soon radioed the French fleet: "The Marshal being no longer able to make free decisions, we can, while remaining personally loyal to him, make decisions which are the most favorable to French interests."[55] Again, after a tough day of negotiations, it seemed Clark and the Allies had achieved remarkable success. But Clark still had a major headache to deal with.

On 12 November, with Torch proceeding nicely and the Allies seemingly on the verge of gaining the French fleet, Clark awoke to a potentially dangerous crisis. Darlan's order to resist the Germans had been revoked. An angered Clark summoned Admiral Darlan, General Juin and English-speaking French Vice Admiral Raymond Fénard. On their arrival Clark ripped into both men: "Both of you keep telling me you want to save France and French colonial territory. Neither of you have given me one single indication of this except in words. All your deeds have been contrary to this aim you both volubly profess to have. Now I learn that the order for French troops to resist Axis moves in Tunisia has been revoked."[56]

Speaking for Darlan, General Juin tried to calm Clark down and told him that the order had only been suspended and would be restored once General Nogues arrived. Clark, who had had enough of Darlan and the ambivalent French, erupted and accused the French officers of working against the Allies, and yet again threatened to deal with someone else. Juin, who would become one of Clark's finest corps commanders in Italy, told the American that he wanted to fight the Germans.[57] At this point Clark was tired of talk and demanded actions. Nevertheless, Juin was adamant; he wanted to wait for Nogues. As Clark grew angrier, Darlan interjected, and announced that the French fleet was prepared to flee Toulon if the Germans entered the city. While this was good news for the Allies, Clark was still at a boiling point. Juin then jumped in and said he would serve under Giraud. This was monumental, because he was the first French officer to agree to serve under him, but he still wanted to wait for Nogues before he issued orders to resist the Germans.[58]

Admiral Raymond Fénard, who spoke English, attempted to calm Clark down and whispered to him, "You are getting what you want if you will only be a little more patient and wait. Don't spoil everything. You almost have solution and a victory in hand."[59] Clark replied that he believed Darlan and Juin were just stalling for time. Fénard, again, attempted to cool the red-hot Clark: "That's not true. I swear it. You are blind, man, you are blind."[60]

Fénard continued to press upon Clark to be more patient, but Clark was adamant and demanded the French act now. As Clark, Darlan, and Juin continued to argue, Clark looked over to Darlan and said he still had not received word what action the French fleet would take. Although Clark realized he had the French where he wanted them, he still requested an immediate order to resist the Germans.

Losing patience with Clark, Fénard jumped in again, telling him to be patient, but Clark replied he would not let up. Despite no immediate order to resist the Germans, the French officers started to negotiate positions in the new alliance. Balancing the egos of the Frenchmen, Clark allowed Giraud to command from Dakar to Bizerte and Juin to command Algeria.[61] With both Darlan and Juin seemingly satisfied, Clark again requested the order.

Darlan and Juin talked outside, while Clark waited in the conference room. Fénard told him, "You don't understand the internal situation. Everyone is behind Darlan. If you will wait you will have everyone with you. If not, you will upset the apple cart."[62] Fénard told Clark that he was with him, and he would back Giraud "no matter what happens." Clark replied, "I can't afford to make any mistakes. The stakes are too high."[63] Darlan and Juin quickly rejoined the meeting and Juin announced that General Barre had orders from Vichy not to resist the Germans, but that he, Juin, had directed Barre to ignore the order and fight.[64]

Finally, Clark relented and allowed the Frenchmen to discuss the situation with Nogues. While the Frenchmen met, Clark received a message that greatly uplifted his sagging spirit; he had been promoted to lieutenant general.[65] After dinner, Clark had one last round with the French, meeting

Nogues for the first time, who demanded a private interview with the American general. A more relaxed Clark told the interpreter, "Tell Nogues that we do not recognize either him or Pétain."[66] He then summoned both Darlan and Nogues into the conference room.

After talking with the two Frenchmen for an hour, Clark brought in General Giraud, and had them all shake hands. With all three of the key French commanders in the room Clark left the meeting, telling his aides, "I'm leaving the boys to battle it out among themselves. I've told them they have to compose their differences or else I will set up a military government. I don't want to be too optimistic, but I think this thing is going to work itself out. Nogues doesn't want Giraud in the military picture. Darlan is now trying to get Giraud and Nogues together. It is no place for me."[67]

Seizing the opportunity, Clark left the scene and received the message he had been awaiting: Eisenhower was en route to deal with the political situation. Happy to be out of picture for a few hours, Clark went to bed for much-deserved sleep.[68] The next day Clark introduced Eisenhower to the Frenchmen and the luck of Eisenhower first emerged: the French had come to an agreement.

Admiral Darlan would head the civil and political North African government; Nogues would remain governor of French Morocco; General Yves Chatel, governor of Algeria; Vice Admiral Jean-Pierre Esteva, governor of Tunisia; and General Giraud, head of the French North African forces. A relieved Clark announced to all, "You have reached an accord that will assist all Allied forces in Africa. I know it has been difficult for you and for me to adjust our differences. I appreciate your cooperation and your help at this time. Now we can go ahead united in our plan of defeating the Axis, restoring France and restoring peace."[69] After the meeting finished, a happy Eisenhower pinned a third star on Clark, telling him, "I've been waiting a long time to do this, Wayne. I hope I pin on the fourth star!"[70]

After Eisenhower left Clark removed the new stars until officially confirmed. In a small press conference he gave before departing Clark half-jokingly told the reporters, "I would have sooner walked into the Germans than into these boys. Politics isn't my line. But I did the best I could and I think I succeeded."[71] The Darlan Deal was now complete and Clark believed he performed brilliantly, writing to his wife later in November, "My negotiations and efforts here will make history. I don't know how the historians will look upon them, but I feel that in the long run the negotiations we are making here will prove to be the right ones."[72] Although the agreement was done, the political blowback from the deal was yet to come.

By 14 November Clark visited the front for the first time and hoped that the French fleet would flee to North Africa. Darlan repeatedly told Clark that he felt the fleet would join the Allies, but Clark was unsure. While he was attending mass at the Holy Trinity Church of Algiers on 15 November the press corps noticed the American general and later asked him why he was praying so hard. Clark told them he was praying for one thing: "Oh, God, let me get the fleet from Darlan!"[73] A week or so after the deal was completed, news of the Allied reaction to the deal began to trickle into North Africa. The news was not good. President Roosevelt labeled the deal a "matter of military expediency."[74] Winston Churchill was also less than pleased in dealing with a Nazi collaborationist like Darlan.

While Clark understood there would be political ramifications, he did not understand why some could not appreciate the military expediency of the matter. Clark tried to explain why the deal was necessary: "If I had not obtained French cooperation we would have had to have kept most of our troops back here watching these fellows while the Hun built up his strength in Tunisia. Because of negotiations the French are fighting with us. Darlan was the only horse we could ride and I think we should ride him to death!"[75]

Clark discussed the situation with Eisenhower, and the commander in chief cabled Clark a detailed memo on how to handle the consequences and avoid future political embarrassments:

> Apparently, we are being rather definitely condemned because we have had the slightest thing to do with Darlan. . . . I am sticking firmly by what we have done as the only possible solution in the circumstances; however, I quite agree that we must do nothing to embarrass our governments in the future from a political angle and must confine our own dealings here to those things that have to do with winning the battle of Tunis. Therefore, we must (a) Have no needless publicity about any dealing with Darlan. (b) We must deal firmly with Darlan to get those obvious advantages that will convince the politicians of the wisdom of our action. . . . (c) We must not allow Flandin, or any other people who are equally odious to the British and American people, to be associated, even in a minor way, with the French Commission. (d) No matter what title or office Darlan or any of his assistants may choose to assume, we must not under any circumstances recognize his authority or his title as extending

beyond French North Africa. (e) Above all, we must get out of him the maximum assistance in winning the battle of Tunisia.[76]

Clark told Eisenhower about the past few weeks: "I know the hell you have been taking, sitting in that damn tunnel, but don't think I haven't had my share of it here. I have never gone through ten days like this before in my life."[77] Later in his life, Clark remarked about Eisenhower that, had he, Clark, "been the commander," he "would have left the deputy at Gibraltar."[78] However, the relationship between the two was fine, and in time the political troubles caused by the deal did down.

The deal was the correct decision, though fighting in Oran was nearly over by its conclusion. The Darlan-Clark Agreement saved countless lives in Morocco and saved the city of Casablanca, which was scheduled to be attacked by forces under General Patton's command.[79] Clark later added that the deal was a necessity: "We needed the cooperation of the French badly. There was only one single-track railroad between Oran and Casablanca. We did not have the forces to patrol this precious iron highway and sabotage, which we would be unable to prevent, could immobilize our vital cargo moving over it."[80] Whether Darlan was the right man to deal with remains a matter of debate; perhaps there was someone else, someone less tainted. As historian A. L. Funk assessed the deal in 1972: Whether or not Darlan had been in North Africa, the deal would have been made with another Vichyite. The uproar in the press might have been less, but the policy would have been the same."[81]

The deal, while politically troubling, was necessary. Other than the thousands of lives saved, the Darlan Deal brought France back into the war against Nazi Germany and Italy. From Torch onwards to Operation Overlord and the fall of Hitler, France proved a supportive ally and helped the Allies to ultimate victory. In the meantime, Clark continued pressuring Darlan to get the French fleet.

On 27 November the Germans entered Toulon, and Darlan, now firmly with the Allies, cabled the fleet to join the Allies. Unfortunately for Clark and the Allies the French fleet was scuttled. Clark's attempt to seize the fleet had failed, but at least the Germans did not take control of it. As for the war in North Africa, Allied forces were moving rapidly, but were beginning to slow due to the German buildup some fifteen to twenty miles outside of Tunis and Bizerte. On the second day of December a resting Clark received joyous news: he was to activate the Fifth United States Army headquarters in the near future.

A few days later, Clark was disheartened, but flattered to learn that his name had been floated about to become the American military advisor to Winston Churchill. Clark thought extremely well of the Prime Minister, writing in his memoirs after the war:

> I consider him to be the greatest man I have ever met—dynamic in the extreme, full of charm, persuasive, with plenty of ability and drive, and a profound understanding of global affairs. He had a surprising knowledge of tactical and strategical problems, but the military factors always were subordinate in his mind to political considerations. Once he had decided that a certain course of action was proper and would produce the best results for the Allied cause—and particularly for Great Britain—he relentlessly pursued that course, ruthlessly eliminating obstacles in his path.[82]

Clark responded to the suggestion: "I don't want this politico-military liaison job with the Prime Minister, but I am pleased that I have been asked to take it."[83] In the end, Clark would command troops after all, but he did not know where or when.

Clark handpicked a girl's school in Oujda, just west of Oran, to become his Fifth Army headquarters.[84] Clark and staff were ordered to plan for Operation Backbone, which was designed to push Fifth Army into Spanish Morocco in case Franco decided to join the war against the Allies. It was during this time that Clark cabled Washington about getting a South American force in North Africa to join Fifth Army: "Consider that it would have an extremely wholesome morale effect if token South American army units, both ground and air, could be sent into the French Moroccan area for assignment to the Fifth United States Army. Their presence in that area, it is believed, would have a fine effect on our relations with the Spanish."[85]

Clark believed South American forces would better relations with the Spanish and that the Western Hemisphere would be more unified against Nazi Germany. While Marshall responded that the idea was a good one, the timing was not right. Eventually South American countries would send troops to North Africa and elsewhere, perhaps the most famous being the Brazilian Expeditionary Force that would fight under Clark in Italy. In the meantime Clark had to figure out what to do with Darlan; keep him or get rid of him. Little did he know that the decision would be made for him.

In the last weeks of December, with the political situation stabilizing, many in the Allied high command believed the time was right to rid themselves of Darlan. Clark believed that he could be replaced with Giraud and that Darlan could be persuaded to leave and move to Warm Springs, Georgia, with his polio-stricken son. In his diary Clark recorded, "As I see it, we will be in a position to diplomatically rid ourselves of Darlan as soon as we take Tunisia. When this is accomplished I think we should go direct to Darlan and tell him that 'our countries [the United States and Great Britain] just won't stomach you.'"[86] On 23 December Darlan invited Clark to a formal luncheon during which he told Clark, "Tomorrow the Axis press will say I gave this luncheon for you because you had a gun pointed at me." Clark, now more at ease with Darlan, laughed and told the diminutive Admiral, "If the rest of the luncheons were as good as this I would get my gun out every week."[87] Their relationship had slowly evolved into not a friendship, but perhaps a type of respect for one another. However, this would be the last time the two would meet.

On Christmas Eve Admiral Darlan was assassinated by Bonnier de la Chappelle, a young de Gaulle supporter who believed he would go unpunished. Around 1545 hours de la Chappelle, a student, somehow obtained a pass to Darlan's office in the Summer Palace. After returning from a late lunch, just as Darlan was about to enter his office, de la Chappelle shot him four times.[88] Darlan's aide tried to tackle the assassin, but was wounded in the leg. De la Chappelle was quickly arrested, sent to trial, and executed. Henri Giraud took Darlan's place and the outcry over the Clark-Darlan deal died with the admiral.

For the Allies the assassination was a blessing, as Clark later wrote: "[His] death was, to me, an act of Providence. It is too bad that he went that way, but, strategically speaking, his removal from the scene was like the lancing of a troublesome boil. He had served his purpose, and his death solved what could have been the very difficult problem of what to do with him in the future. Darlan was a political investment forced upon us by the circumstances, but we made a sensational profit in lives and time through using him."[89]

Darlan's death ended the political outcry. Had he lived, Clark probably would have been proven right. Darlan would have been made financially comfortable for the remainder of his life, and he likely would have lived out his days in Warm Springs or elsewhere in the United States with his son. With his death Clark was now free to move forward with building Fifth Army.

During the last days of 1942 Clark took over the Southern Tunisian front, which consisted of all American and French troops south of the line from Sousse on the Tunisian coast, straight back through Ksour, Algeria.[90] However, Clark's command of the front would be short-lived. On 31 December Marshall cabled Clark that he and his staff should concentrate on planning Operation Backbone while another American would actually command the front. Saddened, Clark knew Marshall was right, as he wrote in his diary: "I knew that that was the right thing to do."[91]

On 5 January 1943 Mark Clark officially activated the United States Fifth Army, the first American army ever activated outside the United States.[92] Fifth Army consisted of forces of the 1st Armored Corps, II Corps in Western Algeria, and XIII Air Support Command.[93] While Clark was still to plan for Operation Backbone there was a possibility that he would return to England and prepare for the European invasion. In taking the army command Clark would leave Eisenhower's side.

The same day he activated Fifth Army Clark penned a very personal letter to Eisenhower:

> In leaving for my new command, I want to tell you how deeply I appreciate all you have done for me. You have brought about all the success that has come to me during the past few months.
>
> I want you to know that to have served under you during the preparation and conduct of the North African operation has been one of the greatest privileges that could come to any solder.
>
> Although I had known you intimately for the past quarter of a century and had always admired you and your ability, it was only during the stress of the past seven months that I really, fully comprehended the depth and strength of your character. Your examples of leadership and character have set for me a goal which I some day hope to reach. Your understanding and consideration for your subordinates has endeared you to all of us.
>
> I hope you will consider my going as only temporary and know that I stand ready and anxious to serve you in any capacity in order to bring you the success which you deserve.[94]

The relationship between Eisenhower and Clark was key to building the United States forces in England and the successful execution of Operation Torch. As Eisenhower wrote of Clark after the war: "He was a relatively young man but an extremely able professional, with a faculty for picking fine assistants and for developing a high morale within his staff. . . . More than any other one person, Clark was responsible for the effective co-ordination of detail achieved in this, the first Allied plan for amphibious attack in the Mediterranean."[95]

In January 1943 Eisenhower wrote Clark thanking him for his service as his deputy: "You have performed brilliantly as Deputy Commander-in-Chief of the Allied Forces and in accordance with my highest expectations, based on intimate acquaintanceship with you and with your record covering the past quarter of a century. Even beyond this, there have been certain instances in which your tact, breadth of vision and clear understanding of basic issues have astonished me."[96]

Though Clark would continue his close relationship with Eisenhower until Eisenhower's death in 1969, the two would never again serve as closely as they did in England and North Africa. Eisenhower would rise to world fame and the presidency of the United States and would further always be remembered for his service, but Clark's role in North Africa was as vital as Eisenhower's had been in Europe.

The Western Allies suffered 70,341 casualties in North Africa: 10,290 killed, 36,688 wounded, and 21,363 missing. The Axis powers suffered 155,000 casualties.[97] As for Mark Clark's role, Winston Churchill believed he showed "daring, sagacity, and power of decision."[98] From his work as Eisenhower's deputy to the submarine mission and dealing with Darlan, Clark was the key figure of Torch. Without him Allied casualties would have been higher, and the whole operation could have become a stalemate or worse, an Allied defeat. Without the operation the Allies would have been forced to wait until 1943 or 1944 to attack the Axis powers, and without a second front the Soviet army would have had to fight the Germans alone until 1944.

The political ramifications of the Allies sitting out the war until the invasion of France would have dramatically changed the war and the peace that followed. However, Clark's courageous behavior, clear judgment, and determination in the face of uncertainty and danger were pivotal factors in the success of the first major Allied offensive operation against the Axis. Had he not played his role so successfully, the outcome for the Allied cause could have been far different, making it much more difficult to achieve the ultimate victory.

Chapter 3

THE BIRTH OF THE FIGHTIN' FIFTH
The United States Fifth Army

W ITH A NEW ARMY TO COMMAND, A MORE CONFIDENT and experienced Clark readied himself for his next tasks: building a new army into a fighting force and planning future operations against the Axis. Clark would command the Fifth United States Army for nearly two years and would experience the highs and lows unique to American commanders in World War II. Under his leadership Clark and his soldiers would successfully land at Salerno, fight their way across some of the toughest terrain in the war, and capture Rome, only to have his forces drained for use in other theaters. By the end of 1944 Clark would once again be stuck in the mountains, forced to conserve supplies and manpower and await final victory on 2 May 1945. Building an army to withstand these heretofore unforeseen circumstances would not be easy, but it fell to Clark to do so. This process reveals much about Clark's character and professional competence grounded in the proving grounds of the North African campaign. His experiences in North Africa from January to September 1943 prepared him well for the burden of combat command in the tough days that he was to confront in the Italian campaign.

Starting immediately, in January 1943, Clark made it clear that he wanted Fifth Army to be ready to fight and to always look for the offensive:

Our duty is clear—to be prepared for battle at the earliest possible moment. All else must be subordinated to that end. Every man and every officer of the Fifth Army, no matter what his job, must prepare at all times for that moment when we march into battle to destroy the enemy. This calls for peak mental and physical condition. It calls for complete devotion to duty, for long, tiring hours of work, for initiative, for resourcefulness, for staying power. Men make the army, and all of you, I know, will make this—the Fifth—a great army.[1]

Extremely careful of how the building of the army would impact its future, Clark told his staff, "I want to get this thing started properly so the men will have the keenest desire to participate. They must have pride in themselves if they are to have pride in their army. We're starting here from scratch and we don't want any strikes on us before we start swinging."[2] Talking to newly arrived officers, Clark further added his beliefs about what the Fifth Army should be: "Remember—our one purpose in life is to make this Fifth Army an effective fighting machine. All our efforts must be pointed toward that one goal."[3]

With his experience under General Leslie McNair and his time as II Corps commander Clark was quickly gaining a reputation as one of the U.S. Army's ablest trainers. By June 1943, with training at full speed, Eisenhower would praise Clark and his methods: "Any soldier who goes through Fifth Army training is going to be much better prepared to meet the initial shocks of actual battle. The training that I have seen is comprehensive, thorough and efficient. I have found the leadership to be excellent."[4] Clark's abilities were becoming famous not only in the Army, but around the world, and he would have some trouble adapting to his fame and growing reputation.

Stemming from his secret submarine trip to North Africa, Clark had attained celebrity status, and numerous magazines and newspapers wanted more on his life and history. Even his son Bill at West Point was having a fun time with his father's fame. Clark wrote to his son in February 1943, "So you have become famous on account of my exploits."[5] Since he was overseas many requests for information on Clark went to his wife and mother. Throughout the war Clark would constantly ask his mother and wife to give him no unnecessary publicity. Writing to his mother in January, after taking over Fifth Army, Clark wrote:

I note what you say about magazines writing to ask you for a boyhood story of me. I sincerely hope that you will not give it. I well understand what the public wants, but there are many people in the Army who resent those things, and there is no use antagonizing them, so please do as you have done and refrain from giving any publicity to me.[6]

While Clark never shied away from the press, he was becoming quite troubled with his growing fame. This reputation stems from the fact that in Italy Clark traveled with a gaggle of reporters and photographers. This was not done entirely for personal gain or attention. Instead it was for the soldiers of Fifth Army who, following D-Day, quickly realized that the Italian theater was no longer viewed as the central battleground of the war and that their compatriots in France were getting much more of the limelight. While not entirely innocent of seeking publicity, Clark wrote to his wife in May 1943 about his growing recognition: "Whereas, as I have told you, I do not seek personal publicity, there are times when families having their sons under my command may be interested in knowing what kind of a bird their loved ones are serving under."[7] Furthermore, after his submarine mission Clark was relieved when the State Department killed a proposed movie, entitled "Advance Agent to Africa" or "Message to Giraud."[8] Clark never rejected publicity, but in this he was no different from Eisenhower, Patton, or even Omar Bradley. For the rest of his life Clark believed his reputation as publicity hound was unwarranted, but he never attempted to defend his actions. Aside from his growing fame and visibility, Clark, spent January helping plan a very secret meeting between the leaders of England and the United States.

From 10 to 18 January Clark spent nearly every waking hour organizing and planning the Casablanca Conference. Clark wanted his headquarters to be spotless and to show off the expanding Fifth Army. On 17 January President Roosevelt visited Clark for the first time since the Darlan Deal had been completed. Reviewing troops and questioning key French officials in North Africa, Roosevelt was pleased to learn how forceful Clark was with Darlan and believed that Giraud was a weak individual and poor commander. Clark, unafraid to express his opinion in front of the president, told Roosevelt that he had been misinformed and that Giraud was a strong leader.[9] The following day, Clark was very much relieved when President Roosevelt admitted to him that he was wrong about Giraud.

Clark again hosted Roosevelt on 21 January as the two reviewed Fifth Army troops and ate lunch together. Following lunch Roosevelt asked a surprised Clark, "May I have my mess kit as a souvenir? I'll have it put in the

Smithsonian Institute." After rushing to find the President's mess kit and finding it already gone, Clark told a soldier to "Give me any mess kit, canteen cup and service."[10] Finally getting a kit, Clark gave the president what he had asked for. Clark's role in preparing the Casablanca Conference was important and while it took away from training and planning Clark was seemingly at ease around the President and other dignitaries. Following the conference he received another letter from Eisenhower, praising Clark for his duty thus far in the war:

> There are things I have told you several times verbally and which I now want to put in writing in an effort to make sure that you can never let any doubt enter your mind on this particular score. It is that never for one second have you lost an atom of the great confidence I have always placed in you, nor has there ever been any diminution in the deep feeling of friendship I have held for you for so many years.[11]

During his remaining time in North Africa Clark would be sidetracked by V.I.P.'s. He often had to take days out of his schedule to meet and dine with such dignitaries as the sultan of Morocco and the pasha of Oujda. Perhaps Clark's favorite trip during his stay in North Africa was in April to Spanish Morocco. Visiting Lieutenant General Luis Orgaz Yoldi, high commissioner and commander in chief of Spanish and native forces in Spanish Morocco, Clark became the first American general to enter Spanish territory.[12] More happily for Clark, in April he managed to hold a small reunion of officers from his West Point class of 1917. Clark took great pride in being the only lieutenant general in his class, as well as the youngest.[13] Graduating with such brilliant commanders as Lawton Collins, Matthew Ridgway, Ernest Harmon, and William Eagles, Clark and his classmates believed their class was the "Class of Destiny" and wrote a small poem about certain members of the class. When the poem got to Clark his verse was, "The *New Yorker* on Opie implied he was dopey, Though the stars on his blouse brightly glean. We bet he was wishing that he was home fishing. And not on that damn submarine."[14] Aside from the Casablanca Conference and meetings with dignitaries and old friends, a majority of Clark's time was spent in planning future operations. He did not know which plan would be executed, and he was forced to deal with cancellations and new plans on a daily basis.

With the surrender of Axis forces in North Africa in May 1943 the Allies had to decide on the next operation. They quickly settled on Operation Husky, the invasion of Sicily. While the Fifth Army would not fight in Sicily, it would train the combat forces for Husky. Obviously not pleased as once again Clark was ordered to train troops, but not command them in battle, the general believed Operation Husky was a mistake:

> This coming move in the Mediterranean [Sicily] will be no great move. In reality, we will get no place by doing it and the result will not be commensurate with the effort and the losses involved. We are going to have to attack the Continent proper and we should decide now how we are going to do it. We are losing time to plan and train for a specific goal.[15]

A month before the invasion of Sicily, Clark and his staff began planning for Operation Brimstone, a proposed invasion of Sardinia.[16] It was believed that the "capture of Sardinia would deprive the enemy of airfields for attacking Mediterranean shipping, would give us bases for air attacks on the continent, and would furnish a steppingstone for future operations against Italy or southern France."[17] Once again, as with Husky, Clark would have no role in executing the operation, only training the troops.

By the middle of July with Husky going extremely well, Brimstone was abandoned in favor of Operation Gangway, proposed as a landing near Naples.[18] A few days later Clark and his planners were further instructed to plan Operation Musket, a landing on the heel of Italy near Taranto.[19] Musket was to be used if the fighting in Sicily toughened. If the fighting in Sicily diminished or the Axis forces quickly collapsed, Clark and his staff planned to go with Gangway, the Naples landing.[20] However, Fifth Army planning was hampered by their British counterparts. They had three plans of their own: Operation Baytown, calling for a landing across the straits of Messina at Reggio di Calabria; and Operations Buttress and Goblet, dual movements calling for landings on the toe and instep of the Italian peninsula.[21] And, as if the Fifth Army planners were not busy or confused enough, a final operation was called for following the removal of Benito Mussolini: Operation Avalanche, a landing near Salerno.[22]

Clark opposed nearly all plans except Avalanche, which he believed was "strategically and tactically much more sound than Buttress and Baytown."[23] The plan called for Fifth Army, made up of the U.S. VI Corps (34th Infantry

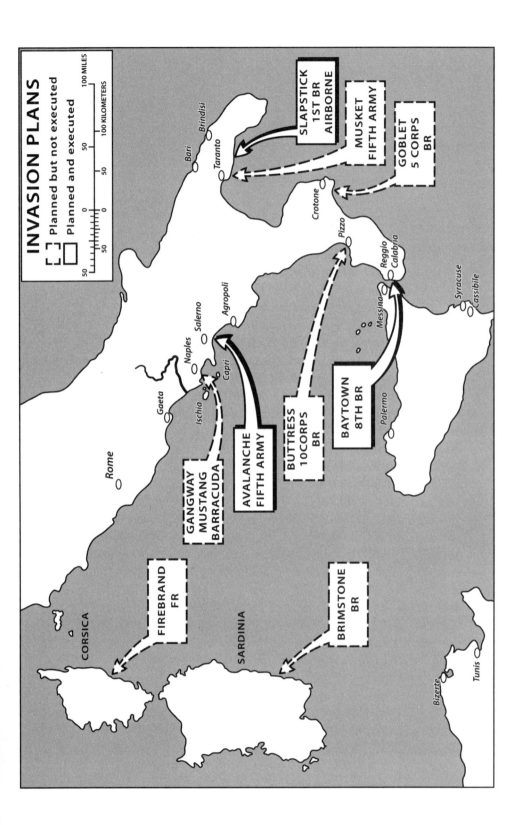

Division, 36th Infantry Division, 1st Armored Division, and 82d Airborne Division) and British X Corps (46th Infantry Division, 56th Infantry Division, 7th Armoured Division, and 1st Airborne Division) to land at the Gulf of Salerno, south of Naples, or the Gulf of Gaeta, north of Naples.[24] Clark, originally favored landing in the Gulf of Gaeta, as the terrain was more favorable with no mountains overlooking the landings. However, the Gulf of Salerno was finally decided upon because air cover could more easily reach that point.[25] D-Day, initially set for 7 September, called for 125 thousand Allied troops to land against 39 thousand German and Italian forces and by D+3 capture Naples and the Foggia airfields.[26] The Allies hoped that the Axis would not be able to build up their forces as quickly as the Allies could. Allied intelligence, believed that the Axis could increase forces to 100 thousand men within days of the invasion.[27] The final decision on what course to take was not made until 16 August when Avalanche was decided upon.[28] The decision to go with Avalanche was one of the most controversial of the war.

While the Allies had decided not to fight a major campaign in Italy, both Winston Churchill and President Roosevelt believed it necessary for the Americans and British to fight somewhere in between the invasion of Sicily and the invasion of France in 1944.[29] The Allies believed that an invasion of mainland Italy would produce numerous advantages. First, it would knock Italy out of the war and break up the Axis. As historian G. A. Sheppard wrote in 1968, the elimination of Italy from the war would result in the loss of two million Axis soldiers.[30] Second, it would eliminate the Italian fleet from the Mediterranean and the war. Third, it would involve German forces that could be otherwise used in the Eastern theater or against the Allied invasion in 1944. Fourth, the invasion of Italy would make a base for a possible invasion of the Balkans. Fifth, the capture of Italian airfields would give the Allies bases closer to Germany and allow for strikes not only against Germany, but the Romanian oilfields at Ploesti.[31] And lastly, not to fight until 1944 could have drastically changed the war and the postwar world. Although unlikely in hindsight, the Germans might possibly have defeated the Soviets on the Eastern Front, resulting in the Allies fighting a stronger Germany in 1944. More likely, the war would have continued past 1945 as the Soviets, following their victory at Stalingrad in early 1943, could have rejected Allied aid and defeated the Germans on their own. The global impact of a vast Soviet victory would have given them near supremacy over Europe and could have dramatically changed the Cold War. Winston Churchill in an address to Parliament understood this well and commented in his address, "We must fight the Germans somewhere, unless we are to stand still and watch the Russians."[32]

The decision to fight in Italy was ultimately correct. It was politically impossible for the American and British governments to sit by and do nothing until 1944 while the Soviets suffered horrible casualties fighting the Germans. The proponents of the idea that fighting in Italy was wasteful miss the notion that an offensive was essential in 1943; invading the Italian peninsula was just that strategic option. Not to have fought between Sicily (9 July–17 August 1943) and the invasion of France (6 June 1944) was impossible, and nowhere else in Europe was there an area in which to fight significant German forces other than Italy.

The major flaw of the campaign was attacking from the south with limited resources and manpower. While landing craft and manpower were in limited supply, the Western Allies could have invaded and taken Sardinia and Corsica and then had a beefed up Fifth Army land in Northern Italy while the British Eighth Army landed in Salerno. This strategy would have deprived the Germans of the rich, industrial Po River Valley and would have forced the German forces to redeploy northward allowing the British to advance up the most difficult terrain virtually unopposed. This bold plan of action could have ended the war in Italy much quicker, but it was never put forward. In reality, the invasion of northern Italy would have been difficult to achieve, but it could have been done, and the war would have been drastically changed. Regardless of the difficult terrain and lack of manpower, the decision to fight it Italy was necessary, but before the invasion could take place the fall of Mussolini would have a drastic impact on Avalanche.

On 25 July King Victor Emmanuel removed Mussolini in favor of Marshal Pietro Badoglio for "administrative purposes and the continuation of the war."[33] Most in the Allied high command did not believe the Italians would continue with the war and during August British and Italian officials met secretly to discuss terms of surrender.[34] A debate between the Allies developed about when and how to announce the surrender. Many hoped that the surrender would aid the landing at Salerno. They believed the Italians would resist the Germans and allow the Allies to land peacefully and easily capture Naples. More optimistic planners believed that after the Italian surrender Hitler would order a retreat into the Po Valley. Hitler and the German high command had already prepared for the inevitable collapse of the Italian government. Operation Alarich called for Field Marshal Erwin Rommel to occupy Northern Italy with thirteen to fourteen divisions and defend the Po

Valley.[35] The German forces already in Italy under Albert Kesselring would retreat northward, where they would join Rommel's command. Regardless, the Allies decided that a few hours before the Operation Avalanche 8 September D-Day, Eisenhower and Badoglio would announce the surrender of Italian forces. To help protect the turncoat Italian government and royal family, Eisenhower decided to drop the 82d Airborne Division into Rome. This greatly changed Clark's plans and would eventually prove to be one of Eisenhower's poorest decisions.

Initially, Clark wanted to drop the U.S. 82d and British 1st Airborne Divisions around Naples during the landings. One would drop on the southern edge of the Naples plain north of Vietri and the other southeast across the Sorrento Ridge. Clark hoped that these two divisions would prevent or at least slow the arrival of two German panzer divisions from opposing the landing at Salerno.[36] However, the 1st Airborne Division was removed from Clark's command and so he decided to airdrop only a regimental combat team less one battalion to allow for more supplies to land in the initial assault. Later the plan was again changed to use the same unit to drop on D-Day minus 1 to seize and destroy the Capua bridge over the Volturno River.[37] The airdrop plan was approved, but on 3 September Clark met with Eisenhower and was told by the commander in chief, "It will be a shock to you, but it has been decided that we'll make the drop on Rome."[38] A shocked Clark protested the decision, "No! That's my division! You know I am going to drop much of it along the Volturno River. The Germans have several panzer divisions south of Rome ready to rush down and block the passes through which we have to go from Salerno to Naples. Taking away the Eighty-Second just as the fighting stars is like cutting off my left arm."

Eisenhower tried to calm Clark by telling him that after the division drops it would pass to his command. This did not placate Clark who, realizing he was not going to win, told Eisenhower, "Thanks, That will be a great help! It will be two hundred miles away from me. Sort of like having a half interest in a wife."[39] With the decision made Clark went about planning and adapted to the loss. In the end, the 82d Airborne Division never dropped on Rome. This was the correct decision as the division would have been surrounded and destroyed, but Eisenhower should never have removed a key element in Clark's plan of operation. The 82d would play a role in Salerno, but it would have been much better for the success of Avalanche had it been used according to Clark's plan.

With the decision finalized, Clark and his Fifth Army readied for their assault on Salerno. The confusion surrounding the surrender of Italy is still controversial. Official histories of the United States in World War II declare that the surrender of Italy helped boost the morale of American soldiers and so was a success.[40] Part of this is true: the surrender did give a temporary boost to the troops, but in the end the surrender hurt the soldiers landing at Salerno. British war correspondent Alan Moorehead believed the Italians were confused by the surrender and could not have done anything more.[41] Historian Ralph S. Mavrogordato believed the surrender of Italy turned the attention of Hitler and the German high command to Naples and Salerno and that it could have played a role in Hitler's decision to fight for Rome.[42]

Perhaps the most damning indication that the surrender of Italy hurt Avalanche comes from Albert Kesselring who wrote in his memoirs that after the surrender of Italy he could "now see the enemy forces and act accordingly."[43] The surrender of Italy, therefore, was a military failure. It resulted in crack German divisions being brought in to defend the Salerno beachhead, confused the Italian army and populace, which was weak and offered little help anyway. With the removal of the Italian Army Hitler and Kesselring quickly brought up additional forces and would nearly drive Clark and his Fifth Army out of Italy. As General Bernhard Montgomery wrote in his memoirs about the situation on the eve of the landings, "The Germans were great in Italy and we were very weak. We must watch our step carefully and do nothing foolish. . . . . I said the Germans could concentrate against AVA-LANCHE quicker than we could build up; that operation would need careful watching."[44] Montgomery's words would be prophetic, but Clark would be up to the task.

Chapter 4

DISASTER AVERTED
The Battle of Salerno

"G REAT OPPORTUNITIES LIE AHEAD OF OUR FIFTH
Army, opportunities which will lead to the complete
liberation of Europe from its present rule of tyranny. It is a great privilege
that we of the Fifth Army can be associated with such an enterprise."[1] The
enterprise Clark mentioned to his troops as they boarded the ships to Salerno
was Operation Avalanche. After months of on-and-off again planning, everything was set for the first American forces to invade continental Europe. The
first Western Allied forces, the British Eighth Army under General Bernard
Montgomery, had already breached the Axis wall on 3 September with Operation Baytown, the landing at Reggio di Calabria on the Italian peninsula.

Clark's Fifth Army consisted of two corps, the United States VI Corps,
under Major General Ernest Dawley, and the British X Corps, under Lieutenant General R. L. McCreery. The VI Corps was made up of six American
Divisions: the 34th Division under Major General Charles W. Ryder, the
36th Division under Major General Fred L. Walker, the 45th Division led
by Major General Troy H. Middleton, and the 1st Armored Division under
Major General Ernest Harmon. The 3d Division under Major General
Lucian Truscott would arrive during the battle, as would the 82d Airborne
Division under Major General Matthew Ridgway. The British corps con-
sisted of three divisions: the 46th Division under Major General J. L. I.
Hawkesworth, the 56th Division under Major General G. W. R. Templer,
and the 7th Armoured Division under Major General G. W. E. J. Erskine.
Defending the Salerno beaches were the newly reconstituted 16th Panzer

Division, which consisted of 17 thousand men and around 100 tanks.[2]

Clark waited aboard the USS *Ancon* with VAdm. H. Kent Hewitt, the amphibious forces commander for Avalanche.[3] The initial plan of attack called for the X Corps to land southeast of Salerno and to capture the vital port of Naples. The VI Corps on the right was to secure a bridgehead, defend the X Corps flank and allow the British forces to attack.[4] More specifically the VI Corps with the 36th Division was to land and make a bridgehead of about twelve miles from Agropole to the Sele River. The British X Corps was to land with the 46th Division on the left and the 56th Division on the right and establish themselves from the Sele River to the town of Salerno. After securing their positions X Corps, along with U.S. Army Rangers, British Commandos, and 82d Airborne Division troopers were to take Naples, while a combat team of paratroopers landed along the Volturno River.[5] However, with the loss of the 82d Airborne Division, the plan was greatly hampered, which had a tremendous impact on the battle.

The initial landings took place at 0330 on 8 September, and soldiers met more resistance than they had in landing in North Africa.[6] The Germans, despite being outnumbered and outgunned, greeted the soldiers with loud-speakers repeating over and over, "Come on in and give up. We have you covered!"[7] Aboard the *Ancon* Clark received the first reports around 1700.[8] Though the fighting was tough—the Germans' defense had stopped some artillery and tank units from being deployed—the Allies were advancing and had secured most of their objectives.[9] On the morning of 9 September, Clark decided it was time to pay his first visit to the beachhead.

Upon his arrival Clark met with General McCreery and both decided that the Italian surrender made the fighting more serious, because instead of fighting weak Italian units, the Germans were defending the beachhead.[10] As the Allied commanders met, German commander Albert Kesselring had already made his decision: refusing to yield ground and retreat northward he ordered XIV Panzer Corps to concentrate at Salerno and drive the Allies into the sea.[11] Kesselring, as he would demonstrate throughout the fighting in Italy, was not afraid to make critical decisions based on limited intelligence. Unfortunately for the Allies and Mark Clark his decisions were usually correct.

On 12 September, as Fifth Army pushed inland from the invasion beaches, Clark decided not to return to the *Ancon*, but to relocate to the beachhead. Clark and his staff committed a minor blunder picking their headquarters site. According to Clark their first selection, "a rather large

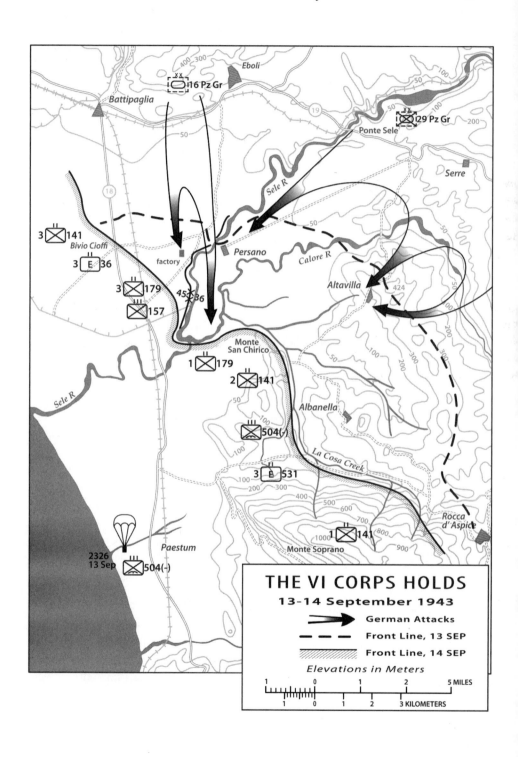

Eboli

16 Pz Gr

Battipaglia

29 Pz Gr

Ponte Sele

Serre

Sele R

3 141
Bivio Cioffi

3 E 36

factory

Persano

Calore R

Altavilla

3 179

157

45 36

Monte
San Chirico

1 179

2 141

Sele R

Albanella

504(-)

La Cosa Creek

3 E 531

Rocca
d' Aspice

2326
13 Sep

504(-)

Paestum

Monte Soprano

1 141

THE VI CORPS HOLDS
13-14 September 1943

German Attacks

Front Line, 13 SEP

Front Line, 14 SEP

Elevations in Meters

1   0   1   2   5 MILES

1   0   1   2   3 KILOMETERS

situation, he acted quickly and wisely in righting the action at Salerno.

With the plans set in motion Clark immediately wrote to 82d Airborne Division commander Matthew Ridgway: "I want you to accept this letter as an order. I realize the time normally needed to prepare for a drop, but this is an exception. I want you to make a drop within our lines on the beachhead and I want you to make it tonight. This is a must."[25] Clark ordered the 504th Parachute Regiment to drop near Paestum during the night of 13–14 September and after dropping enter the defensive line. The following night, 14–15 September, the 505th Parachute Regiment parachute in and protect the right flank of the line.[26] Remembering that Ridgway had been attacked by friendly naval antiaircraft fire on their way to their night drop on Sicily, Clark sent out orders to every one of his units ordering them not to fire. Both drops went off fairly easily, and by 15 September it appeared that the paratroopers had restored the line and the Allied defense.

On 14 September Clark left his headquarters to visit the front lines. The general traveled up to Highway 18 where he came across a tank destroyer battalion and a platoon of medium tanks. After talking with the soldiers of the units, Clark noticed that a group of eight to ten German tanks were in the process of crossing the Sele River. If they succeeded in crossing the river the German tanks would wreak havoc on Fifth Army's already fragile defensive positions. Quickly gathering the commanders of the tank destroyers, Clark led them on an attack that knocked out six of the German tanks, forcing them to retreat.[27] Throughout the day Clark went up and down the lines and helped turn the tide of the battle. While individual leadership in combat can be exaggerated, Clark boosted the morale of his troops and put himself in harm's way during the battle. From personally leading an attack against tanks and yelling at his troops not to give ground, Clark was becoming a splendid battlefield commander and his baptism of fire was nearly complete.

With the situation still in doubt, General Eisenhower, as he often did, wrote a very sincere and complimentary letter to Clark:

> We know you are having a sticky time but you may be sure that everybody is working at full speed to provide the reinforcements you need. . . . You and your people have done a magnificent job. We are all proud of you and since the success of the whole operation depends upon you and your forces; you need have no fear that anything will be neglected in providing you all possible assistance.[28]

Clark did not worry; reinforcements were arriving. Including the 82d Airborne Division airdrop, Truscott's 3d Division had arrived and quickly restored the Allied lines. Still one trouble remained for Clark and his rugged Fifth Army. The only problem, where were the British?

Following Operation Baytown Montgomery and his Eighth Army were slow in linking up with the Fifth Army in Salerno. Though the British faced some resistance, compared to the action Clark's forces were facing the British should have had a much easier go. On 15 September, in the midst of the crisis along the beachhead, Clark received a brief message from Montgomery, "It looks as if you may be having not too good a time, and I do hope that all will go well with you."[29] However, by the next day, Clark wrote back to Montgomery, telling the British general simply, "Here situation well in hand."[30] By 16 September Clark remarked in his diary that for the first time since the landing he felt that everything was going well.[31] Reinforcements from Sicily had bolstered the Allied forces, the XIII Air Support Command had put a tremendous beating on the Axis forces, and naval gunfire from the fleet had turned the tide. Due to this feeling Clark sent out a message to his corps commanders that was to be read to all the troops:

> As your Army Commander, I want to congratulate every officer and enlisted men of the Fifth Army on the accomplishment of their mission of landing on the western coast of Italy. All the more splendid is your achievement when it is realized that it was accomplished against determined German resistance at the beaches. Every foot of our advance had been contested.[32]

Clark's message was well received, and his command received better news on 17 September when Montgomery cabled Clark that their armies had linked up: "we have joined hands delighted to have done so."[33] Though the battle was not yet over Clark had achieved some success, but now had to deal with the first of many changes in command.

Since the VI Corps landing on 8 September Clark almost immediately felt that corps commander Ernest Dawley was in over his head. Clark was not close to Dawley, who was older and more experienced. Clark probably would have removed Dawley prior to the invasion if not for Leslie McNair who believed Dawley would work well with Clark. During the initial phases of the battle and during the crisis period, Clark kept his lack of faith in Dawley to himself. However, on 15 September General Alexander asked Clark how Dawley was performing. Perhaps relieved that someone asked or sensing that Alexander shared the same feeling, he told his superior that he was not entirely satisfied with his performance. Alexander then gave advice to Clark about what to do, "I do not want to interfere with your business, but I have had some ten years' experience in this game of sizing up commanders. I can tell you definitely that you have a broken reed on your hands and I suggest you replace him immediately."[34] With the battle still undecided, Clark took Alexander's advice, but decided the time was not right to act. Clark wrote to Eisenhower on 17 September, and summarized his conversation with Alexander: "I spoke to Alexander about Dawley. He should not be continued in his present job. He appears to go to pieces in the emergencies."[35]

By 18 September, with the arrival of the 3d Division and the withdrawal of Axis forces from the key towns of Battipaglia and Altavilla, Clark believed it was time to remove Dawley. Relieving Dawley on 20 September, Clark wrote in his diary the main reason he decided to remove the VI Corps commander:

> He failed to require strong and deep reconnaissance to the front to determine the enemy situation and probable intentions. When 10th Corps, on his left, left his flank exposed by failure to attain the objective of Battipaglia, Eboli and Ponte Sele, he took no steps to protect his left flank.
>
> When the principal enemy counter-attack occurred on the 13th, he telephoned me and reported a highly critical situation, the first intimation I had received of this. When I asked him what he could do about it, he said: "Nothing, for I have no reserves. All I have is a prayer."[36]

Clark made Major General Dawley deputy army commander until he returned to the United States and eventually John P. Lucas took over command of the VI Corps. By 20 September Clark and the Fifth Army had landed against a determined foe and been pushed to the brink. Rallying his forces and relieving a corps commander Clark had performed admirably, but victory was not yet in his grasp.

By 18 September it was clear to all ground commanders that the tide had turned and the Germans were withdrawing. The Allies had captured airfields, but Naples was still under German control. The Allies in Italy still had not achieved their major objective. From 18 to 27 September Fifth Army pushed the retreating enemy forces outside the beachhead and into the area around Naples. During this advance, Clark met General Montgomery for the first time. Having heard about the temperamental British general, Clark flattered Montgomery by telling him, "The Fifth Army is just a young outfit trying to get along, while your Eighth Army is a battle-tested veteran. We would appreciate having you teach us some of your tricks."[37] Montgomery was very pleased and Clark must have felt relieved that he could work with the British prima donna. Just before leaving Montgomery gave Clark advice that would greatly impact his relationship with Alexander throughout the rest of the war. Montgomery asked if Clark knew Alexander well. After telling Montgomery that he did not, the British general laughed and told Clark, "Well I do. From time to time you will get instructions from Alex that you won't understand. When you do, just tell him to go to hell." A bit surprised, Clark responded, "I've got a better idea, General. If I have trouble, I'll tell you about it and let you tell Alex for me." Just as he pulled away, Montgomery smirked and told the young American commander, "I'll be delighted."[38] This conversation would have little immediate impact, but by January 1944, as the Mediterranean Theater became dominated by the British and as Clark planned for Anzio, his relationship with Alexander and the British worsened. During this time Clark's diaries and his correspondence show a growing bitterness on his part toward the British. By June 1944, with Rome nearly in his grasp, Clark would commit a grave mistake; he ignored Alexander's order to trap and destroy the German Tenth Army, and instead captured Rome. Along with his advice from Montgomery, Clark would receive other news that would turn him slowly against his British allies.

On 22 September, with the Allies progressing nicely, Clark received the first censorship guidance instructions from 15th Army Group. The message infuriated Clark as it read, "First, play up Eighth Army progress henceforth. Second, the Fifth Army is pushing the enemy back on his right flank. Americans may be mentioned. There should be no suggestion that the enemy has made good his getaway."[39] The message infuriated Clark mainly because the Fifth Army had dealt the biggest blow against the Axis forces and had seemingly suffered the most. This message and Clark's conversation with Montgomery foreshadowed what to Clark would become a conspiracy. As the war raged on in Italy, and his forces were stripped for the invasion of France, Clark believed that the war in Italy was becoming a showcase for the dying British Empire. With this belief, and the simple truth that Italy was not as important to the Allies as France, Clark began to fight for publicity for his forces. This was not merely self-serving publicity, but it was for his troops, to boost their morale and keep the families of servicemen informed. Clark could guarantee more publicity for Fifth Army, but first they had to take Naples.

By nightfall of 30 September, Allied forces closed in on Naples and the first major Axis city fell the next day. The first unit credited by Clark with entering Naples was the 23d Armoured Brigade of X Corps.[40] After personally inspecting the city Clark proudly informed Alexander, "Naples has been taken by our troops. I was in the center of the city at noon today."[41] A few days later Clark sent off a quick birthday message to his wife, Renie, "I give you Naples for your birthday. I love you."[42]

Not all was well in Naples; for the next weeks the Allies and civilians had to deal with German time-bombs and booby traps. Clark was shocked by the barbarity of the Germans and wrote in disbelief to his mother, "The Boche left time bombs all over Naples, and we have had many causalities, mostly civilians. That's a despicable way of fighting a war, and he will pay for it dearly. . . . I can assure you there are no holds barred in this war. It is a dirty game."[43] The bombs would cause hundreds of casualties and taught Clark and his Fifth Army that war was hell and that the rest of the campaign would not be easy. With the fall of Naples, Clark and Fifth Army had achieved remarkable success, and for the most part the Battle of Salerno was over. The British captured the Foggia airfields, Naples was captured, but Clark and his forces had one more major obstacle in the way: the Volturno River.

On 21 September, following the withdrawal of enemy forces from Salerno, General Alexander outlined his future plan for Italy: the armies were to cross the Volturno, advance and capture Rome, and eventually capture the northern cities of Leghorn (Livorno) and Florence.[44] While far from Rome, Leghorn, and Florence, the Volturno was the immediate task for Clark and his forces. The Volturno River was about three hundred feet wide, with a fast current and steep banks, so crossing the river would pose some difficulties.[45] Starting on 12 October, with six hundred guns supporting the attack, British X Corps was to begin crossing around 2200 with VI Corps attacking on the morning of 13 October. The task was so difficult that X Corps commander General McCreery argued over the plan of attack with Clark:

I want to make it plain as the commander responsible for British troops and with my experience against Rommel in Egypt, that this is the most difficult job I've faced. You know how I feel about a simultaneous attack. I was opposed to it. We accept your order, of course, and we will go all out, but I have to say that I am embarrassed when an American gives British troops orders that we don't like."[46]

The 3d, 46th, and 56th Divisions, and 7th Armoured Division all faced tough resistance, but in the end Clark turned out to be right, the coordinated attack worked and the river was successfully crossed. The crossing earned Clark high praise from the visiting Secretary of the Treasury Henry Morgenthau who wrote, "I could see that under General Clark's splendid leadership there has been developed a smooth-running machine in which there was in evidence the finest kind of cooperation between the British and American elements. It was very apparent that everything clicked."[47]

By 15 October, with the Allies having crossed the Volturno, Clark pointed out to his chief of staff, Al Gruenther, that for the first time in modern warfare an army that had never fought in combat before had successfully landed against opposition and crossed a major river under similar conditions.[48] By 24 October, Clark moved his headquarters from Naples to Caserta and began planning for an amphibious operation to flank the enemy positions.[49] This plan would never be executed, but it was the first time that Clark and Alexander envisioned a seaborne flanking maneuver. The idea would have to remain stillborn until the Allies advanced further up the peninsula; but that advance would be slowed by strong German defenses that would become known as the Winter Line.

Taking a break in the campaign, on 25 October Clark received an honorary doctorate of political science from Naples University. In his acceptance speech, Clark told the citizens and students of Naples why he was there:

> It is of great significance that you should choose to honor me, a soldier, with an academic degree symbolizing the pursuits of peace and scholarship. I think this most appropriate, for the purpose which brought us to Italy was, in the last analysis, to restore exactly those traditional values of peaceful civilization for which your country has long been removed.[50]

Clark had received his first honor from the Italian people, but he knew the war was a long way from being over.

By 5 November the Battle of Salerno was over and Fifth Army prepared to attack the Winter Line. The Germans had fought well, but suffered less, around thirty-five hundred casualties. As for the Allies, the United States lost about thirty-five hundred men and the British slightly over fifty-five hundred.[51] The battle was one of the most significant of the entire war. This was the first time American forces landed against a German-defended beach, the first capture of a major European city by the Allies, and it marked the first time a United States army had fought against the Germans on the soil of the European mainland. Salerno would teach Clark and the Allies many lessons. First, landings must be made with more men, and second, that the Allies should be careful not to over extend themselves. As for Clark, Salerno was his first taste of battle and he performed well.

In many ways, Salerno was Clark at his best. While the capture of Rome is regarded as the high point of his career, Clark's actions at Salerno were those of an experienced and capable commander, and at times he performed brilliantly. General Eisenhower wrote of Clark at Salerno, "He proved to be a fine battle leader and fully justified the personal confidence that had impelled me to assign him to such as important position."[52]

Historians have long debated the turnaround at Salerno. Though he made plans for evacuation, Clark never believed victory was in doubt. Writing to his mother after the Germans began their withdrawal:

> This has been a real battle. We have done well, and we have learned many lessons. I have to pinch myself sometimes to realize that I am in command of this show which includes large numbers of American troops, as well as British. . . . We are doing alright, and we certainly gave the German a battle. I was rather astounded, from reading the press accounts, that they thought we might pull out. That was never in our thoughts. We would have stayed here until "hell froze over."[53]

Some historians and veterans of the battle believed the advancing British Eighth Army forced the Axis forces to withdraw. While Eighth Army had a significant impact on the battle; by the time they arrived into the Fifth Army area the battle was already well in hand. After the war General Montgomery's chief of staff, Maj. Gen. Sir Francis De Guinard, stated, "Some would like to think—I did at the time—that we helped, if not saved, the situation at Salerno. But now I doubt whether we influenced matters to any great extent. General Clark had everything under control *before* Eighth Army appeared on the scene."[54]

The reasons the battle turned in favor of the Allies were, as mentioned previously, the arrival of reinforcements and Allied air and naval support. Alexander, in his memoirs, wrote, "My conclusion is that if the Navy and the Army had not enjoyed air superiority at Salerno the operation would have failed."[55] These three aspects combined were decisive. What is clear is that the surrender of the Italian government did not help the Allies in Salerno. During the critical period of the battle Clark wrote his wife and explained that the Allies hope that they could walk onto the beaches was wrong:

> . . . we had hoped that Italy's collapse would so upset the Germans that they could not give their full effort to resisting us at the beaches. We had the wrong dope on that, for apparently the German had anticipated such a collapse by Italy and had taken over all the coast defenses and had moved their troops in to meet us.[56]

The landings at Salerno, though behind schedule, had succeeded in achieving every objective. Alexander had issued future plans for Italy on 21 September, but it was not yet clear if the Allies would stay in Italy. However, with the success of the battle and the crossing of the Volturno River, it was evident that the Allies were going to stay. Not all were pleased with this decision as many believed fighting in Italy would drain Allied strength while gaining no major strategic objective. This was inaccurate as *politically* the Allies had no choice but to fight in Italy. If it was not in Italy, it would have had to have been elsewhere, but Italy offered the best chance for the Allies to fight the Germans and prevent them from massing against the Soviets on the Eastern Front. Therefore the decision was made to stay and fight, but it would not be easy, as Eisenhower and Alexander wrote about the future campaign:

> It would therefore appear that we are committed to a long and costly advance to Rome, a "slogging match," with our present slight superiority in formations on the battle-front offset by the enemy opportunity for relief; for without sufficient resources in craft no outflanking amphibious operation of a size sufficient to speed up our rat of advance is possible. There is a danger that a successful conclusion of this "slogging match" might leave us north of Rome in such a state of exhaustion and weakness as not to be able to hold what we have gained, if the Germans bring down from the north fresh divisions for a counter-offensive.[57]

A disgruntled and out of work George S. Patton perhaps said it best about Clark's position in the war following the Battle of Salerno, "I was terribly disappointed not to land at Salerno instead of Wayne but now I think it was lucky for many reasons that I can say."[58] Soon Patton would be running wild across Europe galvanizing the imaginations of the world, while Clark would be stuck in the mud, trolling across the mountains in the winter.

Chapter 5

STUCK IN THE MOUNTAINS
The First Winter

A FTER BURSTING ACROSS THE VOLTURNO RIVER, THE Allied drive began to slow and by 15 November Clark called the offensive to a halt.[1] The Allied armies were exhausted from the constant battle that had lasted since 8 September and needed rest. Also, by this time the weather had turned ugly; constant rain made the roads in the area unusable, slowing the advance. Lastly, the Allies had to stop, gather themselves, and prepare for a tough task: breaking the Winter Line. The formidable line facing Fifth Army stretched north through Monte Camino, Monte Mignano, Monte Santa Croce, and through to the British Eighth Army zone of responsibility.[2] The line protected the gateway to Rome, the Liri Valley. If the Allies could break through, their tanks could run wild across the Liri and take the sacred city. In Alexander's 15th Army Group head-quarters, the intelligence section believed that only a planned, concentrated attack could pierce the line. Further, Alexander and Clark both believed that an amphibious landing would greatly aid the capture of Rome.[3] The Winter Line would test Clark and his soldiers, because not only was the line a tough nut to crack, but the Germans had made a decision to stay and fight.

Hitler's original plan was to have Kesselring's forces retreat north of Rome where they would then come under the command of Rommel and the 14th German Army. However, Kesselring's delay at Salerno and his rosy op-timism slowly persuaded Hitler to stay and fight in central Italy. Hitler, however, like most of the officers of the Oberkommando der Wehrmacht (OKW), believed that the Allies had no intention of fighting to the Alps, but instead would jump to the Balkans.[4] This fear led Hitler to bring in both Rommel and Kesselring for interviews in October 1943. Both commanders argued their viewpoints, with Rommel believing that the original plan to retreat north was proper, while Kesselring believed that would put the Allies closer to Germany and give up great defensive territory. After hearing the two commanders, Hitler agreed with Kesselring, and on 6 November, named him commander in chief Southwest and Army Group C, which consisted of the German 10th and 14th Armies.[5] This decision had a major impact on the war. It meant that the Allies would have to slug their way through Italy for the rest of the war. The decision aided the Allied strategic plans as one of the major objectives of the Italian campaign, other than the capture of Rome, was to engage as many German divisions as possible. With Hitler's decision to stay, the Germans immediately moved in two other divisions to face the Fifth Army and would pour in more throughout the rest of the war.

The Fifth Army now faced five divisions, the 94th Grenadier Division along the Garigliano River to about two miles east of Castelforte, the 15th Panzer Grenadier Division on left of the 94th, the 3d Panzer Grenadier Division located between Mignano and Venafro, the 26th Panzer Division from Venafro to Filignano, and the 305th Grenadier Division on the left of the 26th all the way into Eighth Army's zone.[6] By the end of November, the newly reformed 44th Grenadier Division from Stalingrad would replace the 26th Panzer Division in the line.[7] With the Germans growing in strength, the Americans and British in Italy also received reinforcements that would greatly help in the attack on the Winter Line.

During November 1943, Clark lost the 82d Airborne Division, less the 504th Parachute Infantry Regiment, and the British 7th Armoured Division. This left the British X Corps with two divisions, the 46th and 56th, that held a front of about sixteen miles from the Mediterranean Sea to Capua. The American VI Corps now consisted of the 3d Division, the 45th Division, the 34th Division, with the 1st Armored Division still arriving, and 36th Division in bivouac. The entire VI Corps line ran twenty miles from Caspoli through the Mignano Gap to Venafro.[8] On 18 November, U.S. II Corps under Major General Geoffrey Keyes was established and took over the 3d and 36th Divisions.[9] In addition, the 88th Division and 85th Division would arrive later, but too late to fight in the coming offensive. By Thanksgiving Clark would receive what would become one of his best outfits, the 1st Special Service Force under Colonel Robert T. Fredericks. The unit consisted of American and Canadian soldiers trained in nearly every task of warfare, from ski assault

1 Dec 1942: Clark receives a medal in Algeria with Eisenhower, following the invasion of North Africa. Clark served as Eisenhower's deputy.—*NARA II (Box 157-174426)*

1943: Gen. George C. Marshal walks with Clark and Lt. Gen. George S. Patton in North Africa. —*NARA II (Box 200-186323)*

1943: Clark walks with the Mohammed V, Sultan of Morocco and his son. —*NARA II (Box 164-176503)*

1 Feb 1943:
Clark with
Gen. Auguste
Nogues,
Resident
General
of French
Morocco
in Oujda.
—*NARA II
(Box 510-
273108)*

17 Sep 1943:
Clark and
Eisenhower
shortly after
the landings
at Salerno.
—*NARA II (Box
402-243091)*

20 Sep 1943:
Clark with Air
Marshal Arthur
Tedder, Maj.
Gen. Edwin J.
House and Maj.
Gen. Troy H.
Middleton at
45th Infantry
Division HQ
near Battipagalia.
—*NARA II (Box
807-380220)*

25 Oct 1943: Clark receiving an honorary degree from the University of Naples following the liberation of the city. —*NARA II (Box 184-182069)*

22 Oct 1943: Clark and Dwight D. Eisenhower leaving 3d Infantry Division HQ following a meeting. —*NARA II (Box 204-187484)*

13 Nov 1943: Mark Clark Special Train in Naples, Italy. —*NARA II (Box 501-273162)*

13 Oct 1943: Italian troops cheering news of Italian surrender.—*NARA II (Box 208-188777)*

6 Dec 1943: The British attack the mountainside and capture the town of Capua.
—*NARA II (Box 204-187519)*

Right: 20 Oct 1943: Clark going over a map with Secretary of Treasury Henry Morganthau near 34th Infantry Division HQ. *—NARA II (Box 208-188780)*

Below: 19 Dec 1943: Clark and Ike talk near San Pietro.*—NARA II (Box 204-187522)*

25 Dec 1943:
Clark with Maj.
Gen. Lucian K.
Truscott and Maj.
Gen. Geoffrey
Keyes at II Corps
HQ.—*NARA II*
(Box 204-187524)

1943: Clark con-
gratulates soldiers at
Salerno.—*NARA II*
(Box 53-Folder YY-
AEF-Italy-Salerno)

25 Dec 1943:
Clark and Maj.
Gen. John P.
Lucas near
Roccaravindola,
Italy.—*NARA II*
(Box 204-187523)

19 Dec 1943: Clark and Eisenhower walk away from an antiaircraft gun position. Maj. Gen. Fred L. Walker, CG of 36th Infantry Division and Geoffrey Keyes follow behind.
—*NARA II (Box 234-195976)*

22 Jan 1944: Clark approaching Anzio in a PT boat.—*NARA II (Box 198-185793)*

26 Jan 1944: American forces land at Anzio as seen from the land.
—*NARA II (Box 51-Folder E AEF-Italy-Anzio-Lansing Op)*

26 Jan 1944: American forces land at Anzio as seen from the sea.
—*NARA II (Box 51-Folder E AEF-Italy-Anzio-Lansing Op)*

22 Jan 1944: Soldiers from the 36th Division's 143d Infantry Regiment take shelter from a German sniper following the failed crossing of the Rapido River. —*NARA II (Box 752-356084)*

15 Feb 1944: Allied bombers hit the abbey atop Monte Cassino. —*NARA II (Box 204-187461)*

15 Feb 1944: Same as above, from a different perspective. —*NARA II (Box 204-187460)*

1 Feb 1944: Clark looks nervous as he prepares to land at Anzio with Brig. Gen. Thomas H. Lewis aboard Clark's C-47.
—*NARA II (Box 204–187467)*

6 Feb 1944: The Abbey at Monte Cassino before being destroyed by Allied bombs.
—*NARA II (Box 390–239682)*

20 March 1944: Cpl. Sheldon C. Peterson plants a warning sign at Anzio.
—*NARA II (Box 50–Folder W-2 AEF Anzio-Action)*

7 Mar 1944: Truscott looks over a map soon after taking command of the VI Corps following the Anzio landings.
—*NARA II (Box 415-246592)*

30 April 1944: Sir Harold Alexander pins the Honorary Knight Commander of the Most Excellent Order of the British Empire medal on Clark.
—*NARA II (Box 202-187207)*

Above: 7 Apr 1944: Clark and Lt. Gen. Oliver H.W. Leese at British Eighth Army HQ. — *NARA II (Box 210-189250)*

Left: 9 Apr 1944: Lt. Gen. Jacob L. Devers (left), Deputy Commander Mediterranean Theater, with Clark and Fifth Army Chief of Staff Al Gruenther (center). —*NARA II (Box 693-329919)*

Above: 30 May 1944: Approach to Monte Cassino. The picture shows the excellent line of fire the Germans possessed near the abbey. —*NARA II (Box 709-337120)*

Right: 7 Apr 1944: Clark poses with Col. William O. Darby, CO of 179th Infantry Regiment, 45th Infantry Division. Darby was also the former commander officer of 6615th Ranger Force which lost two battalions following the landing at Anzio. —*NARA II (Box 938-437681)*

Left: 5 June 1944:
Fifth Army soldiers
pass the Roman
Coliseum after
capturing Rome.
—*NARA II (Box
214-190312)*

Below: 5 June 1944:
A father raises his
son to honor the
arrival of American
soldiers in Rome.
—*NARA II (Box
214-190314)*

Above: 5 June 1944:
Clark enters Rome.
—*NARA II (Box
218-191385)*

Center: 3 June 1944:
Clark's office while
at Anzio.—*NARA II
(Box 652-312995)*

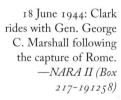

18 June 1944: Clark
rides with Gen. George
C. Marshall following
the capture of Rome.
—*NARA II (Box
217-191258)*

4 June 1944: Clark with II Corps Commander Keyes (left) and Brig. Gen. Robert T. Frederick (right), 1st Special Service Force commander, meet on the outskirts of Rome right before the final push into the city.—*NARA II (Box 908-424727)*

5 Jun 1944: Clark enters Rome surrounded by exuberant Romans.—*NARA II (Box 542-282294)*

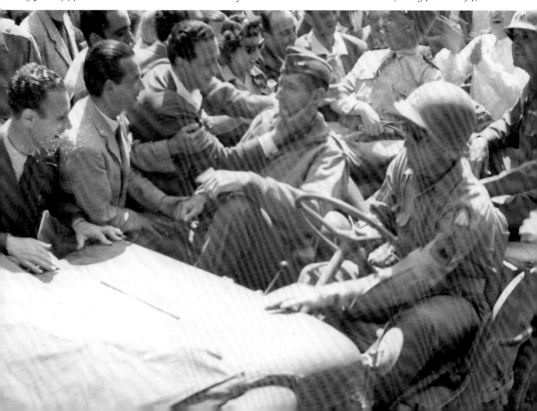

to airborne raids.[10] Lastly Clark would begin to receive his first French and Italian units. By the end of September the Italian government offered to assist in removing the Germans from Italy. On the last day of October the 1st Motorized Group (I Raggruppamento Italiano Motorizzato) under Brigadier General Vincenzo di Pino joined II Corps. The French Expeditionary Corps (FEC), another unit that would become one of Clark's best, would arrive in December under the command of Clark's old adversary General Alphonse Juin. The FEC consisted of two divisions, the 2d Moroccan Infantry Division and the 3d Algerian Infantry Division.[11] By the end of November Clark's Fifth Army had grown from 130,247 men to 243,827.[12] With his army rested and refitted the attack on the fierce Winter Line was about to begin.

On 9 November General Alexander issued his plans to break the Winter Line and take Rome. The attack was to come in three phases. The first called for the Eighth Army to advance in the Pescara-Popoli-Collarmele area and threaten the enemy lines of communication. When Alexander deemed Phase I was working Fifth Army would attack from its positions and drive up the Liri and Sacco Valleys to Frosinone. Phase III would then consist of an amphibious landing south of Rome by a Regimental Combat Team (RCT) aimed at seizing the Colli Laziali (Alban Hills).[13] More specifically, for Fifth Army Clark planned a three phase assault as well. The first assault called for II and X Corps to attack the southeastern end of the Liri Valley and to take Monte Camino, Monte la Difensa, and Monte Maggiore. When these key points were taken, II Corps would shift to the north and take Monte Sammucro, while VI Corps attacked west with one division on the Colli-Atina road and the other division of the Filignano-Sant'Elia road. The final phase would constitute the main attack. The VI Corps would make the main effort to advance north and northwest of the town of Cassino, while the II Corps was to attack to the northwest along Highway 6.[14] The plans were set, and both Clark and the British believed the fighting would be quick. But, just like the entire Italian campaign, the terrain and the well trained German forces would stall any hope of a quick victory.

In a letter to his wife before the battle Clark commented on the terrain of Italy: "Our advance has been steady, but we are hitting some pretty tough resistance right now. I am so anxious to get on with this thing towards Rome. I wish you could see the terrain. It is so mountainous and so easily defended, and the Germans seem to be reinforcing."[15] General Fred L. Walker, commander of the 36th Division commented on the Allied plan of attack on the Winter Line:

The Italian campaign will not be finished this week, nor next. Our wasteful policy or method of taking one mountain mass after another gains no tactical advantage, locally. There is always another mountain mass beyond with the Germans dug in on it, just as before. Somebody on top side, who control of the required means, should figure out a way to decisively defeat the German army in Italy, instead of just pushing, pushing, pushing.[16]

It was becoming apparent that any commander from army-level on down believed that the Italian campaign was going to be a long, slow, slugging match. Italy was not the place for a George Patton or any other hard driving armored commander. Neither the geography of Italy nor the German defenders would have allowed it. The argument that some other American general commanding Fifth Army could have done anything differently ignores the terribly difficult terrain. The Germans were too well trained and too well dug in for another commander to have done anything differently. While perhaps, smaller tactical decisions could have been made differently, the truth of the matter is that Clark and the Allies had no other choice. They either had to fight the hard fight, or leave Italy all together.

Nearing the beginning of the offensive, Clark was growing concerned with the morale and health of his Fifth Army. While the army had been in constant fighting for two months, the soldiers were handling everything well, but with winter and a new offensive coming, Clark issued a memo to his subordinates to give special attention to their troops:

> As our campaign continues I feel that we must give particularly careful attention of the welfare of our troops. . . . I am confident that few of the complaints listed in his report apply to Fifth Army personnel. I also realize that the soldier considers that he has an inherent right to grumble frequently merely for the sake of grumbling. Nevertheless, all such complaints must be carefully examined in order that their basis, if any, can be determined.[17]

By early December the weather had turned worse, and Clark would write in his memoirs that he thought the upcoming offensive was similar to the Eastern Theater.[18] Though not as large scale, the fighting in Italy during the winter of 1943–1944 was similar and would prove some of the hardest of the war.

The Fifth Army attack began on 1 December with the British X Corps assault on Monte Camino. The offensive worked extremely well. During the first nine days of the attack X Corps had taken two-thirds of the Camino hill mass, and II Corps, with the 1st Special Service Force, had advanced well on to Monte La Difensa. By 10 December the entire Camino hill mass was secured and the first phase of Clark's plan was complete.[19]

Phase II of Clark's Fifth Army plan officially began on 7 December; this plan called for a smaller role for the X Corps, as it would consolidate its area, and assist the II Corps in taking Monte Sammucro. The VI Corps, meanwhile, was set to take the high ground around Atina and Sant'Elia, but the main effort in this phase would be made by II Corps, which was to attack and seize Monte Lungo and San Pietro.[20] The hardest task would prove to be San Pietro. Two battles would be fought over the area, the first beginning on 7 December, the second on 15 December.[21] During the second battle Clark visited the front and came across a cold and shivering private. On further inspection Clark noticed that the soldier did not have on overshoes. When he asked the soldier why he did not have them on, the private told the general that his previous pair had worn out, and since his feet were too small he could not find a replacement pair. Clark, surprised at how a soldier could not find a replacement pair, found the soldier's foot size and solved the problem. The soldier's foot size was a small 7A, and as Clark later found out, only sixty-seven pairs of 7A's had been made out of a run of a hundred thousand. Before leaving Clark told the cold soldier, "I'll get you a pair of shoes if there is a pair that size anywhere in the Mediterranean Theater."[22] Ultimately Clark did find a pair for the soldier.

Finally, after weeks of hard fighting, San Pietro fell on 17 December. The battle was costly, and the 36th Division alone suffered 1,200 casualties; 150 killed, 800 wounded, and 250 missing.[23] Though San Pietro had fallen and Phase I of Clark's plan had succeeded, by New Year's Day 1944 the Allied offensive was slowing. The weather and troop exhaustion, combined with the German defense, was too much to overcome. Phase II of Clark's plan was nearly complete, but the VI Corps did not take the high ground near Sant'Elia and Atina. However, by 16 December Clark issued a directive to begin Phase III. As Clark wrote following the battle, "The victory of San Pietro, won chiefly by hard slugging infantrymen against the stiffest kind of resistance, completes the wrecking of the double doors which have blocked our entrance into the Cassino plain."[24] The doors may have been wrecked, but the Fifth Army and the Allies in Italy were in no condition to walk through them.

While the battle raged along the Winter Line, Clark was not only busy planning and observing the action, but dealing with numerous dignitaries. During the initial fighting Clark met, for the first time, a party from the Soviet Union. Clark welcomed the group into his headquarters and was surprised when one Russian general blurted out "We want to see what the Americans are like in action against the Huns. We would like to get right up to the front." A smiling Clark was happy to oblige and as he poured a round of vodka, looked up and told the party, "I'll make certain that you see some fighting."[25] The Soviet delegation was pleased by what they saw and believed Clark was correct in his views that the action along the Winter Line was similar to the battle along the Eastern Front.

On 8 December Clark rushed off to meet a plane of dignitaries. Emerging from the aircraft was General Henry Arnold, commander of the United States Army Air Force, General Carl Spaatz, Admiral William Leahy, General Eisenhower, Harry Hopkins, and finally President Roosevelt. Clark followed the party as Roosevelt handed out numerous decorations. Nearing the end, the President whirled around and pinned a Distinguished Service Cross on Clark's chest for "extraordinary heroism in action" for his performance during Salerno.[26] After awarding the medal, Roosevelt handed Clark a letter that the president had expected would need to be delivered, because he did not believe the two would have a chance to meet:

> I am very sorry to miss seeing you, but much as I wanted to come to Italy to see you at the front and to greet your fighting army there, I was told I just could not go! You and your Fifth Army are doing a magnificent job under the most trying conditions imaginable. Eye witnesses have told me about the fighting, so I know how tough it is.
>
> I also have been told of your personal courage in leading your forces, and especially of your gallantry in those first desperate days after the landing, when by personal example and fine inspiration to your officers at the front line, there was averted a critical situation in which the enemy might have burst through with disastrous results.
>
> Keep on giving it all you have, and Rome will be ours and more beyond!
>
> I am grateful to have such a staunch, fighting general.[27]

Aside from the high praise of President Roosevelt, on 21 December Clark received a message from General Alexander, "I have the pleasure to inform you that His Majesty The King has been graciously pleased to appoint you, LG Mark W. Clark an Honorary Knight Commander of the Most Excellent Order of the British Empire."[28] It seemed that Clark and his performance so far was being applauded, not only in his native country, but in Great Britain as well. The last honor given to Clark in December was an honor that Clark did not want because it would strip him of his beloved Fifth Army. During the last days of December, Clark received a secret message:

> LTG Clark to be assigned to command the Seventh Army effective at a date to be determined later. Effective 1 January 1944 General Clark will be given administrative and operational control of Headquarters Seventh Army and the Seventh Army Headquarters units. . . . General Clark to remain in command of the Fifth Army until such time as he considers it necessary to be relieved to order to devote his time exclusively to Operation ANVIL.[29]

While flattered to receive such an appointment, he did not want to leave his Fifth Army or the Italian theater. During this time, he believed that the best way to put pressure on the Germans was to maintain pressure in Italy, and that Operation Anvil, the invasion of Southern France, was not necessary, as his forces in Italy could achieve the desired results. After receiving the order, Clark sent part of his staff to begin planning for Anvil, but made it clear he would not leave until after Rome had fallen. With the Winter Line unbroken, Clark and the Allies devised a plan to capture Rome. This plan would lead to the greatest controversies of Clark's career and the war in Italy; it would make the Rapido River, Anzio, and Cassino famous around the world and greatly shift Clark's ideas on the British and fighting in Italy.

Chapter 6

BLOODY RIVER
The Rapido River Crossing and the Planning for Anzio

THE OLD MAN WAS SICK AND TIRED. HIS JOB HAD WORN him down, and pneumonia plagued his body. All was not lost—he was recuperating in one of his favorite locations, Marrakech, and enjoying Jane Austin's *Sense and Sensibility*. As Winston Churchill basked in the warm weather his mind went back over past events. Over the last three years the prime minister had risen from what he called "the wilderness" to the leadership of a warring nation. Now the war was advancing and Great Britain was preparing for a cross-channel invasion of France. Yet, something plagued him: what to do about Italy? By the winter of 1943 Benito Mussolini was out of power and Sicily had been freed, but Allied troops were still slogging through southern Italy. With the cross-channel invasion nearing, manpower and supplies were limited, but the wily old man had one last card to play, an amphibious operation to seize Rome. Winston Churchill wanted to send "a wildcat on to the shore" of Italy, but instead he got "a stranded whale."[1]

The "stranded whale" was Anzio. Historians and veterans of Anzio have long debated almost everything about the operation, which entered the planning stage in November 1943. Some question the necessity of the entire Italian campaign while others question the need for an amphibious assault so near in time to Operation Overlord. Most historians place the blame on the VI Corps commander, Major General John P. Lucas. Lucas led his force onto

79

the beaches of Anzio on 22 January 1944, and though the landing was a complete surprise, within a matter of days his force was fighting for its life. The major mistake Lucas made, both historians and veterans argue, was his failure to seize the Alban Hills overlooking the Anzio beachhead. Lucas's superior, Fifth Army commander Mark W. Clark, once wrote: "If we could seize the Alban Hills, we could threaten the Gustav Line defenders from the rear and might force the enemy to give up his powerful defensive line in order to avoid entrapment."[2] (The Gustav Line was the largest line of German defenders in what made up the Winter Line.) However, the failure to seize the Alban Hills and force the Germans to retreat was not due to Lucas's incompetence; it was due instead to wishful thinking, faulty operational planning, and the German army's ability to respond forcefully and aggressively.

By the winter of 1943 Winston Churchill, unchecked by his military advisors at Marrakech, had persuaded U.S. President Franklin D. Roosevelt, Supreme Allied Commander Dwight D. Eisenhower, and other commanders that Anzio was a risk worth taking.[3] Strengthened by Eisenhower's departure from the Mediterranean, Churchill had a freer hand in Italy, and he badly wanted Rome. By November, Churchill had discussed his plan with 15th Army Group commander, General Sir Harold Alexander. By 8 November Alexander issued instructions to Clark to begin planning for an amphibious landing at Anzio, thirty-five miles below Rome.[4] Alexander hoped that the Anzio landing would coincide with Fifth Army's breakthrough of the Gustav Line, which would enable the Allied forces to link up in seven days and move on to Rome. By 25 November Clark and the Fifth Army staff prepared the operation, codenamed Shingle. In their plan, one division would land at Anzio and assist the Fifth Army in its drive on the Alban Hills.[5] Already, the Anzio plan was troubled, as the two plans differed on the Alban Hills. Alexander wanted the Anzio force to seize the Alban Hills and advance towards Rome, while Clark wanted the Fifth Army only to move towards the Alban Hills.

The U.S. VI Corps under Lucas's command would spearhead the invasion. Lucas had commanded VI Corps since September 1943. Older than Clark, he was now fifty-four and, as he put it in his diary, he felt "every year of it."[6] Lucas first garnered attention as commander of the 3d Division at Fort Lewis, Washington, and later as he replaced Lieutenant General Omar N. Bradley as commander of the II Corps. Characterized as having "military stature, prestige, and experience" by General Marshall, Lucas was well respected, but some believed him to be too old and afraid to take risks.[7] Anzio would indeed be a risk, as Lucas knew better than anyone.

Under the VI Corps, the U.S. 3d Division, commanded by Major General Lucian Truscott, and the British 1st Division, commanded by Major General W.R.C. Penney, were to land on the Anzio beachhead. Three Ranger battalions under Colonel William O. Darby, personally trained by Truscott, along with the 83d Chemical Battalion, the 504th and 509th Parachute Infantry regiments under Colonel Reuben Tucker, and one Regimental Combat Team of the 45th Infantry Division would support the two divisions.[8] The plan was for 1st Division to land and hold down the left flank, while 3d Division would land and hold down the right flank of the beachhead. The 509th PIR and the Ranger battalions planned to seize the port of Anzio, while the 504th PIR would drop along the Anzio-Albano Highway, at the base of the Alban Hills to establish blocking positions until the main force arrived.[9] Lucas received his first combat orders from Clark on December 27, which read that the landing force was to:

1. Seize and secure a beachhead in the vicinity of Anzio
2. Advance and secure the Colli Laziali[10]
3. Be prepared to advance on Rome[11]

To support the Anzio landings Clark planned a massive attack by the Fifth Army, hoping to pin down the Germans and prevent them from moving troops to the beachhead.[12] He ordered a four-phase attack. On 12 January the French Expeditionary Corps and the 2d Moroccan and 3d Algerian Divisions were to advance toward the villages of Atina and San Elia and seize the high ground north and northwest of Cassino. Alexander believed the attack was vital to the success of Anzio: "The momentum of our advance must be maintained at all costs to the limit of our resources. The enemy will be compelled to react to the threat to his communications and rear, and advantage must be taken of this to break through his main defences, and to ensure that the two forces operating under Com[man]d[er] Fifth Army to join hands at the earliest possible moment."[13]

On 15 January II Corps, 1st Armored Division, and the 34th and 36th Divisions were to seize and secure Monte Trocchio, the high ground above the Rapido River. With this ground taken the British X Corps, the 5th, 46th and 56th Divisions, and the 23d Armoured Brigade were to attack the main German lines. By 17 January X Corps was to cross the Garigliano River just south of the Rapido and seize beachheads near Sant'Ambrogio and Minturno. After the crossing they were then to seize the high ground that over-

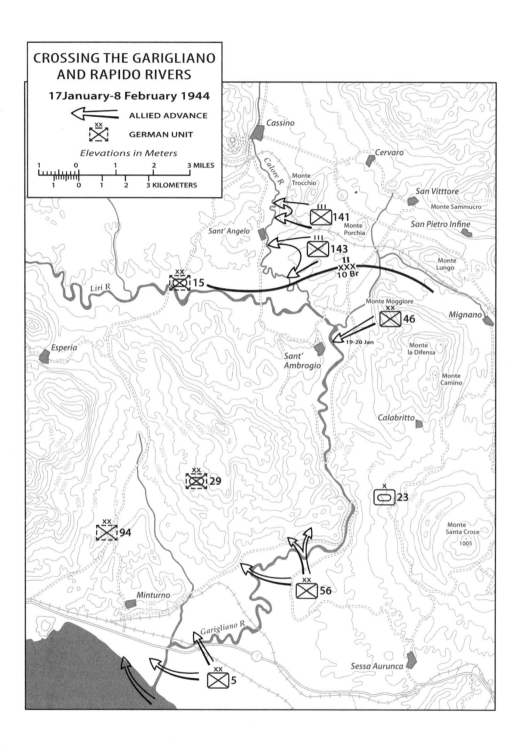

**CROSSING THE GARIGLIANO
AND RAPIDO RIVERS**

17 January-8 February 1944

⟵   ALLIED ADVANCE

⊠   GERMAN UNIT

Elevations in Meters

1   0   1   2   3 MILES

1   0   1   2   3 KILOMETERS

Cassino

Cervaro

Calore R.

Monte
Trocchio

San Vitttore

Monte Sammucro

141

San Pietro Infine

Sant' Angelo

Monte
Porchia

143

Monte
Lungo

11
10 Br

Monte Moggiore

Mignano

Liri R.

15

46

19-20 Jan

Monte
la Difensa

Esperia

Sant'
Ambrogio

Monte
Camino

Calabritto

29

23

94

Monte
Santa Croce
1005

Minturno

56

Garigliano R.

Sessa Aurunca

5

looked the Liri Valley. Finally, on 20 January II Corps would cross the Rapido River near Highway 6 and establish a beachhead near Sant'Angelo. With the Allied armor concentrated, Fifth Army would then break through the Gustav Line about the time that VI Corps was to land at Anzio.[14]

As the plan neared completion, hope for success gave way to quiet fear. The main point of contention was the Alban Hills. When Lucas received Clark's 27 December order he began to believe the operation would be nearly impossible to accomplish. Neither an ardent believer in the plan nor in British supremacy in the Mediterranean, Lucas wrote in his diary: "this whole affair has a strong odor of Gallipoli and apparently the same amateur is still on the coach's bench."[15] Other commanders in the VI Corps came to the same view as Lucas. Third Division commander Maj. Gen. Lucian Truscott, who would play a greater role as the battle progressed, later wrote in his memoirs: "no one below Army level believed the landing of two divisions at Anzio would cause a German withdrawal."[16]

After he issued his 27 December order Clark's fear that Lucas could not seize the hills grew stronger. This concern was not his alone. Eisenhower's G-2, British Brigadier General Kenneth Strong, believed the Anzio landing would not achieve its intended goals. Strong argued that Rome was politically important to Hitler, and the Germans would not withdraw northward. The Germans were going to fight and could move unengaged divisions from France and Yugoslavia to Anzio.[17] Most of this intelligence was ignored, but would prove chillingly accurate.

With the landing growing closer Clark's fear got the best of him, and on 12 January he reissued orders to Lucas that read:

1. Seize and secure a beachhead in the vicinity of Anzio
2. Advance on Colli Laziali[18]

Clark no longer believed Lucas could secure the Alban Hills and changed his instructions from "Advance and secure the Colli Laziali" to "*Advance on* Colli Laziali." To avoid confusion, Clark sent his G-3, Brigadier General Donald Brann, to reinforce his objective and make "it clear that Lucas' primary mission was to seize and secure a beachhead," not to take the hills and stretch his forces.[19] This significant change greatly relieved Lucas and buoyed his spirits in his belief that now the operation might succeed.

In preparation for the landing VI Corps held a rehearsal landing on 18 January. The exercise, codenamed Webfoot, was a disaster and put Lucas in a foul mood.[20] With the landings only three days away Fifth Army had suffered a major setback against the German forces and participated in a miserable training exercise. According to Clark during Webfoot the VI Corps lost forty-three DUKWs; nineteen 105s, including fire control equipment; seven 57mm anti-tank guns; and two 37s.[21] Even hard-charging Lucian Truscott wondered if Anzio would be a "forlorn hope" or a "suicide dash."[22] In his official report to Clark on the exercise it is clear that Truscott believed the Anzio landing was doomed. His most salient points are as follows:

> No military force can hope to assault a defended beach with prospects of success unless it can be landed on shore in tactical order and proper condition to engage in combat.
> * No single battalion landed on time or in formation.
> * Practically no infantry tactical vehicles were landed.
> * No tanks were landed.
> To land this Division on 'SHINGLE' beaches as it was landed during this rehearsal would be to invite disaster if the enemy should counterattack at daylight with 40 or 50 tanks. There is no doubt that the success of the operation would be jeopardized or that the loss of life and material would be excessive.
>
> In my opinion, there is grave need for additional training to insure that assault troops will be landed in condition to accomplish their missions. I recommend a rehearsal.[23]

Regardless of many severe reservations and doubts, final preparations for the landings were made. Prior to 22 January George Patton, Lucas's good friend, wrote him a sarcastic letter: "John, there is no one in this Army I hate to see killed as much as you, but you can't get out of this alive. Of course, you might be badly wounded. No one ever blames a wounded general."[24]

Unlike Patton, Clark sent a more serious note to Lucas as he was set to leave. Greatly affected by the 9 September 1943 Salerno landings, Clark gave Lucas some advice: "Don't stick your neck out, Johnny. I did at Salerno and got into trouble."[25] This comment would later haunt the whole Anzio operation; years later, critics of the landing would say a "Salerno Complex" affected Lucas's leadership and prevented him from seizing the Alban Hills.

Upset by the disastrous rehearsal and the stalled Fifth Army offensive and annoyed with Clark for planning to establish a small command post near the landings, Lucas wrote his most critical condemnation of Anzio:

Army has gone nuts again. The general idea seems to be that the Germans are licked and are fleeing in disorder and nothing remains but to mop up. The only reason for such a belief is that we have recently been able to advance a few miles against them [in the Cassino area] with comparative ease. The Hun has pulled back a bit but I haven't seen the desperate fighting I have during the last four months without learning something. We are not (repeat not) in Rome yet. They will end up by putting me ashore with inadequate forces and get me in a serious jam. Then, who will take the blame.[26]

Like an old Johnny Carson skit, Lucas saw into the future and would be proven right on two accounts. His VI Corps was inadequate and too small a force to seize the Alban Hills, and when the U.S. Army went looking for a scapegoat, Lucas was the perfect candidate.

By this time Fifth Army had begun its preliminary operations towards the Gustav Line to support the landings. Confusion reigned, however, just as it had in most of the planning for Anzio, and Fifth Army failed in nearly every objective. While the French Corps achieved success in advancing towards Cassino, and the II Corps took Mt. Trocchio, British X Corps and 36th Division failed to penetrate the Liri Valley. With a few days remaining until the landing, the 36th Division would be seriously blooded on the Rapido River.

The operations along the Rapido River became and would remain a dark cloud over the reputation of Mark W. Clark. Problems began prior to the river crossing. Under the plan, codenamed Operation Panther, British X Corps was to cross the Garigliano River with the 56th and 46th Divisions and secure a bridgehead near Sant'Ambrogio. This attack would secure the high ground dominating the Liri Valley and the ground near the Rapido River crossing point.[27] The initial attacks by the 56th Division from 17–19 January met with success, but the 46th Division failed in its objective to secure the high ground.

This would have a serious impact on the Rapido crossing. With the Germans still in possession of the high ground, Clark knew full well that the crossing of the Rapido River would be deadly:

The failure of the attack of the 46th Division to reach its objective across the [Garigliano] River[28] towards the San Ambrogio was quite a blow. I was fearful that General Hawkesworth had a mental reservation as to the possibilities of success of his operation. It seems to be an inherent practice with him to attack with minimum forces, with the result that he is repulsed with losses, only to make it necessary to send in heavier forces later to do the same job. It is the question of 'sending a boy to do a man's job'. . . . I flew to II Corps, feeling that it was necessary to discuss with General Keyes the results of this failure, for although the 46th effort would not entirely have protected his left flank, its failure would leave it entirely uncovered during his crossing of the Rapido River. . . . [29]

I maintain that it is essential that I make that attack [the Rapido River crossing] fully expecting heavy losses in order to hold all the [German] troops on my front and draw more to it, thereby clearing the way for SHINGLE. The attack is on.[30]

The failed attack further depressed the mood of Major General Fred L. Walker, commander of the 36th Division, which had been ordered to cross the Rapido. After meeting with General Hawkesworth following the failed Garigliano crossing, Walker described the impact of the failure in his diary. "His [Hawkesworth's] failure, under more favorable conditions than our own, is an omen of the future, and makes it tough for my men, who now have none of the advantages his crossing would have provided."[31] Yet, while the British crossing did not achieve its tactical goals, it did attain strategic success. As Martin Blumenson wrote in his studies of the Rapido River crossing, *Bloody River* and *Salerno to Cassino*, the failed crossing made the Rapido crossing unnecessary, but Clark and the Allied high command never knew it. The British attempt had already helped nail down German forces defending the river and had also siphoned off two divisions from the Anzio area.[32] With the Germans already moving forces away from Anzio, as Clark and the Allies wanted, Clark should have called off the operation.

The idea to cross the Rapido, however, had started in late December 1943. On 28 December Clark asked 3d Division commander Lucian Truscott if he would be willing to cross the Rapido if the heights on either flank were under attack, but not in Allied possession. Truscott told Clark, "Yes, but those attacks should be so powerful that every German gun would be required to oppose them, for only two or three concealed 88's would be able to destroy our bridges. I doubt our capability for making any such attacks."[33] Unfortunately for the soldiers tasked with the crossing, the 36th Division would not receive the help Truscott thought necessary for the crossing.

As D-Day for the Rapido River assault neared, Division Commander Walker wrote privately in his diary numerous times that he believed the crossing was doomed to disaster: "I'll swear, I do not see how we, or any other Division, can possibly succeed in crossing the Rapido River near San Angelo when that stream is included within the main line of resistance of the strongest German position."[34] On 16 January, Walker wrote his most damning entry into his journal about the entire operational plan:

> The 36th Division, in the south zone of the II Corps, is to cross the Rapido on the 20th and establish a bridgehead some 4 miles wide and 3 miles deep, as far as the town of Pignataro. When the bridgehead is established and bridges over the Rapido are in place, the 1st Armored Division is to pass through us, attack up the Liri Valley toward Rome with the hope of going all the way to join Lucas' beachhead. . . .
>
> This is going to be a tough job and I don't like it. There is nothing in our favor. Again I explained the difficulties to both Clark and Keyes and suggested that a greater chance of success could be had by attacking north of Cassino, where the Rapido is fordable and the German defense is weaker. I do not look upon the mountains in that area as impossible obstacles. There, a coordinated attack can be made by a greater initial attacking force, in daylight, with greater surprise, and on a wider front, with the missions of seizing Mt. Castellone, cutting Highway No. 6 west of Cassino, and outflanking the German defense between Cassino and the Liri River. . . .
>
> It seems to me that such an attack, properly planned and executed, promises greater success and fewer losses than a frontal attack on the strongest part of the German defense where, because of German mine fields and limited crossing equipment, we are confined to a few crossing points and where we will have to build up, under fire, a coordinated attacking force by infiltration west of the river, immediately following the disorganization of crossing. Clark and Keyes are not interested. They do not understand the problems and do not know what I am talking about.[35]

While Walker talked about the plan with both Clark and II Corps commander General Keyes, despite his apparent misgivings he never vehemently objected to it. This is not meant as a criticism of Walker, although some historians and readers may wonder why a man so opposed to a plan did not speak up. The answer is simple: this is how the military works. For the division commander to publicly object or refuse to carry out the plan would be insubordination and dereliction of duty, which would have reverberated throughout his entire command. Walker had two choices: either resign his position, which would not cancel the operation and would only hurt the division, or go along with the crossing. As he wrote a few days before the battle: "It appears to me that the defeat of the Germans on the Marne on July 15th 1918, is about to be repeated in reverse on the Rapido in January 1944. Nevertheless, I shall do everything in my power to succeed."[36]

On 18 January a reluctant Walker issued orders for the crossing. His plan was fairly straightforward. The 141st Infantry Regiment was to cross north of Sant'Angelo and drive south and west on the town itself. The 143d Infantry Regiment was to cross south with two battalions and support the advance of the 141st.[37] Aside from the troops on the ground, the XII Air Support Command was to fly 124 sorties in support of the crossings.[38]

With a few hours remaining before the invasion, Walker wrote one more entry into his diary. His lack of confidence in the success of the attack is clearly displayed:

> Tonight the 36th Division will attempt to cross the Rapido River opposite San Angelo. We have done everything we can, but I do not now see how we can succeed. On top of everything else, Army has rushed us into this mission too fast. But even with adequate time, the crossing is still dominated by heights on both sides of the valley where German artillery observers are ready to bring down heavy concentrations on our men. The river is the principal obstacle of the German Main Line of Resistance.
>
> I do not know of a single case in military history where an attempt to cross an unfordable river that is incorporated into the enemy's main line of resistance has succeeded; so according to history, we may not succeed. This mission should never have been assigned to any troops and, especially, when both flanks will be exposed when we get across.[39]

Still, one of Walker's closing sentences suggests that there was some hope or chance of success. "However, if we get some breaks, we may succeed. But they will have to be in the nature of miracles."[40] Sadly for Walker and the men of his 36th Division, the miracle he so desperately looked for would be wiped out by hard German steel in the hands of Kesselring's veterans.

On 20 January at 1800 the 141st Infantry Regiment moved out and immediately ran into trouble.[41] The boats to be used in the crossing were found riddled with bullets, and the white tape that marked the mine fields had been destroyed. Despite these troubles Companies A and B somehow managed to cross the river. Company B, however, was in bad shape. In a single volley of German fire the company lost its commander and executive officer.[42] By the morning of the 21st Walker's headquarters had lost contact with the 141st. The 143d Regiment, south of the 141st, had little success as well, and by 0515 of the 21st Brigadier General William H. Wilbur, deputy division commander, ordered a withdrawal, but Walker refused to give up so quickly.[43] After conferring with Corps Commander Keyes, the two generals decided to send in the 3d Battalion, 143d Infantry Regiment, but by the morning of 22 January, the battalion had only advanced five hundred yards. By nightfall on the same day, with their ammunition nearly exhausted, only forty 3d Battalion soldiers managed to cross the river back to their assembly areas.[44]

A dejected but unsurprised Walker wrote late during the night of 21 January about the river crossing: "The attack last night was a failure. . . . The stupidity of some higher commanders seems to be profound. I agree with General Harmon that, 'There are times when the high command is stupid as hell.' When I heard him say that back in Africa, I thought it amusing. Not today. It's too close to home."[45] Clark, too, wrote in his diary of the attack, perhaps in an effort to rationalize the losses: "As was anticipated, heavy resistance was encountered to the 36th Division crossing of the Rapido River. Accurate enemy artillery fire destroyed bridges as they were erected. It became necessary, later in the day, to withdraw the 143d, but the 141st, north of San Angelo, maintained its position, and efforts to reinforce it were to take place this afternoon.[46]

During the operation across the Rapido the 36th Division suffered 1,681 casualties: 143 killed, 663 wounded and 875 missing.[47] There are numerous reasons for the high casualties, the most obvious being the strong German defensive position. Due to the failure of the 46th Division to take the high ground in the earlier attack, the veteran German soldiers knew exactly where the Americans would cross and had their machine guns and artillery already zeroed in on these locations. The major error of the operation, however, was that the force involved in the crossing, one division with little artillery support, was not large enough. As Lucian Truscott had told Clark on 28 December, the Allies could only succeed if they concentrated enough power into the crossing. Perhaps the entire Fifth Army would not have been enough, but Clark believed the attack had to be made. "I knew it would be costly but was impelled to go ahead with the attack in order that I could draw to this front all possible German reserves in order to clear the way for SHINGLE," he wrote. "This was accomplished in a magnificent manner. Some blood had to be spilled on either the land or the SHINGLE front, and I greatly preferred that it be on the Rapido, where we were secure, rather than at Anzio with the sea at our back."[48]

Although the attack on the Rapido was unnecessary because the Germans had already moved forces from Anzio to help in the defense of the earlier British attacks, Clark could not have known or foreseen this. In hindsight the Rapido crossing should never have been attempted, as Clark seemed to realize on a visit to Walker on 23 January: "It was as much my fault as yours," Clark stated.[49] Looking back sixty years after the battle it is obvious that Clark should never have ordered the assault across the Rapido, but at the time he felt it was better for the Allies to face a critical situation at the Rapido than with their backs against the sea.

For days after the failed crossing tempers boiled and Walker's command post was constantly infuriated by Germans returning the 36th Division's capture carrier pigeons. On 25 January Walker received a message purportedly from a captured soldier stating, "Everybody is giving up pig-wounded. I may as well do the same unless I die first. 3d Bn 141st Inf."[50] Another message received later in the day expressed hope that the Allies would attempt another crossing, "Americans of the 36th Division: Herewith a messenger pigeon is returned. We have enough to eat and what is more, we look forward with pleasure to your next attempt."[51] The last message on which Walker commented was the most venomous:

> To the 36th Division: You poor night watchmen, here is another pigeon No. 2, back so that you won't starve. What do you plan in front of Cassino, with your tin can armor? Your captured syphilitic comrades have shown us the quality of the American soldier. Your captains are too stupid to destroy secret orders before being captured. At the moment, your troops south of Rome are getting a kick in the nuts. You poor nose pickers. The German troops.[52]

On 2 March 1944 twenty-five Texans assigned to the division gathered in a barn to celebrate Texas Independence Day. After a series of cheers for Texas the group voted on a motion to investigate Clark's order that had "caused so many useless and unnecessary casualties."[53] After voting in support of the motion, the soldiers agreed not to begin the inquiry until after the war had ended.

By January 1946, on the second anniversary of the battle, the 36th Division Association in Brownwood, Texas, decided they would try to get the government to investigate the matter. Their appeal to Congress declared:

> Every man connected with this undertaking knew it was doomed to failure because it was an impossible situation. . . . Notwithstanding this information . . . contrary to the repeated recommendations of the subordinate commanders, General Mark W. Clark ordered the crossings of the Rapido. . . . The results of this blunder are well known. The crossings were made under the most adverse conditions . . . [resulting in] a methodical destruction of our troops.[54]

Furthermore, the veterans wanted to "correct a military system that will permit an inefficient and inexperienced officer, such as Gen. Mark W. Clark, in a high command to destroy the young manhood of this country and to prevent future soldiers being sacrificed wastefully and uselessly."[55]

Clark, serving as High Commissioner of Austria, upon hearing of the congressional investigation immediately went to work trying to clear his name. Writing numerous letters to Eisenhower and his former chief of staff Al Gruenther, Clark condemned the action of the 36th Division Association: "I personally am being attacked for inefficiency, inexperience and useless sacrifice of American youth. . . . These charges are absolutely without foundation. The attack of the Rapido and adjacent coordinated attacks were essential to save many times the number of lives which, if we were heavily opposed at Anzio, would have resulted."[56]

As press coverage of the investigation increased, Clark attempted to explain and justify his actions in several letters that perhaps contain the best reasons for the attack:

> Unfortunately battles are bloody and particularly those in Italy where the strength of the opposing forces were so nearly equal and we encountered much unfavorable terrain. At that time in Italy two important reasons existed for pressing the campaign. Firstly we were

definitely contributing to setting the stage for the Normandy invasion of France by holding and attracting large German forces in Italy and secondly in Italy itself in order to secure the success of the Anzio landing which had already been ordered planned and mounted, it was necessary to attract and hold German units in areas removed from Anzio. And that was accomplished. Unfortunately in every large battle one small element may be forced into an extremely difficult role, where chances of success are not favorable. However, these calculated risks must be taken in the interest of the success of the whole battle. The losses sustained at the Rapido were saved many times at the Anzio landing for the enemy troops previously located in the Anzio area had been drawn into the battle to the south. . . . As you [Al Gruenther] well know, the failure of our left Corps to achieve its objective in the opening days of the battle was a major contributing factor to the failure of the Rapido crossing.[57]

A few days later, Clark wrote again to Gruenther, further explaining why he ordered the attack:

First: The attack of the 36th Division had to be made in the sector assigned as it afforded the only approaches to the Liri Valley through which our armored reserve could pass and be exploited.

Second: I was directed to maintain the momentum of the attack at all costs. I needed no such directive for it was obvious that all-out attacks by every element on the 36th Division was in pursuant of this directive, and I am convinced that had the 36th Division Commander inspired his Division that this attack and succeeding one had good chance of success. I am convinced that Walker's mental attitude, that a defeat was inevitable, was a decisive factor in the 36th Division's part in the over-all 5th Army attack.

Third: Until the Anzio landing was absolutely insured, all-out attacks on the south had to be maintained at all costs.[58]

By this time, Clark had begun to believe that Walker was the ringleader of the 36th Division investigation. Clark was wrong; there is no evidence that Walker had anything to do with the 2 March motion or the 36th Division Association letter to Congress. This is not to say Walker believed Clark did nothing wrong. Walker fully participated in the investigation and allowed an interview in which he stated that one failing of the mission was the short notice:

> The division received orders for the attack approximately 2 ½ days in advance. Therefore there was not sufficient time to prepare for a major attack against a determined offense. . . . The situation did not and could not permit of the anticipated exploitations even if the initial river crossing operations were successful. Therefore the secondary objective, namely a breakthrough and a subsequent armored advance down the Liri Valley was visionary and to General Walker seemed to indicate a rather "Boy Scout attitude" on the part of General Keyes, the II Corps commander, and General Allen commanding CCB, 1st Armored Division.[59]

Summarizing the entire crossing, Walker believed "that the War Department's report should show that the attack was a result of poor tactical judgment on the part of the commanders concerned."[60]

As the investigation continued Clark wrote letters to his wife and Al Gruenther, lashing out at Congress and even his friend Eisenhower. Clark decided that if the investigation were to continue any longer he would retire and stated that that those 'low-lives' had better hold on to their chairs for I will blast them plenty."[61] Seeking help from Eisenhower and receiving little feedback, Clark wrote to his wife that he was afraid "he [Eisenhower] is playing politics and not going to bat as he should."[62] As the investigation continued Clark received help from Randolph Churchill, the prime minister's son, who stated in an interview that he believed that the crossing was his father's idea, not Clark's: "My father did order the crossing. What is more, he ordered and helped plan the entire Anzio campaign, against the protests of Mr. Roosevelt and other Allied leaders. And we feel the campaign was justified. While it may be true that the crossing of the Rapido had little chance of success and was costly, it was important to the whole picture. It detracted thousands of German troops and weakened the Nazis elsewhere."[63]

When the investigation concluded, Secretary of War Robert Patterson exonerated Clark and the crossings:

> I have carefully examined the reports in this case and it is my conclusion that the action to which the Thirty-Six Division was committed was a necessary one and that General Clark exercised sound

judgment in planning it and in ordering it. While the casualties are to be greatly regretted, the heroic action and sacrifices of the Thirty-Six Division undoubtedly drew the Germans away from our landings at Anzio during the critical hours of the first foothold, this contributing in major degree to minimizing the casualties in that undertaking and to the firm establishment of the Anzio beachhead.[64]

Though Clark was cleared, the Rapido crossings still hang over his career and achievements. In his memoirs, Clark briefly discussed the crossings and investigations, defending his actions:

Like the guards and tackles of a football team, the 36th was called upon to attack and attack hard in conjunction with other divisions of many nationalities on its right and left, while somebody else made a spectacular end run to Anzio that would have failed if the guards and tackles had not been up to their jobs.

I salute them for their charge and courage. As for myself, I can only say that under the same circumstances I would have to do it over again—and if I am to be accused of something, thank God I am accused of attacking instead of retreating.[65]

To this day the Rapido crossings are remembered for their savagery and brutality. The soldiers of the 36th Division fought bravely and attempted to achieve what many believed and still believe to be the impossible.

After the war, journalist Eric Sevareid, who had been a war correspondent in Italy during the war, wrote about the failed assault across the river:

As the mine flashed off, the Germans poured artillery fire into the flat stretch of ground, and the men screamed and died. Some went out of their heads and ran blindly forward shrieking curses upon the enemy, to perish in shattering explosions. A few men of bravery beyond all words are said to have led their comrades, crawling on hands and knees so that they would catch the mine burst in their bellies and save those behind them. But—though reports were not then permitted to tell this part of it—some two hundred men had refused to enter the minefield. They were not cowards; they were simply worn out, and nothing—not even disgrace and imprisonment for years—seemed so bad to them as what they were ordered to do.[66]

The Rapido River crossing, like the Anzio landing, was symbolic of the entire war in Italy. The Americans and British tried to gain a major victory with limited forces and resources. What happened at the Rapido would happen at Anzio. Just as they had succeeded in crossing the river, the Allies eventually would succeed at Anzio, but only after several critical weeks of hard, touch-and-go combat nearly leading to Allied defeat. With the failed crossing the Fifth Army offensive was stalled. This would have serious implications for the Anzio landing, for without the Allied breakthrough of the Gustav Line the VI Corps would be isolated and left to fight alone.

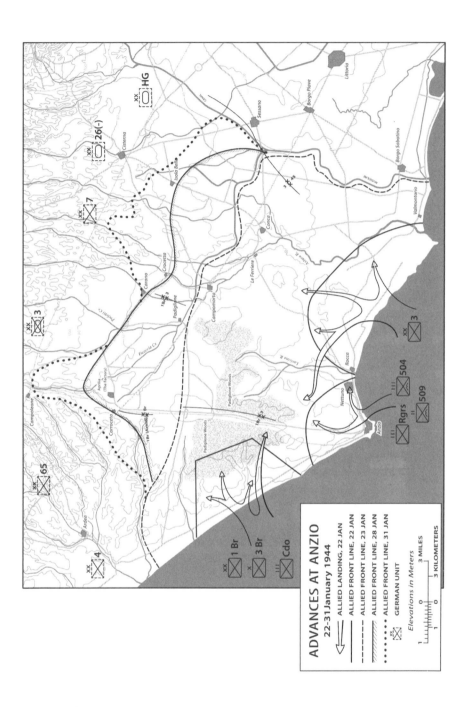

ADVANCES AT ANZIO
22–31 January 1944

Littoria

Borgo Piave

Borgo Sabotino

Sessano

Cisterna

Isola Bella

Valmontorio

Conca

Le Ferriere

Crocetta

Carano

Padiglione

Campomorto

Padiglione Woods

Aprilia (The Factory)

Carroceto

Campoleone

Padiglione Woods

Ardea

Nettuno

Rocca

Anzio

XX ◻ HG

XX ◻ 26(–)

XX ☒ 7

XX ☒ 3

XX ☒ 65

XX ☒ 4

XX ☒ 3

▨ 504

▨ 509

Rgrs ▨

Elevations in Meters

XX ☒	1 Br
x ☒	3 Br
▨	Cdo

→ ALLIED LANDING, 22 JAN
— ALLIED FRONT LINE, 22 JAN
– – – ALLIED FRONT LINE, 23 JAN
– · – ALLIED FRONT LINE, 28 JAN
· · · · ALLIED FRONT LINE, 31 JAN
☒ GERMAN UNIT

0   1   3 MILES
0   1   3 KILOMETERS

Chapter 7

THE WILDCAT THAT
BECAME A WHALE

O N 22 JANUARY 1944 THE VI CORPS LANDED UNOPPOSED
on the Anzio beaches and achieved what Maj. Gen. John
P. Lucas believed was "certainly one of the most complete surprises in history."[1] Moving out at 0500 a day before the invasion, the fleet crossed 120 miles carrying fifty thousand men and fifty-two hundred vehicles.[2] The convoy dropped anchor at 0005 on 22 January. A ten minute naval gunfire barrage, designed to knock out their defensive positions and destroy minefields, greeted the sleeping Germans. The first troops came ashore around 0200 and met little resistance from two depleted battalions of the 29th Panzer Grenadier Division.[3] By midday Lucas established VI Corps on the shores of Anzio. The success of the initial landing was due in large part to the Mediterranean Allied Air Force, which flew over twelve hundred sorties on D-Day with the aim of knocking out German airfields and cutting communications between Anzio and Rome. The air planners believed, and would be proven wrong, that they could "isolate the beachhead from enemy forces by maintaining air superiority over the beachhead, bombing bridges and road transport, and attacking all enemy columns or troop concentrations within striking distance."[4]

On the right of the invasion force the 3d Division landed about four miles east of Anzio on three beaches: X-Ray Beach, Red Beach, and Green Beach, with the 504th Parachute Infantry Battalion assigned to capture the port and clear coastal defenses. The British forces on the left landed on Peter Beach, about six miles northwest of Anzio, and were to strike eastward to establish a road block on the main road above Anzio. The plan called for the Anzio forces to link up and consolidate a beachhead seven miles deep centered on the port.[5] With the landings proceeding at a stunning rate Lt. Gen. Mark W. Clark decided the time was right to pay the beachhead a visit.

Arriving by PT boat at 1407 on 22 January Clark found the landings progressing well as by this time the entire 3d Division was ashore.[6] By the end of the 22d, 36,034 men, 3,904 vehicles, and a large amount of supplies were ashore, accounting for 90 percent of the initial landing convoy.[7] By the end of 24 January the 3d Division had captured the Mussolini Canal and the U.S. forces had taken every objective in the seven-mile deep beachhead.[8] While the operation was going well, Clark was not entirely pleased with the situation. The general was troubled over the fact that Field Marshal Albert Kesselring was not pulling troops from the Gustav Line, and he was constantly bothered by VIP's arriving from Allied Force Headquarters (AFHQ), causing him to lament in his diary, "Never before, in the history of warfare, have so few been commanded by so many."[9] During the first few days of the Anzio invasion Clark's diary entries change from a more positive to a more angry and depressed tone. Though the landings were going well, Clark knew the Germans would not remain inactive.

Starting with the planning for Anzio Clark had slowly grown angry with General Sir Harold Alexander, commander of all Allied forces in Italy. After a planning period with the army group commander Clark commented to his staff that Alexander was nothing more than a "peanut and a feather duster."[10] Aside from terse comments about the British, he began to believe in a conspiracy that the British were attempting to sabotage the upcoming Operation Anvil.[11]

Over the next few days VI Corps advanced slowly. By 25 January the British captured the town of Aprilia, called the "Factory" for its numerous brick buildings.[12] With Allied forces only four miles outside of Cisterna and Campoleone, Alexander, who later would be one of the most vocal critics of Lucas, complimented the initial results saying, "What a splendid piece of work he [Lucas] had done!"[13] Soon after, on 27 January, Alexander told Clark that he was becoming worried over the slowness of the VI Corps attack. Clark, again showing his growing weariness for the British, did not tell Alexander whether or not he agreed with this sentiment. Clark did not say anything because he knew Winston Churchill was urging Alexander to move faster and believed the prime minister was trying to run the war in Italy from his residence at 10 Downing Street.[14] On the same day Clark bickered with Mediterranean Theater chief, Field Marshall Henry Maitland Wilson. Clark believed his Fifth Army had the right to take Rome and that if Anvil became a one division landing, or in Clark's word's a "fart in the dark," he wanted nothing to do with it.[15]

Though slowed by bad weather on 26 January, by 27 January Maj. Gen. Lucian Truscott's 3d Division was outside Cisterna, and the British awaited the attack order to seize Campoleone. However, with the beachhead already ten miles deep, Lucas was weary. Up to this point the landings had cost VI Corps only thirteen killed, ninety-seven wounded, and eighty-four missing. Yet, Lucas had made the command decision not to seize the Alban Hills and instead secure and build up the beachhead.[16] Ultimately Lucas made the correct decision, but until then the VI Corps had to deal with the Germans and their brilliant commander Field Marshal Albert Kesselring.

Nicknamed "Smiling Albert" for his seemingly jovial visage, Kesselring was a former Luftwaffe chief of staff and commander of Luftflotte 2 before being named Commander-in-Chief South in late 1941. Much to the chagrin of his aides Kesselring loved to fly over battlefields to "feel the pulse of the situation."[17] Armed with a brilliant mind and audacious leadership skills Kesselring moved quickly to defeat the Allied invasion at Anzio, what Hitler called the "abscess south of Rome."[18] Surprised and caught off guard by the landings, Kesselring quickly made key decisions to attack the landing force with what he would later call, "a higgledy-piggledy jumble—units of numerous divisions fighting confusedly side by side."[19]

After hearing of the landing Kesselring ordered the 4th Parachute Division along with several units from the Hermann Goering Division to block the main roads from Anzio to the Alban Hills. He then called for reinforcements and received the 715th and 114th divisions from southern France and the Balkans, respectively, while activating the 92d Division. With these units in the process of moving towards Anzio, Kesselring ordered the Fourteenth Army to make units available to resist the landing. Quickly, the 65th and 362d Divisions along with the 16th SS Panzer Grenadier Division were advancing to Anzio.[20] Lastly, Kesselring made a tough decision, he ordered units off the Gustav Line. This was perhaps Kesselring's boldest decision; he was weakening his major defensive line in order to stop the Allies at Anzio. If he made the line too weak, the Fifth Army could break through and force the Germans to retreat north of Rome. Ignoring the consequences, "Smiling Albert" ordered the I Parachute Corps, 3d Panzer Grenadier Division, and more units from the Hermann Goering Division off the Gustav Line and later received the 26th Panzer Division and parts of the 1st Parachute Division from the Adriatic front.[21]

Even with these forces set in motion the Germans were still terribly weak, and Kesselring's chief of staff, Generalmajor Siegfried Westphal wrote:

> On January 22 and even the following day, an audacious and enterprising formation of enemy troops . . . could have penetrated into the city of Rome itself without having to overcome any serious opposition. . . . But the landed enemy forces lost time and hesitated.[22]

Although initially relieved by Lucas's failure to advance, upon reflection Kesselring later came to believe that the American commander had made the right choice. Regardless, Kesselring ordered a general counteroffensive to take place on 3 February, but not before the Allies attacked first.

On the Allied side the VI Corps had achieved initial success, but by 28 January Clark and Alexander were growing concerned with Lucas's lack of audacity. Clark, pressured by Alexander, visited the beachhead on the 28th and wrote:

> I have been disappointed by the lack of aggressiveness on the part of IV Corps, although it would have been wrong in my opinion to attack and capture our final objective [Alban Hills] on this front. [But] reconnaissance in force should have been more aggressive to capture Cisterna and Campoleone.[23]

The seeds for replacing Lucas were already being planted. Yet, Clark's view was that the situation was less than dire, and he even believed Lucas had made the correct decision. In the end Lucas would be relieved for failure to take the hills, even though it had been the correct decision based on the plan and what Lucas knew at the time.

That morning Clark traveled to the beachhead by PT boat. Nearing the shoreline, a friendly torpedo boat accidentally fired on Clark's craft. The accident happened because the torpedo boat captain believed Clark's PT boat was a German E boat, and due to the slanting sun rays of the early morning sun he could not make out the PT boat's markings. Clark managed to escape uninjured, but five of the men around him were hit. After surviving the accident and landing, Clark decided it was necessary to bring up the 45th Infantry Division and the 1st Armored Division less CCB, one of the division's two combat commands.[24] The two divisions would arrive just in time for the planned VI Corps offensive.

Spurred on by Clark, Lucas finally decided to launch his offensive. On 30 January Lucas ordered the British 1st Division to advance to the Albano Road. To their right, the 3d Division and the 504th Parachute Infantry, with the Rangers attached, were to take Cisterna and drive towards Valmontone.[25] As the attack unfolded the British forces succeeded and broke Kesselring's line and secured Campoleone, but the 3d Division's assault left a lasting imprint on the Rangers.[26] Using the 1st and 3d Ranger Battalion to spearhead the assault, the Rangers would attack an hour before the 3d Division. They were to quietly infiltrate the German position and seize Cisterna by surprise. Moving out before dawn on 30 January the Rangers had advanced across the Mussolini Canal; however, they were still eight hundred yards away when daylight revealed their force; and heavy German fire pinned the soldiers down.[27] The attack was a complete failure, and Truscott called a halt to it. Having advanced with more than seven hundred Rangers, only six men returned; the rest were killed or captured.[28] With the VI Corps offensive stalled at Cisterna, Alexander and Clark decided to call off the attack and concentrate on consolidating the beachhead.[29] With the decision to halt the offensive, VI Corps dug in and prepared for another attack. As the Allies decided on what to do next, Clark wrote in his diary about the troublesome situation:

> The situation here is difficult. . . . I think their planning was faulty, although Lucas, Truscott and Darby all expressed their opinions to me that the plans were well thought out. . . .
>
> The German has approximately five divisions confronting us now, with another in sight, against our four. We have no chance, in my opinion, to reach Colli Laziali area against the opposition massed in that vicinity. Should the enemy realize our inability to reach this objective, and with his apparent ability to move divisions from the north whenever required, he may decide that the opportunity is present to give the Allies a reverse.[30]

Clark's troubles would be greatly increased as Kesselring had a surprise for the Allies at Anzio that would turn the beachhead into what the soldiers would later call, "Hell's Half-Acre."[31]

The German three prong attack began on 3 February. The British 1st Division bore the brunt of the thrust. Generaloberst Eberhard von Mackensen ordered his Fourteenth Army to destroy the British salient near Campoleone.[32] Suffering fifteen hundred casualties the British managed to avoid entrapment and withdrew from the town. Four days later, on 7 February, the Germans again attacked the British 1st Division, which had withdrawn towards Aprilia. Three days later the Germans secured the town.[33] With the salient destroyed and the Allied line forced back, the Germans initiated their major attack on 16 February.

Before the German attack began Clark visited the VI Corps area on 6 February and found the situation to be "quiet and fairly well in hand."[34] As he had at Salerno, Clark noticed a weakness in the VI Corps line and discovered a gap between the British 1st Division and the U.S. 3d Division. Clark's discovery came at a pivotal moment in the battle. Filling the hole with two battalions of the 180th Infantry Regiment, these units would eventually help save the Allies.[35] The line was only two miles from the sea. Yet, not all was well with the Allied beachhead. Due to the slowness of the advance and the stalwart German defenses, the Allied schedule to link up with the Fifth Army front was thrown off. To make matters worse, on 7 February, Clark's G-4 told him that there was a critical shortage of ammunition, gasoline and rations.[36] With the VI Corps on the defensive Clark was troubled by the situation. His command was tired and Clark was angry with the British. Clark wrote in his diary, "I think Napoleon was right when he came to the conclusion that it was better to fight Allies than to be one of them."[37] Clark's faith in the alliance would be tested at Anzio, but the battle for the beachhead was not the only fight going on.

*   *   *

By this time Fifth Army had begun its preliminary operations towards the Gustav Line to pull German forces away from the Operation Shingle landing zones. However, the Fifth Army failed to reach nearly every objective. While the French Corps achieved success in advancing towards Cassino, and II Corps took Mt. Trocchio, the British 10th Corps and 36th Infantry Division failed to penetrate the Liri Valley.

The battle for Monte Cassino had been raging since the crossing of the Rapido River. After the landings at Anzio, Kesselring removed some units from the Gustav Line, but not enough to seriously weaken it. By February the Allies were fighting for their lives at Anzio and trying to crack the Gustav Line at Cassino. The Battle of Cassino, like Anzio, would become one of the most controversial actions of World War II. And, just as at Anzio, Clark would be in the center of the controversy, but it was Alexander who had the final decision at Cassino. The controversy to follow came from one event: the bombing of the Benedictine monastery at Cassino. Founded by St. Benedict in 524 A.D. on the former site of a temple for Apollo, the area was a favorite of Emperor Tiberius, who held numerous orgies in the temple. [38] The monastery had survived destruction before, having been destroyed by the Lombards in 581, the Saracens in 883 and finally the Normans in 1030.[39] By February 1944, the monastery had become a critical spot in the German line, as Alexander explained to Winston Churchill:

> The main highway, known as Route Six, is the only road, except cart-tracks, which leads from the mountains where we are into Liri valley over Rapido River. This exit into the plain is blocked and dominated by Monte Cassino, on which stands the monastery. Repeated attempts have been made to outflank Monastery Hill from the north, but all these attacks have been unsuccessful, owing to deep ravines, rock escarpments, and knife-edges, which limit movements to anything except comparatively small parties, of infantry, who can only be maintained by porters and to a limited extend by mules where we have managed under great difficulties to make some mule-tracks.
>
> Further Monastery Hill is cut off almost completely from north by a ravine so steep and deep that so far it has proved impossible to cross it. A wider turning movement is even more difficult, as it has to cross Mont Cairo, which is a precipitous peak now deep in snow. The Americans tried to outflank this Cassino bastion from the south by an attack across the Rapido River, but this, as you know, failed, with heavy losses to the 34th and 36th Divisions.[40]

At the end of January Alexander pulled the 2d New Zealand Division and 4th Indian Infantry Division from the line and used them to create a provisional corps under the command of New Zealander Gen. Bernard Freyberg.[41] The Provisional Corps, which became known as the New Zealand Corps entered the Cassino line on 3 February and two days later General Keyes's II Corps ordered the 36th Division to capture Piedimonte while the 34th Division would attack and attempt to capture the town of Cassino.[42] The attack by the 34th Division began on 7 February with the remainder of the II Corps following on 11 February. For Clark and his Fifth Army the attack was a major gamble. The II Corps, including the 34th Division, was tired, so much so that Alexander put a time limit on how long the division could fight. If the II Corps failed to break through Cassino, Alexander planned to take them out of the line and use the New Zealand Corps.[43] Alexander's plan called for the 4th Indian Division to cross the high ground west of Cassino and establish a bridgehead across the Rapido. Then the division was to attack Monastery Hill during the night of 13–14 February and move south to cut Highway 6 and take the town of Cassino from the west. During this movement the 2d New Zealand Division would lay heavy fire on Cassino from the east and cross the Rapido and aid the 4th Indian Division in taking the town. If all went according to plan, armored units would exploit the breakthrough, crossing into the Liri Valley and moving on to Rome.[44]

One problem occurred before the attack could begin: New Zealand Corps Commander Freyberg wanted dry weather so that his tanks could be better used. It was during this delay that Freyberg came to a critical and controversial decision; the monastery had to be destroyed.

On 12 February Freyberg telephoned Clark's chief of staff Al Gruenther and said, "I desire that I be given air support tomorrow in order to soften the enemy position in the Cassino area. I want three missions of 12 planes each; the planes to be Kitty Bombers, carrying 1000 pound bombs."[45] Gruenther told the New Zealand commander that the air plans for tomorrow were designated for Anzio. Freyberg understood, but believed the air attack was necessary for his ensuing attack. After conferring with other staff members, Gruenther called Freyberg about what targets he had in mind. Freyberg told Gruenther, "I want the Covenant [Monastery] attacked."[46] A startled Gruenther told Freyberg that it was not on his list of targets, but the New Zealand commander would not back down, telling Gruenther, "I am quite sure it was on my list of targets, but in any case I want it bombed. The other targets are unimportant, but this one is vital. The division commander who is making the attack feels that it is an essential target and I thoroughly agree with him."[47] Gruenther said he would check with Clark, but that restrictions prevented the bombing of the abbey. With Clark away, Gruenther turned to Alexander and cabled his chief of staff, General John Harding:

General Freyberg has asked that the Abbey of Monte Cassino be bombed tomorrow. General Clark will not be available for about an hour, so he does not know of this request. Gen. Clark has spoken to Gen. Freyberg on at least two occasions concerning the advisability of bombing the Monastery. He told Gen. Freyberg that after consulting Gen. Keyes, the [II] Corps Commander, and Gen. Ryder, the Commander of the 34th Div. he considered that no military necessity existed for its destruction. Gen. Freyberg expressed to Gen. Clark his considered opinion that the destruction of the Monastery was a military necessity, and that it was unfair to assign any military commander the mission of taking the hill, and at the same time not grant permission to bomb the Monastery. However, in view of the nature of the target, and the international and religious implications involved, I should like to get an expression of opinion from ACMF (Allied Central Mediterranean Force) as to the advisability of authorizing the bombing.[48]

Harding stated he would take up the matter with Alexander, but in the mean time Gruenther got in contact with Clark, who believed the "destruction of the Monastery was not a military necessity."[49] Clark further commented that the entire incident "caused him some embarrassment in view of the extremely strong views of Gen. Freyberg" and that "unless Gen. Freyberg receded from this position it would place Gen. Clark in a very difficult position in the event that the attack should fail."[50] Further down the chain of command, General Keyes did not believe bombing the abbey was necessary, and he further stated that "the bombing of the Monastery would probably enhance its value as a military obstacle, because the Germans would then feel free to use it as a barricade."[51]

Gruenther looked into the available intelligence to see if the Germans had used the abbey in any military way. While there were no definitive pieces of evidence that the abbey was used by the Germans, Keyes's G-2 section had received several reports that the Germans were using the building as an observation point, but that there had been no actual fire. However, evidence did prove that there were enemy strong points close to the building.[52]

At 2130 hours General Harding informed Gruenther of Alexander's decision:

General Alexander had decided that the Monastery should be bombed if General Freyberg considers it as a military necessity. He regrets that the building should be destroyed, but that he has faith in Gen. Freyberg's judgment. If there is any reasonable probability that the building is being used for military purposes General Alexander believes that its destruction is warranted.[53]

Gruenther proceeded to inform Harding that Clark did not believe the building should be bombed and:

[T]hat if the commander of the New Zealand Corps were an American commander he would give specific orders that it would not be bombed. However, in view of Gen. Freyberg's position in the British Empire forces, the situation was a delicate one, and Gen. Clark hesitated to give him such an order without first referring the matter to Gen. Alexander.[54]

Clark further believed the bombing of the abbey would greatly endanger the lives of civilians, of which around two thousand were reported to be hiding and living in the monastery.[55] After discussing the situation further with Harding, Gruenther informed Clark of Alexander's decision and Clark decided to defer to Freyberg's request.

Once more Gruenther discussed the bombing with Freyberg who remained adamant that the bombing take place. After emphasizing the importance and need to help the New Zealand Corps attack, Gruenther arranged the details for the bombing.[56] Later in the day, Clark wrote about the planned bombing of the monastery:

For religious and sentimental reasons, it is too bad unnecessarily to destroy one of the art treasures of the world. Besides, we have indications that many civilian women and children are taking shelter therein. The extent of our air effort which we can put on it will not destroy the building but will merely give the Germans an excuse to use it.[57]

With the decision now made, Clark decided to have leaflets dropped on the abbey to warn the monks and civilians that an attack was coming. The leaflets read:

Italian Friends: Until this day we have done everything to avoid bombing the abbey. But the Germans have taken advantage. Now that the battle has come close to your sacred walls we shall, despite our wish, have to direct our arms against the monastery. Abandon it at once. Put yourselves in a safe place. Our warning is urgent. FIFTH ARMY.[58]

Unfortunately, according to historian Martin Blumenson, no leaflets fell inside the abbey walls and the ensuing battle prevented nearly all the civilians from fleeing the doomed monastery.[59] On 15 February 255 Allied bombers dropped 576 tons of bombs on the monastery, killing three hundred to four hundred civilians.[60] Following the bombings II Corps artillery opened up on the ruined abbey.[61] Many of the bombs were off target, including sixteen that were released early, with one hitting just outside Clark's command post.[62] The worst part, however, was that after the bombing the 4th Indian Division failed to take Monastery Hill. Slowed by the Germans and the fortified hills, the bombings did not help the Allies capture Monte Cassino. Even today the decision to bomb the monastery remains controversial.

While there is no "smoking gun" or hard evidence that the Germans were in the abbey, the Germans were using the abbey. Aerial observations reported a German radio aerial and the movement of soldiers in and out of the abbey.[63] In an effort to placate the monk's fears that the abbey would be bombed the Germans set up a neutral zone around the building. However, by the time of the bombing the Germans had broken the neutral zone. Still, the aerial bombardment unnecessarily destroyed the abbey and killed innocent civilians. Militarily, the rubble made the already defensible terrain even more difficult for the attacking allies.[64] If the monastery was in too vital of a position to remain unscathed, pulverizing it by Allied bombing was overkill. As Alexander wrote in his memoirs about the bombing:

> Whether the Germans took advantage of its deep cellars for shelter and its high windows for observation I do not know; but it was obvious that this huge and massive building offered the defenders considerable protection from hostile fire, merely by their sheltering under its walls ... the enemy fortifications were hardly separate from the building itself.[65]

The Germans were using the abbey to their advantage, but there is little evidence that troops fought in or around the building. Historian Carlo D'Este believes that XIV Panzer Corps commander General Fridolin von Senger und Etterlin, a devout Catholic, would never have allowed German soldiers inside the monastery.[66] In his memoirs Kesselring further commented, "Once and for all I wish to establish the fact that the monastery was not occupied as part of the line; it was closed against unauthorized entry by military police."[67] As for Clark, he never believed the bombing was necessary. Writing in his memoirs:

> I say that the bombing of the Abbey, which sat high on the hill southwest of Cassino, was a mistake—and I say it with full knowledge of the controversy that has raged around this episode. . . . Not only was the bombing of the Abbey an unnecessary psychological mistake of the first magnitude. It only made our job more difficult, more costly in terms of men, machines and time.[68]

The abbey would be rebuilt with American money, and to this day there are no signs in English there.[69] While the controversy over the bombing continues, Clark's viewpoint was probably correct. Unfortunately, the decision to bomb the abbey was not his, but Alexander's. For Clark the trouble over the bombing of the monastery would have to take a backseat, because the Germans were about to launch their counterattack at Anzio.

*   *   *

To help the German offensive Hitler sent his beloved Berlin-Spandau Infantry Lehr Regiment to Anzio.[70] The regiment was one of Hitler's demonstration units that toured Nazi Germany. Although it had never been in combat Hitler believed the regiment could help push the Allies into the sea. As for the other forces, Mackensen ordered the I Parachute Corps, the 4th Parachute and 65th divisions, to attack west of the Albano-Anzio Road. The breakthrough would be led by the LXXVI Panzer Corps, with the Lehr Regiment, which would perform very badly, and the 3d Panzer Grenadier, 114th, and 715th divisions attached. Following the breakthrough on the road, a second wave led by the 29th Panzer Grenadier and 26th Panzer divisions would exploit the breakout and drive the Allies into the ocean.[71]

Initially the attack went well for the Germans as they broke through the Allied lines and drove towards the beachhead. By 10 February the Germans had captured Aprilia, the Factory, and Carroceto.[72] Luckily for the Allies by 13 February the skies cleared and XII Tactical Air Command was able to fly 345 sorties, slowing the German advance.[73] By 17 February the Germans were still near Lucas's last line of defense, but the line held. The night of 18–

19 February was the turning point for control of the beachhead. During this battle the German attack had breached the Albano Road and closed in on the final defensive beach line.[74] During the attack Eisenhower, as he had done at Salerno, sent a morale boosting message for Clark:

> In all the years I have known you, I have never been prouder of you than during the past strenuous weeks. Despite every difficulty, you are obviously doing a grand job of leadership with your chin up. I read the fine message you recently sent to your troops. Together with men like Al [Gruenther] and Truscott, you are writing history that Americans will always read with pride.[75]

The German forces advanced a little farther, but by this time the 45th Division had been reinforced and the VI Corps held the line. By 20 February the major German counteroffensive stalled and Kesselring suspended the attack. A relieved Clark finally had time to write to Eisenhower, and he was pleased to tell the supreme Allied commander: "I believe the Boche has shot his wad today, although I may be wrong."[76] Clark was right, the German attack was finished.

The Germans had pushed the Allies back, but VI Corps still controlled the beachhead. For the Germans the attack was a strategic failure as they endured over five thousand casualties.[77] With the German attack stopped, the Allies held on, but barely. After only a month of fighting the opposing forces had suffered losses totaling forty thousand, and a stalemate ensued.[78]

With the Anzio offensive now bogged down Clark and Alexander lost whatever faith they had in Lucas. Alexander discussed the issue with Field Marshal Sir Alan Brooke, chief of the Imperial General Staff, saying Lucas needed to be replaced. Alexander felt that Lucas was not aggressive enough and wanted to replace him with "a thruster like Lieutenant General George S. Patton."[79] Clark was unhappy with Lucas, but did not want to replace him; however, after talking with Alexander he decided a change was necessary. The decision to remove Lucas began on 16 February, when in a meeting with Alexander, Clark informed his British superior that he was "not 100% satisfied with the hold Lucas has taken."[80] Alexander, as he did with Major General Ernest Dawley in Salerno, agreed with Clark's take on Lucas. He added that he believed Lucas was tired, mentally and physically. Alexander, in an interview after the war, believed he finally convinced Clark to remove Lucas when he told him "I have no confidence in him [Lucas] and in his ability to control the situation. I very much fear that there might be a disaster at Anzio with Lucas in command and you know what will happen to you and me if there is a disaster at Anzio."[81] However, since the Germans were in the midst of their attack, Clark wrote in his diary about the possibility of relieving Lucas:

> I did believe that a change in Lucas would be advisable but under no circumstances would I hurt Lucas, for he has performed well as Commanding General of the VI Corps from Salerno north and in the initial landing at Anzio. . . . I told Alexander that I would put Truscott in as Deputy Commander.[82]

The next day Lt. Gen. Jacob Devers, who was the American deputy to Mediterranean Theater commander Gen. Henry Maitland Wilson visited Clark. In discussing the VI Corps commander Devers told Clark that he agreed with Alexander's criticism of Lucas, "He feels as Alexander does— that General Lucas should be relieved. His estimate of Lucas is that he is extremely tired, mentally and physically, and should be taken out."[83] In order to evaluate Lucas first hand, Clark visited Lucas at his beachhead command post (CP) on 28 January and found the VI Corps commander to be mentally and physically exhausted. With the battle for the beachhead not yet over Clark decided against removing him. However, Lucas's time as corps commander was nearly over, as Truscott prepared to replace him.

On 24 February, Clark finally removed Lucas. Clark later explained his reasoning in his diary:

> I laid all the cards on the table. Told him that Alexander has demanded his release, that General Devers, without talking to me, had visited VI Corps and had come to me and recommended that Lucas be changed. Both thought that he was tired, mentally and physically, had had too much time in combat and needed a rest. I told Lucas he had done a grand job but that, inasmuch as he was not in mental or physical condition to carry on as well as someone else, my course was clear. It was my duty to take him out; that I would make him my Deputy Army Commander.[84]

This is the only explanation Clark ever gave for removing Lucas. Clark's reasoning is weak at best. Every individual involved in the war was tired, but never had that been a reason to remove someone from high command. Perhaps historians will never know, but Lucas's removal had more to do with the failure to take the Alban Hills than from fatigue. With the Anzio landings at a standstill, Alexander and Clark needed a scapegoat and Lucas fit the part perfectly. As for Lucas, he never again commanded troops in combat, but was quickly promoted to Fourth Army commander, a training command back home. For the remainder of his life Lucas believed he could not have seized the Alban Hills or done more to prevent the German counterattack. "Had I done so, I would have lost my Corps and nothing would have been accomplished except to raise prestige and morale of the enemy. Besides, my orders didn't read that way."[85]

A few days after the change of command at IV Corps the Germans tried one more time to destroy the beachhead. Striking at dawn of 28 February the Germans hoped to destroy the 45th Division.[86] The attacks concentrated around Cisterna, and the 26th Panzer and 715th Light divisions attempted to break the Allied line; but like the soldiers of VI Corps, the Germans were exhausted. On 29 February the Germans tried again, this time against the 3d Division. This attack failed to make a dent in the Allied line.[87] By 1 March the German counteroffensive had run its course. A major reason for the failure of the second German counterattack was that the Allies were reorganized and the Germans were simply exhausted. Another deciding factor was the weather. The skies cleared allowing the Allied air force to attack the German positions with 351 heavy bombers on 2 March.[88]

By the end of March the battle for Anzio was over. It would not be until 1 May that the Allies attempted another offensive to break the Gustav Line and reunite the VI Corps with Fifth Army. After having failed in two counterattacks, Kesselring reorganized and rested his forces. The 29th Panzer Grenadier and the 26th Panzer Divisions moved into reserve while the Hermann Goering Panzer Division headed north for Leghorn, the port city on the west coast of Tuscany. The 16th SS Panzer Grenadier Division withdrew to northern Italy and the 114th Light Division withdrew and moved east to face the Eighth Army.[89] The Allies regrouped as well. The British 56th Division was relieved by the British 5th Division, the 504th Parachute Infantry Regiment rejoined the 82d Airborne Division in England, and the 34th Division replaced the 3d Division in Cisterna.[90]

*   *   *

Much debate centers on the failure of the Anzio offensive. Most historians and veterans place the blame on John Lucas who they believe should have taken the Alban Hills, thus seizing the high ground and preventing a strong German counterattack. The two greatest critics of Lucas were Mediterranean Theater chief, Field Marshal Sir Henry M. Wilson and 15th Army Group commander General Sir Harold R. Alexander. Alexander wrote in his memoirs that that biggest mistake of Anzio was naming Lucas to command it:

> The American General John Lucas, missed his opportunity by being too slow and cautious. He failed to realize the great advantage that surprise had given him. He allowed time to beat him.... A younger or more experienced soldier would have been quicker to react.[91]

As for Wilson, he echoed nearly the same thoughts except he believed the operation failed because Lucas did not secure Cisterna and Campoleone earlier. Wilson believed that Lucas had fallen ill to the "Salerno Complex" which he believed led Lucas to put greater emphasis on securing the bridgehead than advancing.[92]

The general belief among historians and former commanders familiar with Anzio was that Lucas was not aggressive enough and that had he been more aggressive VI Corps could have taken Rome within a few days. This belief is filled with errors and ignores the many mistakes made by Churchill, Wilson, Alexander and Clark during planning.

The major mistake was the lack of manpower available for Operation Shingle. As mentioned earlier, Lucian Truscott wrote, "no one below Army level believed the landing of two divisions at Anzio would cause a German withdrawal."[93] The simple fact is that the VI Corps was not large enough to force the Germans northward. With Operation Overlord taking up ever-increasing amounts of manpower and supplies, Anzio was never going to have enough troops or equipment. By 27 January, only five days after the landing, General Brooke believed the operation was not going to succeed: "we have not got a sufficient margin to be able to guarantee making a success of our attack."[94] In a postwar interview Alexander agreed that "the Anzio attack was made too soon—before we had enough strength to make sure of its success."[95]

Historian Martin Blumenson and Field Marshal Wilson have both argued that taking the towns of Cisterna and Campoleone earlier could have prevented a German counterattack and perhaps caused the Germans to withdraw.[96] This is still doubtful; with manpower at a premium Lucas did not feel comfortable enlarging his defensive perimeter. As the Rangers' expedition into Cisterna on 30 January showed, VI Corps was not powerful enough to take the place. By 30 January the VI Corps had grown in numbers, but could still not secure the town. If Lucas had attempted to take the town earlier he might have succeeded only to have been pushed back or surrounded and captured.

Other historians and veterans of the battle believe that Lucas could have advanced and secured the Alban Hills, but this would have been impossible. It is Lucian Truscott who said it best about the failure to seize the hills and walk into Rome:

> I suppose that arm chair strategists will always labor under the delusion that there was a "fleeting opportunity" at Anzio during which some Napoleonic figure would have charged over the Colli Laziali [Alban Hills], played havoc with the German line of communications, and galloped into Rome. Any such concept betrays lack of comprehension of the military problem involved.[97]

If Lucas had seized the hills he might have held them for a few days and even entered Rome for a few hours, but it is clear that Germans would have strongly contested such an advance and that they had the forces to do so. Kesselring's actions on 22 January show that he never thought once about retreating and giving up Rome. Had Lucas taken the Alban Hills and Rome quickly, he would have celebrated this brief victory in a German prisoner-of-war camp. The Germans would have attacked the Allied defensive positions and possibly captured the entire VI Corps. Clark was in full agreement with Truscott's view and explained his beliefs in a letter to his wife at the end of February 1944:

> It is most unfortunate, for you can take my word for it that the troops in this landing have done a magnificent job and have done all that could have been expected of them against the opposition which they have encountered. It is sheer nonsense for these people to criticize them for not having moved on to Rome. The troops would have been cut off.[98]

Clark echoed the same in an interview with Sidney Mathews, who had been a historian assigned to Fifth Army during the war and later served at the U.S. Army's Center for Military History:

With the strength we had we could have taken the Alban Hills but we could not have held them and the result would have been disastrous. . . . Our Anzio forces would have been so extended that the Germans would have cut it to pieces in short order.[99]

Even General Wilson, who believed Lucas should have immediately moved to take Cisterna, believed it would have been impossible for VI Corps to seize the Alban Hills, and blamed the reversal on the failed Rapido crossing: "To have advanced on the first day to the Alban Hills with half built-up force might have led to irreparable disaster; the failure to cross the River Rapido and take Cassino at the same time as the landing upset the whole conception of achieving success."[100]

In regards to Clark's 12 January orders, Lucas was not even ordered to seize the hills. Clark has often been criticized for giving vague orders, but as an army commander he wanted his subordinates to have maximum flexibility. Alexander believed that if the orders had read "advance *ON* Colli Laziali" [Alban Hills] that an aggressive corps commander would have interpreted the order to mean go *TO* Colli Laziali, and that Lucas should have pushed light forces to the Alban Hills.[101] If the opportunity was there to take the hills Lucas had the authority to do so, but the opportunity never presented itself. Instead, he built up his beachhead and did not extend his defensive perimeter.

The Battle of Anzio has long been regarded as a failed operation, led by a failed commander in John Lucas. While the operation did not secure Rome in a timely manner, it ultimately helped win Rome. General Alexander, while harsh on Lucas's performance, later wrote that "Anzio played a vital role in the capture of Rome. . . . Without this I do not believe we should ever have been able to break through the German defenses at Cassino."[102] Anzio in the end helped the Allies capture Rome; where it failed was in its timing. As Dwight Eisenhower explained in his memoirs, "In the final outcome the Anzio operation paid off handsomely."[103]

Anzio also provided two major benefits to the general war against Nazi Germany, one intended, and the other unintended. Following Anzio, Eisenhower and the planners for Overlord realized they needed more forces during the initial landing. To his credit, Alexander realized that Shingle would impact Overlord, and in a cable to Wilson commented, "Nothing I suggest could be worse for OVERLORD than a catastrophe at Anzio."[104]

The planners realized if Anzio had had more troops, it could have succeeded as they had intended it to. Without the experience of Anzio, Overlord could have had very similar results.

As for the intended advantage, Anzio ultimately prevented nearly twenty German divisions and hundreds of thousands of German soldiers from joining the fight against the Normandy landings or against the Russians in the East. Anzio forced enemy divisions from Yugoslavia and France to fight in Italy, not France or Poland. This alone proves the importance of Anzio. Years after the war the German commander Field Marshal Kesselring said, "If you had never pitted your divisions in the Mediterranean, as at Anzio, you would not have won the victory in the West."[105] While an overstatement by Kesselring, Anzio did succeed in eventually capturing Rome and helped in winning World War II.

John P. Lucas was removed from command for his failure to quickly seize Rome. Though he followed orders and made the correct strategic decision not to overextend his forces, the VI Corps commander has been labeled a failure. Instead, the failure should fall on Churchill, Wilson, Alexander, and Clark who were limited by the preparations for Overlord and forced to send an inadequate force into Anzio. The whole Anzio operation was similar to the strategy in Italy; as historian Carlo D'Este writes, "[t]he invasion of mainland Italy was launched in the hope that a brief and limited effort could bring about large gains. As so often seen in the history of warfare, this had proved to be a delusion."[106] After the war Churchill would conclude, "Anzio was my worst moment of the war. I had most to do with it."[107] Instead of planning for victory, the commanders hoped for victory. The operation and John Lucas could never have achieved what the planners hoped.

*   *   *

There would be no more German attacks against the Allied beachhead. For the remainder of March, Clark continued his squabbling with the British. At first events appeared to lighten Clark's mood. With the beachhead secure, Clark was pleased when on 29 February he received a cable removing him from command of Operation Anvil.[108] Never an avid supporter of the amphibious invasion of southern France, his relief meant he would remain with his beloved Fifth Army for the remainder of the war. This also meant that Clark would have to deal with the British for the duration. Already irked over Anzio, Clark radioed Alexander on 1 March and demanded that the Anzio bridgehead be renamed "The Fifth Army Allied Bridgehead Force" instead of the "Allied Bridgehead Force."[109] Clark believed this decision would boost the morale of his troops and that since it was his Fifth Army involved, they should be in the name. While seemingly petty in the midst of a terrible war, Clark was always fighting for publicity, not always for himself, but for his Fifth Army. While the renaming of the bridgehead was somewhat self-serving, Clark believed the name would help his troops. Privately in his diary Clark was more abrasive, calling the decision to name the bridgehead the "Allied Bridgehead Force" was "part of a steady effort by the British to increase their prestige in the Mediterranean area and to exalt in the public mind the part that the British, as contrasted to the Americans, are playing there."[110] By this time in the war, Clark was becoming paranoid about the British. The general was further infuriated, this time by Winston Churchill, who demanded that every dispatch sent to his office must spell "theater," not "theatre" and "through" should not be spelt "thru."[111] Eventually Alexander concurred and the bridgehead became known as the "Fifth Army Allied Bridgehead Force."[112] Clark's battle over the naming of the bridgehead was over, but the battle for Cassino and the Monte Cassino Monastery was not.

*   *   *

After the bombing of the abbey and the failed attack by the New Zealand Corps, Freyberg and Alexander decided to regroup their forces and try one last time. The new plan, to begin on 15 March, called for Freyberg's corps to take Monastery Hill in an attack from Cassino. This meant the town had to be captured. The plan was broken into four phases with the first calling for the 4th Indian Division to capture key points along hills on the western edge of Cassino. When this had been achieved the Allied air force along with ground artillery would bombard the town. After the bombing of Cassino the 2d New Zealand Division with Combat Command B of the 1st Armored Division would take Cassino, form a bridgehead across the Rapido along Highway 6, and then take Monastery Hill. The final phase called for exploitation into the Liri Valley with the 4th New Zealand Armoured Brigade and other forces.[113]

The attack began 15 March and the Allies appeared to be making some gains into Cassino. However, the bombing of Cassino hurt the New Zealander's drive as their armor was slowed by the huge craters left from the impact of the bombs; some craters even had to be bridged.[114] The bombing, while devastating, was not terribly accurate. Clark believed half the bombs missed the target area entirely, while 60 percent of the remaining bombs were in the prescribed area and effective with the rest falling with no damage.[115] The planned assault to take Monastery Hill and the abbey were checked by the Germans on 19 March, and again the next day.[116]

With the New Zealand Corps unable to take the hill Alexander and Clark had to make a decision: whether to call off the attack and reorganize the entire front or proceed with it for another twenty-four to thirty-six hours. Alexander's plan of reorganization called for the entire Fifth Army to move to the Anzio bridgehead, with the remaining British forces spreading out along the Cassino front.[117] General Alphonse Pierre Juin, commander of the French Expeditionary Corps, wanted the attack cancelled immediately and wanted the Allies to cut the German supply line and starve the enemy out.[118] Juin's plan was ignored, but his advice was beginning to influence both Alexander and Clark. By 23 March Clark wrote in his diary that he believed the New Zealand Corps's attack was finished. "I hate to see the Cassino show flop. It has been a most difficult situation that I have been in, due to the fact that all troops involved were British. . . . I am most anxious to start the reorganization, for I am sure that with the Americans and French together we will advance."[119]

Reluctantly, Alexander and Clark decided to proceed with the attack. By 25 March the attack on Cassino was stopped by Alexander, Clark, and the Allied high command. The battle for the abbey and Monastery Hill would have to wait. The battles for the Anzio beachhead and Cassino were finished until May 1944. From 22 January to 31 March, the dual campaigns inflicted 52,130 casualties: 22,092 British and Commonwealth, 22,219 American, and 7,421 French.[120] While the Germans had suffered tremendously, the Allied high command and the press believed the two operations were failures. Writing to Devers at the end of March, Clark explained why the offensives had proceeded so slowly:

> You mention being shocked with the slowness of the attack. I am too, but probably not to the extent that you are, for I have seen for the past eight months, and had impressed upon me, the reasons for the slowness of our progress in Italy. They are: Terrain, weather, carefully prepared defensive positions in the mountains, determined and well-trained enemy troops, grossly inadequate means at our disposal while on the offensive, with approximately equal forces to the defender.[121]

Clark's statement explained not just Anzio and Cassino, but the entire war in Italy. With limited resources and troops, the Allies fought against some of Germany's best soldiers, in some of the toughest terrain of the war. The fact is that the Allies tried to achieve a major breakthrough in Anzio and Cassino with limited resources. The lessons of Anzio and Cassino taught Alexander and Clark that only a fully coordinated assault would break the German defenses and open the way to Rome.

Chapter 8

ROME: *The Prize?*

FTER MONTHS OF AGONY AT ANZIO AND CASSINO, CLARK and his Fifth Army prepared for the capture of their ultimate prize: Rome. By April the Allied Armies in Italy (AAI) were reorganized and waiting for warm spring weather to launch their assault. (Allied Armies in Italy was the name given on 9 March 1944 to the Allied ground forces that had formerly been known as the 15th Army Group.) The capture of Rome, according to Mark Clark's wife, was the high point of his career.[1] While Clark believed the same, the fall of the eternal city was, like Anzio and Cassino, shrouded in controversy. Unlike Anzio and Cassino, blame for the controversy falls squarely on the shoulders of General Clark. Angered over the rise of British dominance in Italy, Clark's relations with Alexander and the British high command were perilous. On the verge of annihilating the German 10th Army in late May, Clark's pride and prejudice towards the British would cloud his vision. The capture of Rome was not his high point; instead it was Clark at his very worst.

In preparation for the battle and to crack the vaunted Gustav Line, following the New Zealand Corps' last battle for Cassino, Alexander decided to shift the Allied forces. The British V Corps shifted to the eastern sector of the Allied line with the Eighth Army relieving the Fifth Army at Cassino and along the Rapido. Clark's Fifth Army squeezed into a thirteen-mile stretch from the Tyrrhenian Sea to the Liri River.[2] The British Eighth Army under Gen. Oliver Leese consisted of the XIII Corps under Gen. Sidney C. Kirkman on the left, astride the Liri Valley with four divisions, and X Corps on the right of the British line.[3] At the Anzio bridgehead Lucian

Truscott commanded the VI Corps' five and a half divisions: the British 1st
and 5th Divisions; the American 3d, 34th and, 45th Divisions, with Combat
Command B of the 1st Armored Division, along with the 36th Engineer
Combat Regiment and the powerful 1st Special Service Force.[4] All together
the Eighth Army had 265,371 men and the Fifth 350,276 for the offensive.[5]

Facing the Allies, Field Marshal Kesselring and his Army Group South
consisted of the Tenth and Fourteenth Armies. The Fourteenth Army under
General Eberhard von Mackensen faced the Anzio bridgehead and consisted
of two corps, the I Parachute Corps and LXXVI Infantry Corps, which
totaled eight divisions. The 92d Grenadier Division was in reserve near Civitavecchia, the 29th Panzer Grenadier Division was near Lake Bracciano, and
the 26th Panzer Division just to the east at Sezze. The 4th Parachute Division, 65th Grenadier Division, 1027th Panzer Grenadier Regiment, the
Infantry Lehr Regiment, and the 3d Panzer Grenadier Division, were all
located on the north flank of Anzio, while the 362d Grenadier and the 715th
Light divisions were on Anzio's southern flank.

General Heinrich von Vietinghoff's Tenth Army was situated on Germany's southern front in Italy with the LI Mountain Corps (334th Grenadier
Division, 305th Grenadier Division, and units of the 114th Light Division)
along the Adriatic coast. The XIV Panzer Corps consisted of the 94th, 71st,
and parts of the 44th Grenadier divisions; the 15th Panzer Grenadier Division in the Liri Valley; the newly renamed1st Parachute Panzer Division
Herman Goering, and the 44th Infantry Division near Cassino; the 5th
Mountain Division in the central mountains; and the 90th Grenadier Division in reserve northwest of Cassino outside of Frosinone.[6] Though under-
strength, Kesselring's forces consisted of twenty-two divisions, about the same
number as the Allies.[7]

Before the offensive began, Mark Clark took a well-deserved break, leaving Italy on 9 April 1944 for the United States. After relaxing with his wife
in Sulphur Springs, West Virginia, Clark returned to Italy on 23 April.[8] On
5 May the rejuvenated Fifth Army commander received plans for the upcoming offensive from Alexander. The British general's goal was not to capture
Rome, but to destroy the German 10th Army. Codenamed Diadem, Alexander's plan called for the destruction of the German Tenth Army as well as
an Allied push to drive the German Fourteenth Army to the north of Rome
and then to pursue the enemy to the Rimini-Pisa line, inflicting maximum
losses on the fleeing German forces.[9]

According to the plan Clark's Fifth Army was to capture the Ausonia
defile and advance south of the Liri and Sacco Rivers. At Alexander's choosing VI Corps would attack out of the Anzio bridgehead. The breakout was
to be along the Cori-Valmontone axis with the objective of cutting Highway
6 in the Valmontone area. Cutting Highway 6 was vital to Alexander's plan
for this would cut off and surround the German 10th Army.

This aspect of Alexander's order was, like most British orders, vague,
allowing Clark to interpret it as he pleased, and he interpreted it to mean
that capture of Rome, not the destruction of the Germany Tenth Army, was
his major objective. However, while the order was vague on how to cut the
line or how much of his forces to employ, it is clear that Alexander wanted
Highway 6 to be cut. After the fall of Rome the Allies were to pursue the
retreating Germans and capture the Viterbo airfields and port of Civitavecchia. The last phase of the plan called for the Allies to advance on the city of
Leghorn.[10]

With D-Day set for 11 May, victory fever swept through the Fifth Army
ranks. On 5 May Clark held a news conference and warned of overconfi-
dence:

> Now I want to say a word as to over-optimism. I have every confi-
> dence in the success of this attack but I must emphasize that we must
> not let ourselves look into the crystal ball and by wishful thinking
> realize that we are going to join up or capture Rome within a few
> days. We should join up—we will join up—and we will march on to
> the north in reasonable time.[11]

The Allies had reason to be optimistic. Their forces were experienced,
well trained and rested, and had a small numerical advantage. Much of Clark's
anxiety was centered on Highway 6 and getting to Valmontone. Clark was
worried, and wrote in his diary before the invasion, "in order to get to Valmontone the beachhead forces would more or less by-pass the Alban Hills,
leaving the enemy holding high ground that was vital to us if we were to
enter Rome."[12] Clark was not sure his VI Corps was powerful enough for
the attack and was again angry with Alexander, who was solely responsible
for the decision to launch the attack out of the bridgehead.

Clark, as he had at Salerno, believed that a commander should think of
every possible outcome and plan accordingly. According to his memoirs Clark
spoke to Alexander about the rigidity of the army group plan: "I doubted it

because there were other roads over which they could withdraw. I pointed out that I merely did not want to have to follow any rigid preconceived ideas in the breakout, and that if we played our cards right we had a chance for a great victory."[13] After discussing this with Alexander, Clark ordered the VI Corps to plan for three possibilities. The first plan, codenamed Plan Grasshopper, called for the VI Corps to attack and hold the high ground near Sezze and advance to Frosinone or Terracina, depending on the situation. The second plan, codenamed Plan Turtle, called for the VI Corps to attack on the left to reduce the Factory salient and more north and northwest to break the right flank of the German defensive line. The last plan, and the one VI Corps commander Lucian Truscott recommended, was Plan Buffalo, which called for the VI Corps to drive through Cisterna, take the high ground near Cori, and attack towards Artena with the final objective of cutting Highway 6 near Valmontone.[14]

Meeting Truscott on 5 May to finalize plans for the critical Anzio breakout Alexander told Truscott "very quietly and firmly that there was only one direction in which the attack should or would be launched and that was from Cisterna to cut Highway 6 in the vicinity of Valmontone in the rear of the German main forces."[15] Plan Buffalo *would* be used. After reading Truscott's report Clark exploded in anger over his belief that "Alex [is] trying to run my army."[16] Infuriated, Clark wrote in his diary a condemnation of Alexander's leadership and further professed the growing British conspiracy to have Eighth Army gain the glory for liberating Rome:

> I told Alexander that if Truscott's report was correct I resented deeply his issuing any instructions to my subordinates; that if he did not like the manner in which I was carrying on the functions of the VI Corps he should issue any orders to the contrary through me and that under no circumstances would I tolerate his direct dealings with subordinates.... I know factually that there are interests brewing for the Eighth Army to take Rome, and I might as well let Alexander know now that if he attempts anything of that kind he will have another all-out battle on his hands; namely, with me.[17]

Still in a frenzy Clark met with Truscott the next day and told the VI Corps commander that, "the capture of Rome is the only important objective."[18] Clark was laying the groundwork for switching the axis of attack out of the bridgehead towards Rome. Under direct orders from Alexander,

Truscott, who believed that Alexander was right, told Clark that the VI Corps was "prepared to do the BUFFALO Operation under conditions now existing on the beachhead on 7 days notice."[19]

Clark remained very angry with Alexander, and continued to berate him in his diary, but he had no choice but to go along with Plan Buffalo:

> I told Alexander that I wanted to attack out of the beachhead with everything I had; that if conditions were right I wanted to attack towards Cori but that what I was guarding against was pre-conceived ideas as to what exactly was to be done and that he felt that he and Harding had much pre-conceived ideas. I told him that I thought there was a chance for a great victory if we played our cards right and did not attack prematurely. He kept pulling on me the idea that we were to annihilate the entire German Army and did it so many times that I told him that I did not believe that we had too many chances to do that; that the Boche was too smart. . . . I told him that inasmuch as the attack was to be all-American I would strongly recommend that we sit tight, maintain our flexibility and under no conditions should we permit the main attack to be stalled and then try to save our face by a premature attack out of the beachhead. I told him that I had directed Truscott to give first priority to the Cori attack but that he would continue plans for the attack to the west of Colli Laziali. I wanted to have plans prepared to meet any eventuality, keeping my mind free of any definite commitment before the battle started.[20]

Along with Alexander's offensive, Clark and the French Expeditionary Corps planned to secure Monte Majo in order to help break the Gustav Line in the mountains. Monte Majo was an ideal spot for the highly skilled mountain warriors of the French Expeditionary Corps to attack. As the Germans did not believe the Allies would attack such a rugged spot in the line, the hill was weakly defended.[21] The plan was championed by French Expeditionary Corps commander Alphonse Juin and II Corps commander Geoffrey Keyes, and called for two divisions of the French Expeditionary Corps to take Monte Majo with the II Corps advancing on Monte Scauri, Castellonorato, and Monte dei Bracchi. Following the capture of Monte Majo, one division of the French Expeditionary Corps would mop up the Germans northward to Sant'Ambrogio, while another division would take the high ridge running northwest from Mount Major to Castellone Hill, with the II Corps ordered to clear the Ausonia Valley.

The next phase of the operation called for the entire French Expeditionary Corps to attack Esperia and Monte d'Oro and then for the II Corps to pass through and exploit the advantage northwest to Monte Leucio and Pico.[22] Clark cheerfully approved the plan, and it would be the success of Juin and the French Expeditionary Corps that would greatly aid Alexander's offensive. The brilliant maneuver of the French would be one of Clark's most important decisions of the spring offensive.

With the plans set and the forces ready for battle, the two stalwarts of the Italian campaign separately issued statements to their troops for the upcoming battle. Alexander's letter discussed the troubles the Allied Armies in Italy had already faced: "Throughout the past winter you have fought hard and valiantly and killed many Germans. Perhaps you are disappointed that we have not been able to advance faster and farther, but I and those who know, realize full well how magnificently you have fought amongst these almost insurmountable obstacles of rocky, trackless mountains, deep in snow, and in valleys blocked by rivers and mud, against a stubborn foe."[23]

Clark, on the other hand, realizing that Operation Overlord was mere weeks away, boosted the morale of his troops and told them that their actions so far were helping win the war. "It may appear to you, since the Fifth Army's progress in terms of territory gained during the past few months has been slow, that our campaign is no longer a major one or that it is not having significant success in the war as a whole. Nothing could be further from the truth."[24] Six hours after the pep talks, at 2300 hours on 11 May, twenty-three hundred guns opened up on the Germans: the Battle for Rome had begun.[25]

The initial attacks on 12 May went extremely well. The Gustav Line was not yet cracked, but the German position was nearing collapse. On the third day of the attack the French Expeditionary Corps captured Monte Majo and with the capture of Monte Revole on 16 May the Gustav Line was breached.[26] A delighted Clark praised the French Expeditionary Corps and General Juin in his diary on the success of the French attack: "The Fifth Army attack has been characterized by great aggressiveness and dash on the part of the French Expeditionary Corps. Our plans were well conceived and have been executed as previously planned."[27] While the II Corps attack was advancing slower than that of the French Expeditionary Corps, Alexander's offensive was working. On 18 May the abbey at Monte Cassino finally fell to the 3d Carpathian (Polish) Division. The Liri Valley, the gateway to Rome, was open.[28] The time was nearly ripe for the VI Corps breakout from Anzio.

Realizing that the Germans were about to crumble, Alexander and Clark met on 17 May to decide when to launch the VI Corps attack. After discussing the ongoing battle Alexander believed it was time for VI Corps to break out. Clark, still unsure of the direction of the breakout, asked the British commander, "Where will Truscott go from there?" Alexander refused to budge from the objectives of Buffalo, as Clark later recorded in his diary:

> I then brought up the subject of direction of attack out of the bridge-head on Cori and Valmontone. He remains adamant that that is the correct and only direction of attack, regardless of the enemy situation. . . . I replied that in getting to Valmontone I had gone over the mountains, had absolutely no roads and would only have foot troops and pack equipment. He brushed this aside. I pointed this out because I want him to evaluate the situation when the time to attack approaches, in order that we can attack in the right direction, and the Cori-Valmontone may be the wrong direction.[29]

Alexander believed that the attack toward Cor-Valmontone would cut the German lines to the east and entrap the German Tenth Army between the VI Corps and the British Eighth Army.[30] After Alexander declared that Plan Buffalo would be used he left the meeting believing that Clark was in full accord with the mission to destroy German Tenth Army, not to capture Rome. Even at this early date, it was clear Clark wanted Rome for the Americans and was afraid that the British might get there first.

Still unconvinced of the validity of Alexander's Plan Buffalo-only, Clark decided to meet with Truscott on 19 May. The day before the meting Clark cabled Truscott and told him, "At conference please be prepared to discuss feasibility of following operation as an alternative plan."[31] If he could not convince Alexander to change the direction of the attack, Clark would push his subordinates, under the cloak of flexibility, to change directions. During their meeting Clark pushed Truscott for an alternate plan, telling him that "Plan BUFFALO would be carried out as planned but that he wanted General Truscott to be flexible in his plans and be prepared to change the direction of the attack north from Cori-Valmontone to an attack to the northwest toward Rome. Much depended upon the German reaction to the attack on the main Allied front."[32]

Although it was appropriate for Clark to have alternate plans, it is clear

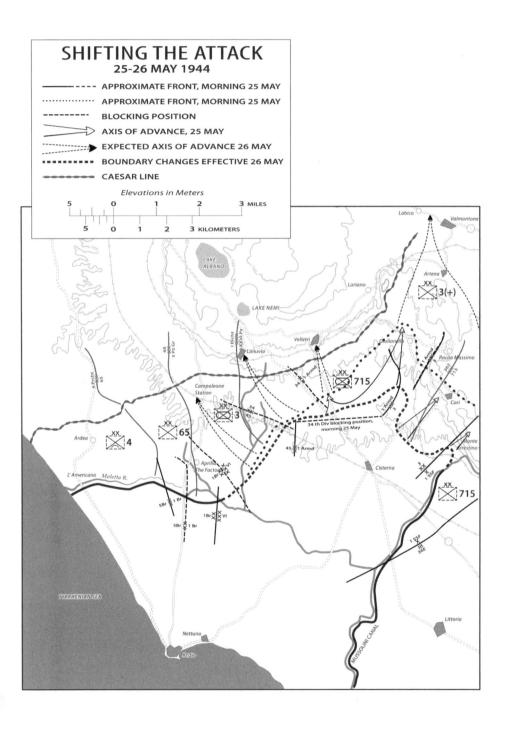

SHIFTING THE ATTACK
25-26 MAY 1944

———— -----	APPROXIMATE FRONT, MORNING 25 MAY
··················	APPROXIMATE FRONT, MORNING 25 MAY
---------	BLOCKING POSITION
▷	AXIS OF ADVANCE, 25 MAY
▶	EXPECTED AXIS OF ADVANCE 26 MAY
■■■■■■■	BOUNDARY CHANGES EFFECTIVE 26 MAY
●●●●●●	CAESAR LINE

Elevations in Meters

in Clark's diaries that he was never convinced of the efficacy of Plan Buffalo and was prepared to use any excuse to switch the axis of the VI Corps attack away from Valmontone and on to Rome. Clark's eventual wanton disregard for Alexander's orders was not a spur of the moment decision, but the result of a month-long plan to cover his tracks and have Fifth Army capture Rome.

Clark would grow even more upset with Alexander, whom he believed was trying to run his Fifth Army. On 20 May Alexander decided that the VI Corps attack would begin on the night of 21–22 May or the morning of 22 May. Clark recorded his fury in his diary: "I was shocked when I received it to think that a decision of this importance would have been made without reference to me. I sent that word back to General Alexander, who made the weak excuse that he felt that we had discussed it for the past three days."[33] Clark had no real reason to be upset with Alexander; after all, he was the commander of all Allied forces in Italy and was senior to Clark. Alexander did nothing wrong in not telling Clark. The reason he was so upset was not that Alexander was running his army, but that he disagreed with the direction of the VI Corps attack. After learning the date of the attack, Clark requested a delay of twenty-four to forty-eight hours to better prepare his forces.[34] The attack was now set for 23 May.

The American VI Corps attack began as scheduled on the 23d and moved towards Cisterna.[35] Truscott's plan was for the 1st Armored Division to push along the Le Mole Canal and cut the railroad line northwest of Cisterna and then proceed to Highway 7. After getting onto the road the division would cross the corridor between the Alban Hills and the Lepini mountains. Truscott's old division, the 3d, was to concentrate on Cisterna and capture the town.[36] The VI Corps attack began fairly well, and only the lack of Allied artillery support prevented the 3d Division from seizing Cisterna.[37] The next day the fortunes of the VI Corps improved with the 1st Armored Division exploiting its success from the first day and the 3d Division encircling Cisterna the following day. On 25 May Truscott was ready to break out of the bridgehead and ordered the 1st Special Service Force to take Monte Arrestino, the 3d Division to capture Cisterna and drive on Cori, and the 1st Armored Division to drive on Velletri and proceed northwestward to Valmontone while the 45th Division anchored the left flank of the assault.[38] Cisterna fell on the 25th; Valmontone was a mere ten miles away, and with it the destruction of the German Tenth Army. With the offensive proceeding well, Clark prepared plans for the link-up of the VI Corps bridgehead forces with the rest of the Fifth Army.

This successful link-up was one of the proudest moments of his life. Much later war correspondents and historians alike became disgusted with how Clark handled the situation. Traveling with twenty-five photographers and correspondents, Clark was trying to get publicity for the long sought-after link-up not just for himself, but for his forces and their families.[39] Yet even at his moment of triumph, Clark was still angry with the British, as his letter to Gruenther on the importance of the link-up reveals:

> As you know, the joining up of my two Fifth Army forces will be one of the highlights of the Fifth Army's career. It is primarily a Fifth Army matter, and I want you to tell General Alexander that I want authority given me immediately to issue a simple communiqué from here as soon as II Corps troops have moved overland into the bridgehead. The rebuttal they may give you—that a temporary joining up does not mean a permanent one—is unimportant, for the story, and the big argument, is when Fifth Army main front troops move overland into the bridgehead.[40]

On 25 May the Anzio force united with the rest of Fifth Army and Clark issued a special communiqué of the moment to his entire force: "Patrols from the Fifth Army main front made contact with patrols from Fifth Army allied bridgehead in the early morning of 25 May. This brings to a climax the spectacular advance of Fifth Army of more than sixty miles in only fourteen days."[41] According to Clark, the juncture took place a few miles southeast of the beachhead along the coastal highway between Terracina and Anzio.[42] The forces that met were the 36th Engineer Regiment and advance elements of II Corps, the 48th Engineer Regiment and 91st Reconnaissance Regiment.[43]

Though proud, Clark was mildly embarrassed by the way journalists and the public viewed the link-up. Writing to his wife after the juncture, Clark wondered if he came off looking like a glory hound: "It may have sounded dramatic in the papers the way I rushed to witness the joining of the two forces, but it meant more to me than anything since our success at Salerno. The way some of the correspondents expressed it may have sounded as though I was looking for publicity. Did you get that impression? At any rate, I had to be there when the two forces joined up. It meant too much to me."[44] A few days later, Clark wrote to his wife that they should be more careful with the press and warned her, "We must be very careful not to overdo on publicity, for there are still those who resent deeply my publicity."[45] Most of all, Clark was proud of Fifth Army and its achievements. With the Anzio bridgehead now behind him for good Clark believed it was not time to follow Alexander's orders and destroy the German Tenth Army; it was time for the Americans to take Rome.

On 25 May Clark decided to change the axis of the VI Corps attack. He told his G-3, Donald Brann: "We will capture Rome ... it is just a matter of time."[46] The day before Clark issued the directive he had discussed briefly with Truscott about switching the attack northeast toward Rome. Truscott believed that his VI Corps could do it, but only if the German Fourteenth Army shifted the I Parachute Corps from the Alban Hills to Valmontone.[47] The simple fact, according to Truscott's statement, was that Plan Buffalo was the correct move, but that if the Germans moved a large force into the Valmontone, then and only then should Clark change the axis of the attack.

On 25 May Clark issued instructions to Brann. The order was not only about the direction of the attack, but also for Brann to placate Alexander by assuring him that his instructions were being followed:

> Have directed VI Corps to attack as follows prior to noon tomorrow. 3d Division and Special Service Force push vigorously from Cori area on Valmontone via Artena, elements of 1st Armored Division in support. 34th and 45th Divisions attack northwest, followed by 36th Division echeloned to right rear. . . . I am launching this new attack with all speed possible in order to take advantage of impetus of our advance and in order to overwhelm the enemy in what may be a demoralized condition at the present time. You can assure General Alexander that this is an all-out attack. We are shooting the works.[48]

Later in the afternoon, Clark sent Brann to Truscott's command post where the Fifth Army G-3 told the VI Corps commander, "The Boss wants you to leave Highway 6 and mount that assault you discussed with him to the northwest as soon as you can."[49] As Truscott's memoirs recount:

> I was dumbfounded. I protested that the conditions were not right. There was no evidence of any withdrawal from the western part of the beachhead, nor was there evidence of any concentration in the Valmontone area except light reconnaissance elements of the Her-

man Goering Division. This was no time to drive to the northwest where the enemy was still strong; we should pour our maximum power into the Valmontone Gap to insure the destruction of the retreating German Army."[50]

Clark's diary further explains his decision to change the direction of the attack. Clark believed the new plan posed a "direct threat toward Rome," that the Germans were in a bad position, and that the attack would gain the high ground north and south of Velletri, which Clark hoped would force the Germans to withdraw and leave the road to Rome open.[51] On 27 May Clark again tried to explain his decision. His diary entries about switching the attack were meant less for himself and more for historians:

> As I have often indicated, the direction of the attack assigned me for the Anzio effort was in the direction of Cori-Valmontone. This was due to a long-standing, pre-conceived idea by Alexander, instigated by this Chief of Staff, Harding. It was based on the false premise that if Route #6 were cut at Valmontone a Germany Army would be annihilated. This is ridiculous, for many roads lead to the north from Arce, Frosinone and in between. I was forced into this attack, but it had a good feature in that it took Cisterna and gave us observation in the area of Cori. If the going became tough on Valmontone I could shift the weight of my attack to the northwest. Exactly this has happened . . . we will capture Rome. It is just a question of time now.[52]

After ordering Truscott to make the necessary changes in the attack on 25 May, Gruenther informed Clark that Alexander thought the decision to change the direction of the attack was wise: "I explained the plan of today's attack in the bridgehead as outlined in your radio, and as further amplified by you while you were here yesterday. General Alexander agreed that the plan is a good one. He stated, 'I am for any line of action which the Army Commander believes will offer a chance to continue his present success.' About five minutes later he said, 'I am sure that the Army Commander will continue to push *toward Valmontone* [emphasis added], won't he?'"[53]

Always the gentleman, Alexander displayed a cool demeanor to Gruenther, but in reality he was furious at Clark's insubordination. By the time Alexander was informed of Clark's decision to change the direction of the

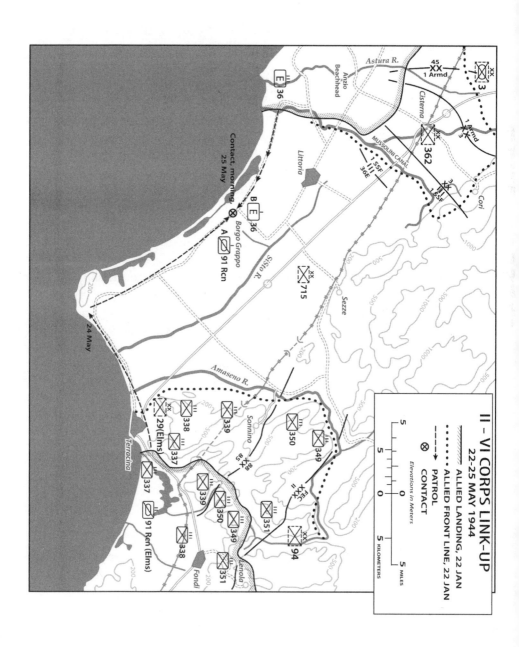

II – VI CORPS LINK-UP
22-25 MAY 1944

ALLIED LANDING, 22 JAN
ALLIED FRONT LINE, 22 JAN
PATROL
⊗ CONTACT

Elevations in Meters

5   5   0   5 MILES
5   5   0   5 KILOMETERS

attack there was little he could do. He had no choice but to go along with it.

In an interview after the war Alexander stated he believed Clark had misinformed him about why he switched the direction of the attack. "At the time Clark decided to shift the axis of attack from Cori-Valmontone to an attack up the Albano Road-Lanuvio Line on 25 May 1944 Alexander was told by Clark that the thrust towards Valmontone was being stopped by German reinforcements and that he was shifting the axis to break through quickly."[54] As his memoirs reflect, for the remainder of his life Alexander believed that Clark erred in his decision. "[F]or some inexplicable reason General Clark's Anglo-American forces never reached their objectives. . . . If he had succeeded in carrying out my plan the disaster to the enemy would have been much greater; indeed, most of the German forces south of Rome would have been destroyed. True, the battle ended in a decisive victory for us, but it was not complete as it might have been."[55]

In an interview with Sidney Matthews, Alexander stated that Clark's decision came at a critical time and that, "if the Germans [did not block] us at the time the axis of attack was changed [then] it was a mistake to shift the axis of attack, for it ended the chance of cutting off the 10th Army on the southern front."[56] The only answer Alexander could ever come up with to explain Clark's decision was that "the immediate lure of Rome for its publicity value persuaded him to switch the direction of his advance."[57] Alexander was right: the allure of Rome, caught Clark's imagination and persuaded him to change the direction of the attack. With Operation Overlord and the invasion of Southern France about to take place, Clark knew he and his Fifth Army had one last chance for fame and publicity: the liberation of Rome. While Clark had been careful with the press and concerned over his growing fame, Rome clouded his decision-making and the Allies lost an excellent chance to destroy a large portion of the German ground forces in Italy.

For the rest of his life, Clark stuck to his decision to change the direction of the attack. According to Sidney Matthews, who interviewed Clark about his decision to switch the axis:

General Clark had never favored the BUFFALO attack 23–25 May 1944. The Germans had too many roads parallel to Highway No. 6 for that effort to succeed in cutting off the Germans in the Liri Valley. In addition, General Clark regarded the Anzio force as not strong enough to cut Highway No. 6. . . . Clark said that he always had to be careful about making it possible for the British Eighth Army to get an easy victory by 5th Army's efforts and swinging along on the successful offensive of the American Fifth Army. General Clark indicated that this was at least one factor in his preference for an attack against the Alban Hill Line rather than against Valmontone on Highway No. 6.... When General Clark changed the axis of the beachhead attack on 25 May 1944, he did so because he did not believe the attack against Valmontone would cut off the Germans and he thought that the Germans in the Alban Hills had weakened their front so that the attack in that direction would succeed. Also, General Clark had received information from his G-2 that German reserves were likely to move down and block us at Valmontone. Therefore, he decided to change the axis of attack.[58]

Clark's memoirs, however, basically admit that it was the lure of Rome that caused him to switch the direction of the attack:

I should point out at this time that the Fifth Army had had an extremely difficult time throughout the winter campaign and that we were now trying to make up for our earlier slow progress. We had massed all of our strength to take Rome. We were keyed up, and in the heat of battle there was almost certain to be clashes of personalities and ideas over this all-out drive. We not only wanted the honor of capturing Rome, but we felt that we more than deserved it; that it would to a certain extent make up for the buffeting and the frustration we had undergone in keeping up the winter pressure against the Germans. My own feeling was that nothing was going to stop us on our push toward the Italian capital. Not only did we intend to become the first army in fifteen centuries to seize Rome from the south, but we intended to see that the people back home knew that it was the Fifth Army that did the job and knew the price that had been paid for it. I think that these considerations are important to an understanding of the behind-scenes differences of opinion that occurred in this period.[59]

The trouble with this statement is that it is not true. Alexander's offensive was designed to destroy the German forces, not to capture Rome. Clark knew this and on 22 May, a few days before he ordered Truscott to switch the direction of the attack, he held an off-the-record meeting with the press and informed them that the plan was to cut Highway 6 and to destroy as many Germans as possible.[60] Even after the decision had been made, Clark told the reporters at a 31 May press conference: "This attack does not have Rome as its primary objective but to kill and annihilate as many of the Germans as possible in our front." In his diary, however, Clark revealed that he hadn't lost sight of the fact that the City of Rome might be gained as a result of this attack.[61]

By this time Clark's fear of a British conspiracy in Italy had fully taken hold. In his diary Clark wrote down his worries about the upcoming capture of Rome: "First, the British have their eye on Rome, notwithstanding Alexander's constant assurance to me that Rome is in the sector of the Fifth Army. They have drawn the Army boundary south of Route #6 just to the outskirts of Rome and then veered it to the north. . . . Second, my French Corps is being pinched out. A more gallant fighting organization never existed. . . ."[62]

Clark's fear of losing Rome and his fear of a British conspiracy are equally absurd. Clark's Fifth Army was going to capture Rome; Fifth Army was in the best position to do so, but the saddest part of Clark's decision was that *his* plan did not work. The change of direction did not lead to Rome, but into the heart of the German defenses.[63] On 29 May, Clark ordered II Corps to capture the Valmontone Gap.[64] In the end it was Plan Buffalo that opened up Rome, not Clark's decision to switch the axis of attack.

Overall, Clark's decision was a grave mistake and the worst decision of his career. While there was no certainty that the German Tenth Army would have been destroyed, Plan Buffalo offered the greatest hope. Historian Sidney Matthews believed: "that General Clark did not see the Valmontone attack itself as an excellent opportunity for quick advance to Rome is puzzling. Terrain, the nature of the enemy's defenses, and the enemy's lack of substantial forces to halt a drive on Rome via Valmontone, all favored the adoption of this course."[65]

Clark willingly and with full knowledge switched the direction of the attack to gain Rome, not because the Germans forced him to change plans, but because he wanted it for himself and his Fifth Army. It was the first time in his military career that Clark's ego and lust for success got the better of him and led him to a wrong decision. With Overlord just weeks away and Allied resources in Italy on the wane, Clark knew that this was the last chance to steal the headlines.

While the capture of Rome was a remarkable success, it was nothing more than a symbolic victory. Kesselring still had a large force in Italy, and the mountainous and hilly terrain meant that the war in Italy was far from over. Regardless, in his speech to VI Corps on 30 May Clark was convinced he had made the right decision. "We stand now on the threshold of Rome. Before many days have passed we shall have freed this first of the European capitals from Nazi domination."[66] Clark was right, but the capture of Rome was not worth the price.

*   *   *

As the liberation of Rome grew closer, Clark and the British again squabbled over publicity and credit for the capture. Clark made it clear that, "With reference to the publicity on Rome, they left with me a copy of the following letter. I agreed to it and made it plain that when troops entered Rome I would radio 'Fifth Army troops have entered Rome.'"[67] Further complicating matters was whether or not Clark planned on a formal entry into the city. On 3 June, with the fall of Rome hours away, Clark received a message from Alexander that he wished for a detachment from the II Polish Corps to participate in the entry of Rome. Clark, still at odds with Alexander, mockingly told Al Gruenther that he had no formal plans for the entry of Rome: "See if you can get me a couple of thousand Swedes to run through the weeds in Rome, then I'll be all set. You politely tell them that I am not framing the tactical entrance of troops in Rome. God and the Boche are dictating that. . . . Tell Alexander I concur in his idea to have a big parade about a week later, but let's get through and exploit our success to the north and Civitavecchia before we think of parades."[68]

Later, Clark would be nearly insubordinate again, after the British commander asked for the Eighth Army to participate in the capture of Rome. An upset Clark told Alexander "if he [Alexander] gave him [Clark] such an order he would refuse to obey it and if the Eighth Army tried to advance on Rome, Clark said he would have his troops fire on the Eighth Army."[69]

On the verge of entering the city, on 3 June an ecstatic Clark wrote Fifth Army chief of staff and good friend Al Gruenther: "You can yell 'whoopee,' the news is great."[70] However, a worried Gruenther informed Clark that, "The Command Post has gone to hell. No one is doing any work here this afternoon. All semblance of discipline has broke down."[71] On the same day the Germans appeared to be having similar problems. After talking with the Vatican the OKW issued a joint declaration naming Rome an open city.[72] As for the German forces, Kesselring was ordered to hold his front south and southwest of Rome long enough to aid the withdrawal, and then they were to retreat north of Rome to the next defensive line.[73]

With the capture of Rome only hours away, Clark wrote a message to his forces:

> Fifth Army forces are approaching rapidly the city of Rome. The intentions of the enemy are not known; he may decide to fight within the city or withdraw to the north. It is my most urgent desire that Fifth Army troops protect both public and private property in the city of Rome. Every effort will be made to prevent our troops from firing into the city; however, the deciding factor is the enemy's dispositions and actions. If the German opposes our advance by dispositions and fires that necessitate Fifth Army troops firing into the city of Rome, battalion commanders and all high commanders are authorized to take appropriate action without delay to defeat the opposing enemy elements by fire and movement. Such action to be reported immediately to this headquarters.[74]

Around the time of Clark's message an infamous event is reputed to have taken place on the outskirts of Rome. II Corps commander Geoffrey Keyes met with 1st Special Service Force commander Robert Frederick to discuss the final push into the city. General Keyes asked Fredericks what was slowing the drive. "The Germans, sir," the startled Fredericks replied. Inquiring how long it would take Fredericks "to get to across the city limits," Keyes learned it would take "the rest of the day" due to "a couple of SP guns up there." He then informed Fredericks: "General Clark must be across the city limits by four o'clock" because he "must have a photograph taken," to which Fredericks replied, "Tell the General to give me an hour."[75]

While this conversation likely did occur, Clark, with all his inadequacies, would not have allowed his soldiers to be killed or put into a dangerous position for a photograph. While it was clear to all that Clark wanted Rome before the announcement of the Overlord landings, he would not have foolishly rushed his forces into the city. He had erred in switching the direction of the attack away from Valmontone, but that attack could have succeeded if it had been applied in force. A plunge straight into Rome would have been disastrous, and Clark never would have allowed it to happen, no matter how badly he wanted to take the city.

Finally, at 0800 on 4 June, the first Allied forces rolled into Rome. The first official unit was the 88th Reconnaissance Troop of the 88th Division.[76] Entering Rome the next day Clark traveled in a jeep and got lost. Trying to find Capitoline Hill to meet with his corps commanders, Clark was interrupted by an English-speaking priest. Clark asked him, "Where is Capitoline Hill?" The priest responded, "We are certainly proud of the American 5th Army. My name is _____."[77] Clark, looking down from his jeep, responded, "My name is Clark."[78]

Meeting with Keyes, Truscott, and Juin at the top of Capitoline Hill, Clark and his commanders were surrounded by reporters and well-wishers. According to a disgusted Eric Sevareid, Clark looked to the reporters and told them, "Well, gentlemen, I didn't really expect to have a press conference here—I just called a little meeting with my corps commanders to discuss the situation. However, I'll be glad to answer your questions. This is a great day for the Fifth Army."[79] Sevareid, who did not get along with Clark, was probably overreacting; Clark did nothing egregious in meeting with his corps commanders. During the next few days the Fifth Army continued to clear out Rome and advance north of the city. For Clark the capture of Rome by his Fifth Army was only a front-page headline for a day. On 6 June the Overlord landings took place.

After the fall of Rome Clark received numerous congratulatory messages from everybody but one—his spouse. Clark radioed her: "I have received radiograms of congratulations from practically everybody you ever heard of, but none from my wife."[80]

Eisenhower, who was obviously busy with the on-going Overlord invasion, took time to write to his friend: "Your accomplishments have more than justified your high reputation and my great confidence in you and your ability."[81] President Roosevelt's message read: "You have made the American people very happy. It is a grand job well done. Congratulations to you and the men of the Fifth Army."[82] And finally, Winston Churchill, the individual who had the most to do with the entire Italian campaign, wrote: "We rejoice with you in the splendid exploits, comradeship and tireless energy of the United States, British and other Allied troops under your command and it gives me the greatest pleasure to congratulate you once again on your brilliant leading."[83]

There was even a song written for Mark Clark and the capture of Rome, entitled "The General Clark Liberator of Rome March":

Marching forward / Ever forward / We hit the beach at Salerno, /

We jumped the brink at Volturno, / We broke through at An-zi-o. / Just the job for GI Joe. //

  Fighting Vino, / Or Cassino, / Nothing's ever alarming / To the Fighting Fifth Army. / We will fight / For long or brief / For our daring six-foot chief. //

  . . . Mark Clark has won it, / Italy's Capital. / None ever did it / Even Hannibal. / Hitler, Gothic, any Line / Nothing can stop us now. / We've got the man, / With the guts and plan, / Who'll lead us to Vict'ry and Home again. . . . [84]

There was, however, one somewhat troubled reaction to the fall of Rome. On 8 June, just days after the city fell, Clark had a short meeting with Pope Pius XII to discuss the war in Italy and the future of the conflict. The Pope was puzzled by the American reaction: "You know, I think your American soldiers do not like me," he told Clark. The Pope continued: "Well, I appear for these audiences after the soldiers have assembled in the courtyard. Now when Italians or other Europeans attend such audiences, I follow about the same procedure, and when I appear, they break into cheers and shouts of greeting and similar expressions of enthusiasm. But when I appear before your American soldiers, they do not utter a sound. They do not say one word."[85] Perhaps Americans were not used to cheering high religious authorities; it might have felt disrespectful.

  Clark's decision to take Rome, while strategically poor, did have two advantages. First, it did raise the morale of all the Allied troops, and secondly, as Clark described in his diaries, the capture of the city shortened the very long Allied supply lines.[86] However, the capture of Rome drastically changed the war in Italy. It had been decided previously, that after the fall of Rome, some divisions would be pulled out of Italy. While expected, the loss of these units would be devastating to Clark and his remaining forces. On 15 June the VI Corps was relieved by Gen. Willis Crittenberger's IV Corps.[87] Clark was surprisingly happy to lose the VI Corps. His best unit was hard to handle, as he wrote in his diary: "Am glad to get VI Corps out of the line. It was the most difficult corps my staff had to work with, for Truscott is not a cooperator, nor is his Chief of Staff. As a result of their Anzio experiences, the whole gang [has] become . . . prima donnas. I would sooner release that corps before any others."[88]

  By the end of July, Clark would also lose the 3d, 36th and 45th Divisions, and the entire French Expeditionary Corps. Clark was saddened to lose the

French, who had spearheaded the breakthrough of the Gustav Line. Furthermore, Clark was angry over the decision to proceed with Anvil. His diary records his belief that, if given the proper manpower and supplies, the forces in Italy could achieve more than Anvil could:

> I assume that the Combined Chiefs of Staff making these decisions know what they are doing and if ANVIL is launched feel that it will contribute . . . to the invasion and the second front more than our continued effort in Italy. I am convinced that the CCS are wrong, for they made their decision to prepare for this operation without realizing the great success the Fifth Army and Eighth Army were to have in Italy. The morale of the Fifth Army is sky high. The Boche is defeated, disorganized and demoralized. Now is the time to exploit the success. Yet, in the middle of this success I lose one Corps Headquarters and five divisions—three immediately and two within another two weeks. In other words, to prepare for the eventuality of ANVIL they are sacrificing a great victory here. It just doesn't make sense. . . .
>
> The depressing part of this is the case of General Juin. He is a superlative commander and leader. He has performed magnificently in combat, has cooperated 100% with me, and we have mutual admiration and respect for the other, as do all our troops.[89]

Ironically, Clark's dislike for Anvil would change. On 19 June Clark discussed Anvil and the war in Italy with Generals Henry Arnold and George C. Marshall. Clark's disagreement with Anvil vanished when he learned that Eisenhower wanted the invasion of Southern France. He wrote to Eisenhower after the meeting: "You know you can have every single unit I have, and they will leave here the minute the request is made. I have told my staff to give the best we have, but don't forget the rest of us, if you take most of my outfit, for we want to get back with you and wind this thing up as fast as possible."[90] In time, Clark's disagreement with the operation, that Anvil was a mistake, would return, but his friendship with Eisenhower overruled his opinion of it during the war. Even if Clark had protested Anvil in his meeting with Marshall and Arnold, it would not have mattered: Anvil was on . . . at the expense of the Italian campaign.

By the end of June the Allies were north of Rome and approaching the Arno River. During the battle for Rome, Clark's Fifth Army suffered 35,014 casualties: 5,938 killed, 26,450 wounded, and 2,626 missing.[91] In the end it seemed that Anzio had in fact paid off. It did not achieve success as quickly as hoped, but the landings set the stage for the liberation of Rome and the subsequent advance to the Arno. Alexander wrote in his memoirs: "Anzio played a vital role in the capture of Rome by giving me the means to employ a double-handed punch—from the beachhead and from Cassino—which caught the Germans in a pincer movement. Without this, I do not believe we should ever have been able to break through the German defences at Cassino."[92]

General Wilson agreed with Alexander's sentiment, as he wrote years after the war: "The pay off of Anzio lay in the drive and strength of the attack on the Alban Hills which otherwise would have been impossible without a pause to rest the troops and get up ammunition, whereas fresh troops, with all requirements, including fuel, were on the spot."[93] Wilson took the argument even further, stating that the march towards Rome and the full on pursuit of the war in Italy would have been better than the invasion of southern France and the campaign up the Rhone: "By slogging it out in Italy we could produce a far better diversion for Eisenhower's operation than by a landing in southern France using up ten divisions."[94]

In the end Clark's decision to switch the axis of attack away from Valmontone towards Rome was a mistake, but the Allied spring offensive was a success. According to the Fifth Army History of the battle:

The German Fourteenth Army was destroyed and part of the Tenth badly mangled. A few conclusive figures tell a story of their own. With some 24,000 enemy captured, an estimated 15,000 killed and a probable 35,000 wounded, a conservative total of approximately 75,000 of the enemy's strength was rendered non-effective. Our armored elements accounted for a minimum of 100 enemy tanks destroyed while the total of enemy field guns of different calibers captured runs to well over three hundred pieces.[95]

The German forces in Italy had taken a tremendous hit, and victory fever swept the Allied forces. Unfortunately for the troops the war was far from over. With dwindling supplies and manpower the Allies would have to spend another winter in the mountains of Italy while the Germans under Kesselring continued a brilliant defensive campaign.

Chapter 9

STARVING TIME
The Failed Advance
and the Second Winter

R OME HAD FALLEN, THE GERMANS WERE ON THE RUN, and Hitler wanted it stopped. Kesselring refused to do so, and told Hitler:

The point is now whether my armies are fighting or running away. I can assure you they will fight and die if I ask it of them. We are talking about something entirely different, a question much more vital: whether after Stalingrad and Tunis you can afford the loss of yet two more armies. I beg to doubt it—the more so as, if I change my plans to meet with your ideas, sooner or later the way into Germany will be opened to the Allies. On the other hand I guarantee— unless my hands are tied—to delay the Allied advance appreciably, to halt it at latest in the Apennines and thereby to create conditions for the prosecution of the war in 1945 which can be dovetailed into your general strategic scheme.[1]

Kesselring had reason to be optimistic: although his forces were retreating across the Arno, he knew the Allies in Italy were dangerously weak. With the Normandy beachhead now well established and the ground forces being built up for a breakout, Allied divisions in Italy were going to be removed for Operation Dragoon. Kesselring had another reason to be confident that he could continue to slow the Allied advance in Italy; that reason was the Gothic Line.

Fewer than two hundred miles north of Rome, the Gothic Line rested high in the Apennine Mountains and protected the invaluable, industrialized Po Valley. The line, anchored in the west of the mountains north of Pisa, stretched easterly to Rimini on the Adriatic coast.[2] Just south of the line was the Arno River. Flowing westward to the Tyrrhenian Sea through Florence and Pisa the river was about two hundred to two hundred and fifty feet wide and could rise to over thirty feet during flood stage.[3] The Germans needed a strong defensive line, because just like the Allies, they were exhausted and short of everything.

Alexander's Diadem plan had nearly wiped out the German forces in Italy. From 11 May to the fall of Rome on 4 June the Germans lost over 1,500 vehicles, 110 field artillery pieces, 125 propelled self-propelled artillery pieces, 122 tanks, and over 15,000 prisoners captured. The German Fourteenth Army had nearly been destroyed, and only the Hermann Goering Panzer Division remained combat ready. The other German divisions had been severely depleted by their earlier battles: the 71st, 305th, 362d, and 715th Grenadier divisions were annihilated, and the 15th, 29th, and 90th Panzer Grenadier divisions, along with the 44th and 92d Grenadier divisions, were partially destroyed. Directly after the fall of Rome General von Mackensen was relieved of command and replaced with Lt. Gen. Joachim Lemelsen.[4] Kesselring managed to rebuild his forces by moving the 20th Luftwaffe Field Division from Denmark, the 19th Luftwaffe Division from Holland, the 16th SS Panzer Grenadier Division Reichsführer from Hungary, and the 356th Grenadier Division from Genoa.[5] As the Germans were struggling to rebuild, Clark and the Allies were having an equally tough time.

On 5 July Alexander received a message from AFHQ, Mediterranean Theatre, informing him that, "an overriding priority for all resources in the Mediterranean Theatre between the proposed assault on southern France and the battle [in Italy] is to be given the former to the extent necessary to complete a buildup of ten divisions in the south of France."[6] This meant that support for the war in Italy was going to be further cut. By the middle of July Clark's Fifth Army had been reduced to the IV and II Corps, with only five divisions: the 34th, 85th, 88th, and 91st divisions, and the 1st Armored Division.[7] By 1 August his forces totaled only 153,323 men; two months earlier Fifth Army had 248,989 soldiers on its roles.[8] By this time the Allies in Italy had lost the VI Corps headquarters, the 45th and 3d divisions, the 1st Special Service Force, 509th Parachute Infantry Battalion, and the entire French Expeditionary Force.[9] By the end of June Clark's army had been augmented by the 91st Division, which included the hard-charging Japanese-American 442d Regimental Combat Team. Later in the campaigning north of Rome Clark also received, the 92d Division, an African-American unit. Clark did not believe this division was ready for action and in July informed Gen. Jacob Devers that he did not "feel that it is wise to count on its offensive ability in a slugging match with the Germans to the same extent as a white division. You can rest assured that I will give it every opportunity to develop its full 100% effective offensive power if it has the inherent capability of doing so."[10] The condition of Clark's forces grew even more deplorable after the fall of Leghorn on 18 July. Clark believed the 34th, 91st, and 88th divisions were used up and that the Fifth Army only had enough support troops for one corps of three divisions, two attacking with the other in reserve.[11] Some help did come from the unlikely source of Brazil.

The 25 thousand-man strong Brazilian Expeditionary Force (BEF), which included the Brazilian 1st Division along with air and naval forces, arrived in early August under Gen. J. B. Mascarenhas de Morales, and came under Clark's command.[12] The Brazilians, like the 92d Division would learn to fight and performed admirably. They were especially close to Clark as it was his idea, following the invasion of North Africa, to get Latin American countries more involved in the war. Clark scribbled a quick note into his diaries after the war praising the Brazilian Expeditionary Force: "Only Latin Americans to fight in war. . . . Great thing—always cooperative—I am very proud of them."[13] While his forces were being rebuilt, supplies and support were still lacking. Even with the new divisions the Fifth Army and the Allied drive north of Rome stalled due to exhaustion and lack of manpower. Sidney Mathews relates that Clark told him after the war that:

> Between Rome and the Arno he could have used more divisions—not deployed more at one time, but he could have alternated them and rest the most tired divisions. With more divisions than he was left he was sure he could have kept the drive north of Rome going better and could have pressed the Germans back more rapidly.[14]

Clark later commented in his memoirs, that he believed the decision to go ahead with the invasion of southern France at the expense of Italy was a terrible decision:

> A campaign that might have changed the whole history of relations between the Western world and Soviet Russia was permitted to fade away, not into nothing, but into much less than it could have been. . . . The weakening of the campaign in Italy in order to invade southern France instead of pushing on into the Balkans was one of the outstanding political mistakes of the war.[15]

Clark further added:

> I am firmly convinced that the French forces alone, with seven divisions available, could have captured Marseilles, protected General Eisenhower's southern flank, and advanced up the Rhone Valley to join hands with the main OVERLORD forces. The VI American corps, with its three divisions, could then have remained in Italy. The impetus of the Allied advance in Italy would thus not have been lost and we could have advanced into the Balkans.[16]

Unfortunately, the decision was out of Clark's hands and on 14 July Alexander issued orders for the next step in the campaign.

Alexander's forces were to continue to drive the Germans toward the Gothic Line while attempting to inflict maximum losses on the enemy. Then the Allies were to break the defensive barrier between Dicomano and Pistoia and exploit the breakthrough over the Apennine Mountains and into the Po Valley.[17] Alexander decided that the main attack to crack the Gothic Line would be at the Futa Pass, one of the lowest points in the mountain chain.[18] The Fifth Army attack was to take place on 7 August, but Clark postponed the attack until 19 August to make minor changes in the plan. It was during this time, however, that Alexander made a bold decision; he decided to shift the main attack up the eastern, Adriatic coast.[19] Alexander came about the decision after Allied intelligence reported the Futa Pass had been strengthened. Alexander believed that by attacking up the Adriatic coast, Kesselring would be forced to draw his forces to that area, which would then allow the weakened Fifth Army to strike northward along the Florence–Bologna axis.[20] Clark's forces in the center were to be aided by the British XIII Corps. Alexander's plan troubled Clark, who wanted more control of the British force, not only to help in the attack, but to bolster his army.

Meeting in mid-August, at General Leese's Eighth Army headquarters Clark and Alexander discussed the plan. Agreeing at least in part with Alexander, Clark said, "General Alexander, I think that your change in plans with respect to the timing of the two attacks is sound. . . . It furthermore seems to me that the two forces should be under single operational control. In that way, and in that way only, can we strike an effective blow."[21] Leese, who was listening to the conversation while relaxing on the ground, was startled by Clark's suggestions and told Alexander that he, Leese, wanted to "control the ultimate destinies of the divisions of the Eighth Army."[22] Clark calmly and coolly responded, telling Alexander:

> General Alexander, you have heard my argument; you have heard General Leese's. It is a matter of considerable embarrassment for me to suggest that a British corps should pass to command of Fifth Army. I make this recommendation only because it is my sincere belief that it is the only logical and correct decision in this situation. I shall say no more about it; the decision is yours. I shall cheerfully abide by any decision which you reach.[23]

Leese at first wanted Alexander to sleep on the decision, but before Alexander and Clark departed the Eighth Army commander relented, and passed the British XIII Corps to Fifth Army. Clark's army was greatly strengthened with the arrival of the 6th South African Armoured Division, the 6th British Armoured Division, the 8th Indian Division, 1st British Infantry Division, and the 1st Canadian Army Tank Brigade.[24] While Allied manpower in Italy was still critically short, these veteran forces gave Clark reason to be optimistic about the upcoming offensive. The plan was ready, and just like all the battles in Italy, it would take longer than expected.

By the end of August and the beginning of the Allied offensive the Germans had halted their retreat at the Gothic Line. At this time Kesselring had twenty-seven divisions under his command, which due to shortages and casualties were the relative equivalent of fifteen Allied divisions.[25] The 16th SS Panzer Grenadier Division, 65th Grenadier Division, 26th Panzer Division, and 3d Panzer Grenadier Division, along with infantry regiments of the 362d Grenadier Division and 20th German Air Force Division, faced the Fifth Army to the west. On the east and facing the Eighth Army were the 29th Panzer Grenadier Division, 4th Parachute Division, the 356th, 715th, 334th,

305th, 44th, and 114th Grenadier divisions, as well as the 5th Mountain Division and 71st and 278th Grenadier divisions, with the 1st Parachute Division, and the 162d Grenadier Division reforming near Ravenna.[26] Kesselring's forces were tired, but not beaten, and they would make the Allies fight for every foot of territory facing the Gothic Line.

The Allied attack began with a bang. Beginning on the night of 25–26 August, the Eighth Army moved out and immediately made progress toward the Gothic Line. Reeling from the attacks, Kesselring did exactly as Alexander had planned: the German commander shifted three divisions to the British front, which allowed Fifth Army to launch its attack. The IV and II Corps moved out and easily crossed the Arno River. After passing the river Clark decided to break the Gothic Line at the Il Giogo Pass, just east of the well defended Futa Pass, which Alexander originally wanted to attack.[27] With the fall of Rimini on 21 September Clark decided to divert a portion of the II Corps to attack northeast into the Santerno Valley with the hope of reaching the Imola plains. This movement was made against weaker German defenses, offered the shortest route into the Po Valley, and would greatly aid the main attack of Eighth Army.[28] With the fall of the Il Giogo Pass and Rimini the Gothic Line was, for all purposes, destroyed. The Allies had gained a great victory and a quick end to fighting in the mountains seemed likely, but by the beginning of October Mark Clark and his Fifth Army were exhausted and faced massive shortages.

Writing to Jacob Devers in early October, Clark tried to explain just how dangerous the situation was: "Infantry replacement situation in Fifth Army is so critically serious that current operation may be endangered."[29] At the same time Clark tried to explain to General George C. Marshall just how precarious the mountain fighting was and the toll it was taking on his troops: "My troops have been negotiating the most difficult mountainous terrain we have had to face it Italy, involving the bitterest fighting since we landed at Salerno."[30] Perhaps Clark best explained the situation to his mother:

> We are fighting desperately in the Apennine mountains. It seems so strange that it should be our role to fight it out until the last Hun is killed while in other sectors the going is so much easier with greater means to do the job. . . . I am forward every day, looking at these damnable mountains and wonder that any man could ever fight through them. We will, but not without the price.[31]

The toll of Anvil and the continuous fighting over rough terrain against a well trained foe had finally caught up with Clark and the Allies in Italy. Their fall offensive had broken the line, but manpower shortages and a lack of supplies and equipment doomed the Allies to another winter in Italy. Clark tried in vain to get more troops, but the political and military situation would not allow it. Clark's anger, just as it had during the planning of the Anzio landings, got the better of him. This time his anger was directed not at Alexander, but Jacob Devers. Writing in his diary, Clark believed Devers was purposefully holding out troops to better his, Devers's, position: "Devers, due to his dual capacity, has diverted troops badly needed in this theater for his own use in France, guided entirely by a selfish interest, in my opinion."[32] Clark further added on 15 October:

> My efforts to bring to the attention of the War Department my replacement situation apparently were futile. I am positive that Devers never properly represented my case to General Eisenhower.... My only alternative is to discontinue the attack and remain in the Apennine Mountains for the winter. Such a solution is entirely unsatisfactory to me.... I am faced with the necessity of almost destroying the future usefulness of four infantry divisions.[33]

With the Allied offensive bogged down by exhaustion, lack of supplies and bad weather Generals Wilson, Alexander, and Clark decided to call a halt to the attack for reorganization and rest. During this pause Alexander would planned for further operations in Italy and Clark would grew more infuriated with the British. Writing in his diary of the decision Clark wrote, "Decision to end drive was probably the toughest I made during war—we were so close to Po Valley it seemed terrible not to get there—I had lost my French Corps and 3 divisions of 6th Corps and ammo shortage—we just couldn't make it."[34]

On 27 October, Clark received Alexander's proposed attack into the Balkans. General Alexander planned on using the Eighth Army to spearhead the attack, while the Fifth Army held down as many German divisions as possible and force the enemy northeastwards. The army group commander's plan called for the British Eighth Army to cut German communications through Ljubljana and capture the port of Fiume. Alexander believed that this pincer movement would converge on Gorizia and Trieste, not only annihilating Kesselring's forces, but also allowing the two armies to advance into

Austria.[35] Alexander's plan was bold, but impossible due to the political situation in the Balkans and more importantly the lack of manpower and supplies for his forces. Clark opposed the plan because it would leave his Fifth Army to bear the brunt of Kesselring's forces, while Eighth Army would be well out of range. Peeved at the instructions Clark damned the project in his diary and pointed out just a few problems of the plan:

> The Germans have 15 Divisions on my Fifth Army front—13 massed in front of II Corps. Their infantry strength is greater than mine. My restrictions on ammunition and replacements make a prolonged attack out of question. . . . I am convinced that Eighth Army and Alexander are more interested in Balkan operation than in the capture of Bologna. A Balkan operation by the Eighth Amy would permit a landing behind Tito's forces without opposition. Great ballyhooing would follow for the British Empire, leaving the bulk of Kesselring's Army opposing me.[36]

No decision had yet been made on Alexander's plan, but by the beginning of December it was clear the Allies were going to have to suffer another winter in the Italian mountains. By this time Fifth Army was facing nearly twenty divisions, and with manpower at an ebb a major offensive was out of the question.[37] From 16 August to 15 December, Clark's forces had sustained 30,458 casualties: 5,061 killed, 22,556 wounded and 2,841 missing.[38] During this time the Fifth Army was 7,000 men under strength and all were tired from constant fighting. Although the Allies attempted small scale attacks, on 26 December the German Fourteenth Army launched Operation Wintergewitter astride the Serchio River and achieved enough success to end all Allied offenses until the spring of 1945.[39] Much of the blame for the German success was placed on the 92d Division. Clark believed the unit was inadequate and wrote in his memoirs, "the 92d gave ground and some units later broke, falling back in a state of disorganization. This left a gap adjacent to the river and made a more general withdrawal necessary."[40] Clark further condemned the 92d Division's performance in his memoirs:

> This performance by the 92d—and it was a bad performance—has since been used on various occasions in an effort to argue that Negro troops cannot be depended upon to fight well in an emergency. Having commanded the only Negro infantry division in World War

II, which was continuously in battle for over a period of six months. I feel I should report factually on its performance during that period. Of the ten American infantry divisions in action in the Fifth Army in Italy, the 92d Division's accomplishments were less favorable than any of the white divisions. . . . I must reiterate that it would be a grave error now for the Army to attempt the indiscriminate mixing of white and Negro soldiers.[41]

While Clark's conservative viewpoints would land him in trouble after the war and lead to a smeared image, Clark did write in his memoirs that, "There were colored officers who distinguished themselves in Italy—You can find good negro officers."[42] Race relations aside, the German attack seriously hampered Allied offensive action for the remainder of the winter. With his men shivering in the mountains, Clark decided to move his headquarters nearer his men, as he believed, "The men of those divisions are going to spend the winter in the mountains. So is my headquarters."[43] However, Clark's stay with his troops was about to end.

With the passing of Field Marshal Sir John Dill, head of the British Military Mission in Washington, Clark received notice on 25 November that he would take over command of the Allied Armies in Italy, which was renamed the 15th Army Group.[44] General Wilson, the supreme commander of Allied forces in the Mediterranean, was designated to replace the late Dill, so Alexander moved up to replace Wilson. Clark would leave the Fifth Army to Lucian Truscott, who would become the only American to command a division, corps, and army in the war. Though Clark's role would be strictly tactical, he proudly accepted the promotion:

> I will be deeply honored to command the 15th Army Group. I fully realize the responsibility this assignment entails and the compliment H.M. Government has paid me in consenting to place your glorious Eighth Army under my command. Please rest assured that its welfare will be carefully guarded.[45]

Moving to the army group headquarters in Siena, Clark's promotion was bittersweet. Both the American and British governments respected Clark well enough to give him the position, but it meant Clark would leave the Fifth Army that he had built from nothing. Leaving Fifth Army on 16 December Clark gave his troops a final speech:

When I assumed command of the Fifth Army two years ago upon its activation in North Africa on 5 January 1943, it was with pride and confidence. I was proud of the organization I had been appointed to lead, and I had confidence in its ability to accomplish the great mission assigned to it. Subsequent events have fully justified by feelings. Much has been demanded of you in this difficult campaign. No commander could have received a more gratifying response.

In assuming command of the 15th Army Group in Italy, I do so with those same feelings. Side by side, through the bitterest fighting and against the most difficult obstacles in the history of warfare, the Fifth and Eighth Armies have driven a strong, resourceful and fanatical enemy from the extreme south of Italy to the Valley of the Po.

Your contribution to an Allied victory does not rest upon the mere liberation of an Axis-dominated land. Far more important has been your effect upon the enemy's forces and your destruction of thousands upon thousands of his troops and their equipment. It is our campaign that holds in this theater many of the enemy's best divisions which could otherwise be used against the Eastern or Western fronts. We shall continue to defeat them and eventually shall destroy them. Never underestimate the vital and continuing importance of your role in the Italian campaign.

I can wish my successor, General Truscott, no finer heritage than the loyalty, courage, determination, and combat skill you have always shown me. We shall continue to form a powerful Allied force of ground, sea, and air power, dedicated to the defeat of our enemies.

I am happy that I remain in Italy to continue the fight with you. My affection for the Fifth Army will never diminish, nor will my interest in your welfare and achievements. I could not have hoped to command finer men or better soldiers.

And now, I wish to thank each of you for what you have done—and for what you will do. A great and even more glorious future lies ahead for the Fifth Army,

Good luck and God bless you.[46]

Clark left Fifth Army and began to plan with Alexander the final offensive in Italy. Though the 15th Army Group was short of men and supplies, both Alexander and Clark were determined to win the war in Italy and help bring defeat to Germany.

Chapter 10

VICTORY AT LAST

Dear Mr. Truman, let the boys come home,
They have conquered Naples, they have conquered Rome.
They have beat the master race
And spit right in Herr Hitler's face
Oh, let the boys come home
Let the boys at home see Rome.[1]

D URING THE WINTER OF 1944–45 THE AMERICAN SOL-
diers stuck in the Italian mountains had a reason to sing.
They were winning the war, but the Italian theater was no longer paramount
to Allied goals, and the Germans still refused to quit. General Mark W. Clark,
now 15th Army Group commander, believed one last major offensive would
end the war in Italy and aid the Allies in the war against the Nazis. On 12
February Clark issued Operation Instructions Number 3. The three-phased
plan called for the capture and establishment of a bridgehead around Bologna. Bologna offered the Allies a great jumping off point to invade the Balkans. Even though Alexander's plan for a Balkan invasion had been scrapped,
the capture of the city would still be valuable.[2] After capturing the city, Clark
wanted the Allies to develop positions along the Po River and then finally
cross the river with the object of capturing Verona, which would prevent the
Germans from escaping into Austria through the Brenner Pass in the Italian
Alps.[3]

By the beginning of 1945 the Fifth Army consisted of the IV and II
United States Corps along with the British XIII Corps. The 92d Division

was left directly under army headquarters control and IV Corps, under Willis Crittenberger, consisted of Task Force 45, the 1st Brazilian Infantry Division, 6th South African Armoured Division, and the recently arrived U.S. 10th Mountain Division under Maj. Gen. George P. Hays.[4] The II Corps consisted of the 1st Armored Division, the 91st, 34th, and 88th divisions. The XIII Corps included the British 1st and 78th divisions, the 6th Armoured Division, and the 8th Indian Division.[5] Stretched along the Apennine Mountains with IV Corps on the left, II Corps in the center, and XIII Corps on the right, the entire Fifth Army front was fifty miles long, and blocked by numerous crack German divisions.[6]

At the same time, the Eighth Army, still the larger of the two armies, stretched from the Adriatic coast east of Bologna and extended west to where it met the Fifth Army south of Montecaldero. By February, the Canadians left for Northern Europe, causing the V Corps to move into their place alongside the Adriatic. West of V Corps the XIII Corps held the area east of the Fifth Army. The Polish Corps, despite their disagreement over Yalta, remained a sizeable force for the Eight Army and remained in the southernmost British sector.[7]

The Germans clung to Northern Italy not only because it was a gateway to southern Germany and the Balkans, but because it was the most productive area in Italy. This heavily industrialized region produced, 139,000 tons of steel a month, 3,800 tons of zinc, 9,000 tons of aluminum, and 80,000 bottles of mercury. The area produced textiles for the Germans that amounted to 23 percent of the Third Reich's total output.[8] Aside from industrial materials, the northern region of Italy also produced substantial amounts of wine, boots, rice and fruit. Twenty-eight divisions defended the region, which included sixteen or seventeen German divisions. Thirteen divisions alone faced the Fifth Army.[9] Though tired and worn out, the Germans in Italy were not beaten and planned to hold out for as long as possible.

From January to March 1945, Clark and the 15th Army Group rested. While there were minor engagements, due to manpower and supply shortages the Allies decided to await the spring and recommence offensive operations in April. During this time the Brazilian Expeditionary Force (BEF) was trained and, under the guidance of Lucian Truscott, American divisions were rested. Under Truscott's plan, major units would be taken out of the line for a period of four weeks, with at least one week dedicated to rest.[10] The British Eighth Army also took advantage of this period to rest and reorganize. Rest centers popped up seemingly everywhere, the most popular in Rome and Florence. In Rome, the Excelsior Hotel was setup for officers and the Foro Italia for enlisted men. The goal of the rest was to "make the men feel like civilians while they are here."[11] The second winter for the Allies in Italy was tough, but proved invaluable, as they were rested, refitted and trained for the 1 April offensive.

After getting used to his new job as an army group commander, Clark was growing tired of the war, and of high command. Writing to his mother in early February, Clark told her, "I certainly wish this war would get over. It is quite a strain to have a job like I have had without relief. Of course, I want to continue until the Pacific war is over, but I am afraid it will take me some time to get rested up after we finally do win the peace we deserve."[12] Although understandably tired, Clark wanted to join the fighting in the Pacific. However, like other high commanders in the European theater, Clark would not go to the Pacific. While his forces rested Clark was once again drawn into a political battle. On 2 March Clark had to convince Gen. Wladyslaw Anders, commander of the Polish Corps, to stay and fight. Following the announcement that the Soviets would gain take over some territory of eastern Poland, Anders was furious and according to Clark's diary:

> Anders' first violent reaction was to send a letter to the Commanding General of the Eighth Army requesting that his Corps be relieved immediately from front line duty. He even intimidated that it would be better to accept the Polish Corps as prisoners of war. He felt that under the circumstances he could not be responsible for holding a sector with mixed emotions as prevailed among his men. . . . The gist of my conversation was "What are you going to do about it? If you turn in your suits now you lost the respect of the Allies, your only friends. Your men are going to follow the cue you indicate to them. If you become a defeatist and indicate that all hopes are lost to your men, you will have failed in your duty as their commander."[13]

While Clark understood Anders's anger, he was correct in what he told the Polish commander and in his handling of the situation. Clark eventually was able to calm Anders and the Polish forces served honorably for the rest of the war. Later Anders would be promoted to commander in chief of the Polish army in exile and died in London in 1970 after refusing to return to Communist Poland. Clark respected Anders, and the spring offensive would have been seriously hampered had the Polish forces refused to fight. Again, Clark's political skills aided the Allied cause.

Happy news reached Clark a little over a month later, on 15 March, Clark received the news that he had been nominated to receive a fourth star, becoming a full general.[14] The promotion made sense as he was now an army group commander and his performance, for the most part, had been commendable. In the meantime, Clark watched as his armies participated in limited attacks in February and March. Designed to regain lost territory from the German attack in late December 1944, the operation began on 4 February. The attacks were immediately successful, and by 11 February, all the ground lost in late December was recovered.[15] Days later, on 18 February, the 1st Brazilian Division, and the 10th Mountain Division began operations to capture Monte Belvedere, Monte della Torraccia and Monte Castello.[16] By 4 March, the operation wrapped up and the 15th Army Group was well in position for the spring offensive. Further adding to the strength of the Allies, on 15 March the Italian Legnano Group joined the Fifth Army's II Corps.[17] The Eighth Army continued its advance and readied itself for a larger attack in April and May.

At the end of March, and for the first time wearing his fourth star, Clark gave a well received speech to his forces, congratulating them on their performance of the last few months and to prepare them for the upcoming battle:

> You and the other magnificent Allied troops of the Eighth and Fifth Armies have defeated and kept down here and chewed up over twenty-five of the best German divisions in the German army. Suppose those Germans were now opposing our troops in the West! Suppose they were in the East opposing the Russian Army! It would be a different story. You have kept them here, and their home, Germany, is being invaded from all sides. Their homes are being destroyed and their morale is at its lowest ebb.[18]

With the winter coming to an end, and the troops rested and refitted, Clark issued Operation Instructions Number 4 on 24 March 1945. The instructions outlined the spring offensive. Beginning on 10 April the 15th Army Group was to launch an all-out drive against the enemy to destroy their forces south of the Po River, to cross the river, and capture Verona. (The attack actually kicked off on 9 April.) In the first phase the Eighth Army was to breach the Santerno River and, along with the Fifth Army, capture Bologna. Next the armies would cross the Po, encircle the enemy forces, and finally take Verona.[19] The Fifth Army would launch the main effort of the attack into the Po River Valley.

In March General Heinrich von Vietinghoff took over command of Army Group South West from Kesselring, who was ordered to the Western front. Facing the Fifth Army was Lieutenant General Joachim von Lemelsen's Fourteenth German Army made up of the LI Mountains Corps and the XIV Panzer Corps. The LI Mountain Corps consisted of the 148th Grenadier Division (reinforced), the 232d Grenadier Division (reinforced), the 114th Light Division, and the 334th Grenadier Division. The XIV Panzer Corps included the 94th Grenadier Division, 8th Mountain Division (reinforced), and the 65th and 305th Grenadier divisions.[20] The Germans were ready to fight, and with superior numbers could prove to be a tough adversary, but the Allies would be more than ready for the challenge.

On the eve for the attack, Clark issued a statement to the 15th Army Group:

> As never before we now have an opportunity to deal a decisive blow. With our enemy weakened by recent severe blows on other fronts the shock of a severe attack here will do much to speed his defeat, with consequent saving of lives and hastening of the day of victory over all our enemies. . . . It is my greatest hope that this will be the last major offensive that will be conducted by 15th Army Group.[21]

On the same day the last Allied offensive in Italy began. Advancing quickly the Eighth Army moved out and immediately made gains. On 13 April, a day before Fifth Army's attack, Clark received news that President Roosevelt had passed away the previous day. Having worked with Roosevelt, Clark issued a public statement to his troops to inspire them before battle:

> The death of Franklin Delano Roosevelt represents a tragic loss to the nation, and a personal loss to me and every soldier serving with 15th Army Group. Though the President has passed on, he has left to us a legacy of the finest and most soldierly qualities. As our Commander-in-Chief he charted us a course for battle. We will continue unswervingly to devote ourselves to the fight for complete victory.[22]

After recovering from the shock of Roosevelt's death, the Fifth Army was ready to attack. With the Allies closing in on Berlin, Clark and his forces in Italy were about to help drive the final nail in Hitler's Third Reich.

Advancing on 14 April the Fifth Army made quick progress, and by the end of 17 April the Germans were badly hurt.[23] By the next day, enemy forces in front of II Corps had retreated, but the Allies had yet to make a breakthrough. The turning point of the attack was on 20 April when the German XIV Panzer Corps broke, and Fifth Army's IV and II corps broke through towards Bologna.[24] The next day, Bologna fell as troops from the 3d Battalion, 133d Infantry riding on tanks from the 752d Tank Battalion entered the city.[25] An excited Clark wrote in his diary on the same day, "The capture of Bologna is a victory that belongs to every Allied fighting man—soldier, sailor and airman—in the Italian Theater."[26] The Eighth Army continued advancing and crossed the Santerno River and completed the first phase of their operation. The door to the Po River valley was now open.

During this time, the Allies were aided by Italian partisans, who were much more numerous in the Po River Valley than in any other region of Italy.[27] Making matters more difficult for the Germans, on 24 April elements of the 10th Mountain Division crossed the Po River.[28] Clark visited the river and, like Patton at the Rhine, urinated in the Po, writing in his diary: "I went across the Po in small boat while engineers were building bridges—Took leak in the Po."[29] On the same day of the crossing of the Po River, Clark wrote to his wife and expressed his frustration of the past winter and to partly justify the offensive:

> For many months I have wanted to attack, but during these months repeatedly troops have been taken from me for other fronts. First I lost many divisions for the Southern France show. For months after that all my heavy artillery went away. Then, with the difficulties in Greece, I lost several divisions. Each time I recovered from a shock and went ahead and counted my resources and planned another attack only to be hit below the belt another time. Air was taken. Then the Canadian Corps of two divisions and many supporting troops went to Montgomery. That was the last blow that almost kept me down. Ammunition was diverted to other theaters so that my winter attack had to be postponed. I had a scant superiority over the enemy. He had more divisions than I had. I did not have ammunition to carry the fight for a sufficient number of days....

So reluctantly, I gave up the attack in February. There was much snow in the mountains. The air could not support me because of the weather. I would have had slim chances of victory, so I rested my troops, saved the ammunition, built up replacements, trained and trained, and planned, and raised the morale so that when proper weather came I might hit a successful blow. . . .

Before my attack I was confronted with many war correspondents; their papers asking, 'Why do you attack?' I gave them the answer that Hitler and his mob were moving into a southern fortress of which Italy was a part.[30]

While the attack was going extremely well, most of the German forces had escaped capture, but had to leave their equipment on the north side of the Po. With victory nearly within reach, Truscott urged his Fifth Army to continue the push and finish the job:

The enemy now seeks to delay our advance while he reassembles his broken and scattered forces in the mountains to the north. You have him against the ropes, and it now only remains for you to keep up the pressure, the relentless pursuit and enveloping tactics to prevent his escape, and to write off as completely destroyed the German Armies in Italy. Now is the time for speed. Let no obstacle hold you up, since hours lost now may prolong the war by months. The enemy must be completely destroyed here. Keep relentlessly and everlastingly after him. Cut every route of escape, and final and complete victory will be yours.[31]

Truscott's words along with the might of Allied soldiers did the job, and by 28 April Verona fell and with it all hopes of German escape.[32] A day later 15th Army Group troops entered Milan and forces from the United States Third and Seventh Armies crashed into Austria, destroying any chances of a German redoubt.[33]

On the same day as troops entered Milan, surrender negotiations began. Odd talks of ending the war had begun earlier in the year when in January 1945 Italian businessman Baron Parrilli traveled to Switzerland to meet with Dr. Max Husmann, director of a private school near Lucerne. The two men discussed German plans and decided to attempt to bribe key SS officers in Italy to not only end the war in Italy, but to get the United States to join them and fight against the Soviets.[34] Little came from these talks as the Americans would not turn on their Soviet allies. After a series of negotiations Kesselring authorized a cease fire effective 2 May at 0430.[35] The next day, Clark issued orders stating, "Enemy forces under command of Commander in Chief Southwest have surrendered unconditionally," and that "Fifth Army will cease firing forthwith except in event of overt hostile act on the part of the enemy."[36]

Meeting Clark on 4 May at 1030 hours Gen. Fridolin von Senger und Etterlin officially surrendered the German forces in Italy. The war was finally over except for one minor detail. After saluting Clark, as von Senger was leaving the room the American general noticed that the X1V Panzer Corps commander was still armed. Clark immediately yelled for someone to stop von Senger:" Get him back here. Get rid of that gun," Clark then told an aide "Get me that gun under the tree, I can use that among my souvenirs."[37]

Writing to his troops about the final offensive in Italy, Clark stated:

> One of the most complete and decisive victories in military history has been recorded by their two armies in a period of approximately three weeks. Approximately 145,000 prisoners have been taken, and the Ligurian Army, consisting of two German and two Italian divisions is hopelessly pinned in the Turin area will all exits to the north blocked. . . . Troops of the 15th Army Group have so smashed the German armies in Italy that they have been virtually eliminated as a military force. . . . Twenty-five German divisions, some of the best in the German army have been torn to pieces and can no longer effectively resist our armies. . . . You have demonstrated something new and remarkable in the annals of organized warfare. You have shown that a huge fighting force composed of units from many countries with diverse languages and customs, inspired, as you have always been, with a devotion to the cause of freedom, can become an effective and harmonious fighting team. . . . Men of the 15th Army Group, I know you will face the task ahead with the same magnificent, generous and indomitable spirit you have shown in this long campaign. Forward, to final victory. God bless you all.[38]

A day after the surrender on 5 May, Clark's experience in World War II came full circle with another letter from Eisenhower:

In a way, of course, I feel slightly proprietary interest in you. This is always the case when anyone does extremely well and so I am just voicing a sentiment that probably a thousand others are doing this minute. . . . Your accomplishments, since you landed at Salerno, are among the notable ones of the war and I realize more keenly than most, how difficult your task has often been.[39]

The two soldiers had traveled to England together, and now finished the war together, though in different theaters. For Clark his war was over. While there was talk of using Clark's forces to liberate Trieste, the 15th Army Group deserved a rest, and this mission was assigned to units from Eighth Army's New Zealand Division and partisans.[40] By 9 May, it was becoming increasingly apparent that Clark would not fight in the Balkans or the Pacific; instead he would become high commissioner of Austria.[41]

*   *   *

The campaign in Italy lasted 601 days, beginning on 9 September 1943 and ending on 2 May 1945. The Allies had used twenty-seven divisions, seven corps, and the Fifth Army alone suffered a total of 188,546 casualties: 31,886 killed, 133,825 wounded, and 22,835 missing.[42] More specifically for the United States, 19,475 soldiers were killed, 80,530 wounded, and 9,637 missing for a total of 109,642 casualties.[43] The British suffered 47,452 casualties, the French 27,671, the Brazilians 2,211, and the Italians 1,570 casualties.[44] Altogether the Allies in Italy suffered 312,000 casualties. The Germans sustained worse losses, which totaled 434,646: 48,067 killed, 172,531 wounded, and 214,048 missing.[45] The war in Italy was finally over, and on 31 May, Clark left the peninsula and traveled to the United States for rest and celebration. Writing in his memoirs about the success of his forces in Italy, Clark stated, "In the Italian campaign we had demonstrated as never before how a polyglot army could be welded into a team of allies with the strength and unity and determination to prevail over formidable odds."[46]

CONCLUSION

THE ITALIAN CAMPAIGN UNDER MARK W. CLARK'S LEAD-
ership succeeded over formidable odds, yet historians have
long debated the career of Clark and the necessity for fighting in Italy. With
the end of fighting in Europe, Clark's command quickly vanished. By the
middle of July the II Corps left for Austria, and the IV Corps had become
non-operational. Finally, on 2 October 1945, U.S. Fifth Army, which Clark
had started and built into a formidable force, was deactivated.[1] According to
his memoirs, Clark "slept all through it" as his command disbanded or left for
other regions.[2] Since landing in Salerno in September 1943 Clark and his
forces had advanced 480 air miles northward up the Italian peninsula, approximately the same distance as Eisenhower's forces fought from Normandy to
the Elbe River.[3] Therein lays the debate over the Italian campaign in World
War II. While Eisenhower, Bradley, and Patton rolled over the Nazis in
France, Clark and his soldiers slogged through mountains, rivers, and German lines. Although the Italian theater did not have the larger-than-life personalities or the glory of the campaigning across France and into Germany,
it was nevertheless of major importance to the Allied war effort in Europe.

Politically the Western Allies could not have sat on the sidelines while
the Soviets lost millions of soldiers and civilians in their brutal struggle with
Nazi Germany. The Allies had to fight somewhere, and at the time Italy
offered the best conditions and possibilities. More importantly, the fighting
in Italy achieved its purpose. The two strategic objectives in fighting in Italy
were the surrender of Hitler's ally, achieved before Salerno; and second, to
keep as many German divisions tied down as possible. In both objectives the
war in Italy was a success; it just took longer than planners envisioned. Prime
Minister Winston Churchill was the leading proponent of attacking the "soft

underbelly" of the Axis Empire. While the Italian campaign proved to be far more difficult than anticipated, the "Third Front," according to Churchill, "attracted to itself twenty good German divisions. If the garrisons kept in the Balkans for fear of attack there are added, nearly forty divisions were retained facing the Allies in the Mediterranean."[4]

In September 1943 there were only six German divisions in Italy; by the end of the war in May 1945 Germany had used thirty-six divisions, three of which were Italian and one Russian.[5] By fighting in Italy the Allies tied down over thirty more Axis divisions. Aside from the sheer number of divisions pulled in, the Allies introduced during the fighting in Italy a number of inventions that helped win the war. Mulberries or artificial harbors made famous in Overlord were first used in Sicily as were proximity fuses for artillery shells. Furthermore, as Lucian Truscott wrote in his memoirs:

> It eliminated the Axis menace in the Mediterranean; from its inception it removed one Axis partner from effective participation in the war; occupied thirty-five or forty divisions which the Germans desperately needed elsewhere; inflicted heavy losses in men and material and imposed enormous strains upon an already overburdened economy; and provided bases from which the Allied Air Forces carried the air war over all of German-held territory from Rumania to Poland.[6]

Even Field Marshall Kesselring said the Allies were correct to fight in Italy. In his memoirs Kesselring said the Germans had no choice but to defend Italy as it would have left the Allies "untrammeled freedom of movement in the direction of France and the Balkans."[7] Perhaps unsurprisingly Kesselring agreed with the rationale the Allies used for fighting in Italy, that it tied up enemy divisions. "The Italian theatre pinned down Allied forces which," Kesselring wrote, "if they had been engaged on decisive fronts, might have powerfully influenced events in the east or in the west adversely for Germany."[8] Fighting in Italy did not win the war, but it certainly helped bring the war to an end. Both politically and militarily, the decision to fight in Italy was the right one.

The major criticism of the war in Italy was that it took too long and that equipment and manpower could have been used effectively elsewhere. First, the campaign in Italy, like most operations in the theater, was too weak to sustain an offensive and yet too powerful to stay on the defensive.[9] The reason it took so long was that Kesselring and his highly skilled forces were brilliant defensive fighters who used every inch of Italian terrain to their advantage. Their ability to withdraw when necessary in order to maintain a strong defensible line added months, if not years, to the war. As to the supply question there are two difficulties with this argument. First, what other theater would the supplies be used for? In fact, there was no other theater. There was nothing more the Allies could do in North Africa; invading France in 1943 had been ruled out as impracticable; while increasing troops and aid to the China-Burma-India Theater would have been laughed at. There was simply no other place to fight that would both somewhat placate and relieve the pressure on the Soviets, and damage the Germans.

Second, the Allied forces in Italy had never received enough supplies to begin with. Clark and his forces were constantly short of ammunition, vehicles and other equipment. More importantly, there were never enough soldiers or service troops in the campaign. The shortage became particularly apparent and troublesome after the fall of Rome when Allied troops were siphoned off from Italy for Anvil. With troops and equipment tough to come by, Clark and the forces in Italy could have done little to finish the war more quickly. While he and other Allied commanders in Italy could have made different tactical decisions, such as crossing at a different spot along the Rapido River, or launching Anzio after the Fifth Army was closer, strategically Clark and the Allies performed wisely and admirably in Italy.

As for Clark, following victory in Italy the general was selected to command United States Forces in Austria and did so ably. Administrative duty seemingly suited Clark. On 4 May 1947 Clark left Europe and returned to duty in America for the first time in seven years. With Eisenhower retired and Omar Bradley chairman of the Joint Chiefs of Staff, Clark was assigned as chief of the Army Field Forces at Fort Monroe, Virginia.[10]

By 1952, the Korean War had been raging for two years, and Clark privately advocated bombing "military targets in Manchuria and China."[11] Following Matthew Ridgway, Clark was appointed commander in chief, United Nations Command in Korea. For his final act in uniform Clark signed the armistice ending hostilities in Korea. He later wrote that the event "capped my career, but it was a cap without a feather."[12] Like most World War II commanders the world had passed him by; no longer was total victory needed or wanted. The Cold War brought a new era of diplomacy and military strategy, one that threatened nuclear war, but did everything possible to avoid it. Clark and others would never understand the purpose of limited warfare, and they never wanted anything to do with it. For him it was time for a change. He eventually found that change as head of the Citadel in Charleston, South Carolina.

Appointed president of the college on 1 March 1954, Clark improved the Citadel, brought more money in, and raised professor's salaries. More importantly, however, he used the Citadel and the city of Charleston as a forum to spread his ideas. Always a firm anti-Communist, Clark echoed Senator Joseph McCarthy's claim of Communist penetration into American councils of state. He even went as far as to say that the United Nations was a place that gave the Soviet Union a sounding board for propaganda and a haven for spies and saboteurs.[13] Further adding to his ultra-conservative views was his work with the Hoover Commission that recommended measures to correct perceived American weaknesses, while improving the quality and efficiency of the nation's electronics, nuclear weapons, and supersonic planes.[14] The report was published around the time of the downfall of McCarthy, and Clark's ideas were rejected. Clark also proved outspoken in regards to race relations in the United States, blaming the Communists for fostering "intermarriages of the races."[15] Always a conservative figure, some likened his political views to Genghis Khan.[16] Just as the political and military world had changed after World War II, so had views on race. His views alienated most Americans, and, following the 1960s and Vietnam, Mark Clark and his accomplishments were forgotten.

One major criticism of Clark has been his zeal for publicity. Lucian Truscott went as far as to argue that Clark's ego hurt his military ability, writing in his memoirs:

> His concern for personal publicity was his greatest weakness. I have sometimes thought it may have prevented him from acquiring that "feel of battle" that marks all top-flight battle leaders, though extensive publicity did not seem to have that effect on Patton and Montgomery.[17]

Truscott makes a point, but Clark was always near the battle, and his personal leadership at Salerno not only helped turned the tide of battle, but won him high praise from his superiors. Much of this criticism stems from journalists who never truly understood him. Many war correspondents believed he traveled with a large contingent of media to better publicize his career. Clark was aware of his situation, but reporters never gave the other side of the story. Clark realized the Italian theater was not the Western Allies' primary effort and that because of this he felt he had to do more to get media attention. The media attention was not just for him, but for his soldiers. He wanted the parents and loved ones of his soldiers to know what they were doing, and he believed they deserved the same attention that soldiers in Western Europe were receiving. The only time in the war that Clark's ego got him in trouble was Rome. His desire to capture the city, and the need to give the soon to be even more secondary theater additional publicity, was just too tempting for the general. Many postwar writers, including Clark and his son William, believed the capture of Rome was the high point of his career; it was also Clark at his worst. Rome was not the main objective of Alexander's offensive, and while the plan may not have destroyed a large part of the German Army, it offered the Allies the best opportunity. The Allies would have taken Rome eventually, but Clark wanted this to occur before the landings in Normandy, which would have overshadowed it. Not only would the liberation of the Sacred City boost the morale of the Allies and inflict a significant symbolic loss on Hitler and Germany, it would bring Fifth Army and its commander great acclaim. Ironically, Clark and his army only seized the headlines for one day; the next day Overlord bumped Rome from the front pages.

Another criticism of Clark is that he was not a great combat leader. It is true that Clark was outperformed by George S. Patton and, to an extent, Lucian Truscott, but this is not really an indication of Clark's ability. After the war, in a conversation with historian Sidney Mathews, Field Marshal Alexander said he believed Clark was "extremely ambitious," but that he was a "good Army commander."[18] In many regards Clark was given a tougher task than his flag-officer brethren in other theaters. He fought with limited manpower and supplies against a skilled and determined foe on ground that did not suit the United States Army or its military doctrine. Perhaps World War II hero Paul Tibbits of *Enola Gay* fame says it best about Clark:

> [Clark was a] great, great general. . . . A southern gentleman. Very soft spoken, never got riled. Never got upset—or if he did, he didn't show it. He had innate politeness. He was more than a good general. He was a good man. Of all the military leaders in World War II, Mark Clark is the one who never got the proper credit publicly. He didn't seek it—and somehow he didn't get it. But we all knew. We knew what kind of a man Mark Clark was.[19]

Clark was a good field commander and a *brilliant* combat commander, as he demonstrated at Salerno, although like most people, he had his faults.

Clark performed well in World War II: along with Dwight Eisenhower he helped establish United States Forces in Europe; he was the first American general to command a field army in combat, and was the first to fight in continental Europe; and under his leadership his forces were the first to liberate an Axis-occupied capital. Though stripped of troops and equipment, he led his forces through an unbearable winter in the mountains and successfully defeated a large portion of the German Army. Without Mark W. Clark and the fighting in Italy, the war would have been fought much differently, and victory would have been more prolonged and more costly.

APPENDIX A

Transcript of meeting between Maj. Gen. Mark W. Clark and Admiral François Darlan at St. George Hotel in Algiers, 9 Nov 1942

CLARK: Explain to Admiral Darlan the necessity of coming immediately to the point. We have work to do to meet the common enemy. Is he ready to sign the terms of the armistice? It will cover all French North Africa. It is essential that we stop this waste of time and blood.

DARLAN: I sent a resume of the armistice terms to Vichy. Laval was absent from Vichy. There will be no reply until the Council of Ministers meets this afternoon.

CLARK: Do you understand that diplomatic relations between France and the United States have been broken off within the past 24 hours.

DARLAN: There is no official statement or confirmation of this rupture but I want to see hostilities stopped as soon as possible. I have been given strict orders to enter into no negotiations until I have received orders from Petain or the Council of Ministers. All my associates and I feel hostilities are fruitless.

CLARK: I am negotiating with you as commander of the troops on the ground. I am not prepared nor do I propose to await any further word from Vichy.

DARLAN: I want to make it clear that I am not here in a capacity of the French government. I can simply obey the orders of Petain.

CLARK: Then I will have to break off negotiations and deal with someone who can act.

DARLAN: It is up to you to take whatever means necessary. It is regrettable. You have the guarantee of security here in Algiers.

CLARK: The problem is bigger than that. Will the French troops east of Algiers resist as we pass through to meet our common enemy?

DARLAN: I have asked Vichy to give me an answer to your terms as soon as possible.

CLARK: What you propose is not possible. I will end this conference in thirty minutes.

DARLAN: I understand what this means and I want to tell my government of what has happened.

CLARK: This is impossible. It will be necessary to retain you in protected custody. I hope you understand. We must move east. I proposed to negotiate with someone who can issue orders to the troops. Can you not take the same steps as you have taken here without the approval of Vichy? Why can't you do the same thing in other parts of North Africa.

DARLAN: The situation is different.

CLARK: What answer do you expect to get from Vichy in view of the severance of relations?

DARLAN: I am giving Petain my opinion that it is stupid to continue hostilities here. I urged acceptance of the terms, I am confident that Petain will agree.

CLARK: That is fine, but do you understand that we cannot sit here while governments agree and ministers debate? If the Admiral will not issue instructions for the cessation of hostilities, I will go to General Giraud. He will sign the terms and issue the necessary orders.

DARLAN: I am not certain the troops will obey. This will only mean the loss of more time and there will be more fighting.

CLARK: Are you so sure of the decision from Vichy? Petain has already informed President Roosevelt that he considers our landings aggression. If you think Petain will agree with you that hostilities must cease why can't you issue that order now?

DARLAN: I can't assume the responsibility for such an order. It would result in the immediate occupation of Southern France by the Germans.

CLARK: We all agree concerning the great danger of the occupation of Southern France, but it will not be because of this order. What you are doing now means more killing of French and Americans. This all boils down to one question. Are you going to play with the Vichy government or go with us?

DARLAN: I am simply bound by an oath of fidelity to the Marshal to obey

28 July 1944: Clark and Britain's King George VI at Fifth Army HQ. Clark's cocker spaniel Pal is running in front, keeping the king company. —*NARA II (Box 322-220441)*

6 July 1944: Clark poses, l-r, with Secretary of War Henry L. Stimson, Maj. Gen. Charles W. Ryder, CG 34th Infantry Division, and Maj. Gen. Ernest W. Harmon, CG 1st Armored Division.—*NARA II (Box 324-220956)*

8 June 1944: Soldiers read about the successful landings at Normandy. —*NARA II (Box 53-Folder HH-AEF-Italy-Rome)*

11 Aug 1944: Clark inspects troops of the Brazilian Expeditionary Force with their commander, Maj. Gen. Joao Batista Maecarenhas de Moraes, near Cecina, Italy.—*NARA II (Box 226-193648)*

9 Aug 1944: Clark inspects Japanese American soldiers of the Hawaiian National Guard's 100th Infantry Battalion with Secretary of the Navy James V. Forrestal. —*NARA II (Box 223-192733-S)*

19 Aug 1944: Clark inspecting troops with Prime Minister Winston S. Churchill near Vieda, Italy. —*NARA II (Box 231-194952)*

14 July 1944: Clark with Stimson, Devers, and Maj. Gen. Harry H. Johnson, Military Governor of Rome. —*NARA II (Box 53- Folder KK-AEF- Italy-Rome)*

Below: 19 Aug 1944: Clark sits with Winston Churchill and Capt. Robert McKenzie near Leghorn, Italy. —*NARA II (Box 231-194953)*

13 Aug 1944: Clark reads scripture, as Maj. Charles E. Brown, Assistant Fifth Army Chaplain, looks on.—*NARA II (Box 231-194955)*

3 Sep 1944: Clark visiting the Leaning Tower of Pisa.—*NARA II (Box 231-194956)*

1 Sept 1944: Clark works outside as Sgt. Geraldine Horne, WAC, answers the phone. —*NARA II (Box 227-194027)*

Below: 27 Sept 1944: Clark and Maj. Gen. Geoffrey Keyes looking over a map near Firenzuela, Italy. —*NARA II (Box 233-195582-S)*

No date: Clark talks with Heavyweight Champion of the World, Joe Louis.—*NARA II (Box 228-194352-S)*

8 Sept 1944: Clark with his cocker spaniel, Pal. Pal had a Fifth Army ID around his collar.—*NARA II (Box 229-194377)*

8 Sept 1944: Clark with Crown Prince of Italy Umberto. —*NARA II (Box 229-194376)*

13 Oct 1944: Clark earned a poor reputation from the press, but here he presents journalists from *Stars and Stripes* with a Fifth Army plaque of merit.—*NARA II (Box 237-196714)*

27 Oct 1944: Men of the 1st Armored Division's 16th Armored Engineer Battalion remove bridge after heavy rains along the Gothic Line.—*NARA II (Box 244-198693)*

25 Oct 1944:
Clark with
Alexander,
Lt. Gen.
Joseph T.
McNarney,
Deputy
Supreme
Allied Com-
mander. Lt.
Gen John
Harding and
Maj. Gen.
Lyman L.
Lemnitzer
look on in
the back-
ground.
—*NARA II
(Box 339-
225402)*

25 Oct 1944: Same meeting from different view.—*NARA II (Box 339-225403)*

15 Nov 1944: Clark shakes the hand of Maj. Gen. Ivan A. Sousloparov, Red Army, after receiving the Military Order of Suvsrov, 1st Degree. The Russian contingent that visited Clark believed the fighting in Italy closely resembled the fighting in the Eastern Front. —*NARA II (Box 237-196718-S)*

26 Nov 1944: Clark, now 15th Army Group Commander, with Maj. Gen. Alfred M. Gruenther pose with Lt. James E. Jones in Florence, Italy. —*NARA II (Box 256-201938)*

26 Nov 1944: Clark, l-r, with; Maj. Gen. John K. Cannon, CG 12th Air Force; Sir Harold Alexander, Lt. Gen. Richard McCreery, CG Eighth Army, and Vice Marshal W. F. Dickson in Florence, Italy. —*NARA II (Box 256-201939)*

8 Dec 1944: L-R; Maj. Gen. Willis D. Crittenberger, VI Corps commander; Brig. Gen. Donald D. Brann, Clark, Maj. Gen. W.H. E. Poole inspect troops captured by South Africans near Bologna. —*NARA II (Box 244-198628)*

15 Jan 1945: A jazz band from the Brazilian Expeditionary Force hits the road.—*NARA II (Box 467-261164)*

9 Jan 1945: Aerial view of Italy's Apennine Mountains. This rugged mountain range includes two peaks that exceed 9,000 feet in elevation.—*NARA II (Box 759-359118)*

29 Jan 1945: Clark with Maj. Gen. R. W. Foster, CG 1st Canadian Division. —*NARA II (Box 375-235363)*

6 Dec 1944: Lt. Gen. Lucian K. Truscott right before taking over Fifth Army from Clark. Truscott was one of the best commanders in the entire war, having commanded a Division, Corps and Army.—*NARA II (Box 244-198700)*

Below: 3 Feb 1945: Clark looking commanding with Lt. Gen. W. D. Morgan and Maj. Gen. T. S. Airey.—*NARA II (Box 414-246321)*

June 1945: Clark poses after the end of the war in Europe.—*NARA II* (Box 929-433924)

Below: 3 Apr 1945: Clark inspects Indian troops in Florence.—*NARA II* (Box 929-433911)

4 May 1945: Soldiers from the Fifth and Seventh armies link up near the Brenner Pass at the end of the war.—*NARA II (Box 802-377888)*

April 1945: Aerial view of the Liri Valley.—*NARA II (Box 673-321010)*

Sep 1945: Aerial view of Anzio/Nettuno.—*NARA II (Box 673-321020)*

Dec 1945: Aerial view of Monte Cassino.—*NARA II (Box 673-321012)*

4 May 1945: German General Fridolin von Senger und Etterlin, XIV Corps commander surrenders to Clark while Maj. Gen. Benjamin W. Childlaw, CG Twelfth Air Force looks on.—*NARA II (Box 929-433915)*

12 Sep 1945: Eisenhower and Clark, now CG US Forces in Austria visit the Roman Coliseum with Lt. John Eisenhower.—*NARA II (Box 325-221455)*

his orders. I can't take the responsibility of giving an order to cease hostilities.

CLARK: This is the time when [we] lean on our inclinations and not on our orders. You are under domination. Here is an opportunity for all Frenchmen to rally and win the war. Here is your last chance.

DARLAN: I am willing to send an urgent message to Marshall Petain, recommending an armistice for Algiers and Morocco.

CLARK: You have already done that.

DARLAN: I have not done so in specific terms.

CLARK: We haven't time. I am going to stand firm. All Frenchmen and all Americans have the same interests at heart and here we are fighting among ourselves, wasting time. I know that the Admiral wants—deep down in his heart—to stop this fighting between our troops. We all want to do the same thing and we must get an order for cessation of hostilities this morning. We have the means. We have 150,000 Americans and British troops in French North Africa. We have the means of equipping the French army and making this the base from which we can go into France. How anybody can fail to join us in an operation that can mean the liberation of France is against my understanding.

DARLAN: I am completely in accord with your point of view, but I still can't act until I hear from Petain.

CLARK: Giraud will sign the terms of armistice.

DARLAN: Giraud has no authority in Morocco where [Auguste] Nogues is in charge or in Algeria where General Georges Barres is in charge. I would like to send a message to Vichy.

CLARK: We can't put up with delay. We have seen what delay has meant before. This cannot go on. I will have to take you into protective custody without communication. We will have to do business with the commanders on the ground.

DARLAN: The army is still with me.

CLARK: We will make is as easy as possible for you.

DARLAN: I would like five minutes with my staff, for discussion.

CLARK: You understand that no one is to leave here or communication with anyone outside.[1]

Following the meeting of the French officers Clark rejoined the discussion:

DARLAN: Will you accept this order?

Darlan laid down a copy of the order on the table. In substance it said that the Americans would not accept his refusal to declare an immediate armistice, that further battle will be fruitless, and that blood will flow. Darlan wants to tell Marshal Petain that as a result of fighting they will probably lose their African colonies. He wants to cease hostilities and take an attitude of complete neutrality.

CLARK: What I want is orders to the troops.

DARLAN: Then I will pass an order to Juin, Nogues, Barres, the Air Force, and the Navy.

CLARK: Under our instructions each commander will decide the terms of the armistice. These officers will negotiate with the French commanders concerned. General Patton will meet with General Nogues and offer terms to him. When they cease firing they will enter into terms for the whole territory.

DARLAN: What about Tunisia. There will be no hostilities to Americans there?

CLARK: That is right.

DARLAN: Then the question of the status of Giraud comes up.

CLARK: What Giraud wants is to help France in this big set up and there is room for everyone. Right now I am trying to stop fighting.

DARLAN: Nogues may hesitate on the validity of this order if it is radioed to him. What are we going to do about that?

CLARK: Let me see the order first. [The order gives all land, sea, and air forces in North Africa orders to cease firing against American troops upon receipt of the order and to return to their bases and observe strict neutrality.] This will stand unless otherwise changed by the Allied Commander-in-Chief. It may be necessary later to make changes and for that reason I have asked you to insert "for the present." You understand that there are some British troops, but that all of them are under American supreme command.

DARLAN: Then I will change it to American troops or their Allies.

CLARK: All right.

DARLAN: What dispositions will be made of the French generals who disobeyed orders? I mean Mast and two others. I think they should be given no French military command.

CLARK: That is one of the things I want to discuss with Admiral Darlan.

DARLAN: I don't want to treat with those men. It is in your own interest to agree that I can't tolerate these men not obeying my orders. The other officers don't want them to have anything to do with French command.

CLARK: I think I can handle this soon and investigate. As I understand it, you do not want these men under your command?

DARLAN: Yes!

CLARK: I don't understand. They helped us so much. However, I do understand your resentment against their not obeying orders. We must see that these orders to cease hostilities are carried out. The order is not worth the paper it is written on unless carried out."[2]

CLARK: Both of you keep telling me you want to save France and French colonial territory. Neither of you have given me one single indication of this except in words. All your deeds have been contrary to this aim you both volubly profess to have. Now I learn that the order for French troops to resist Axis moves in Tunisia has been revoked.[3]

CLARK: Not once have you shown me that you are working in our interests. You say that until you have Nogues backing you don't know if the troops will obey your orders. If that is the case—and I have no doubt it is—you are not strong enough to hold the positions you do. We will get someone strong enough; someone whom the troops will obey. I don't recognize Nogues. To us, he is not the Commander-in-Chief in North Africa. We are in a position where we don't have to accept any individual. Those that we recognize must guarantee that they will fight on our side against Germany.

JUIN: I'm willing to fight the Germans.

CLARK: You must not only say you are willing to fight. You must show, by your actions, that you are fighting. You haven't done that and I'm sick and tired of the way you have been conducting yourself. I think you are weak!

JUIN: One of the great difficulties is that I am subject to the order of Nogues. He is Commander-in-Chief by the order of Marshal Petain. Wait until Nogues comes and I confer with him. Then I will issue the orders to resist in Tunisia. I can't do that until I talk to Nogues. If he refuses to let me issue the order, I will do it anyway. But first, for my honor, I must consult him.

CLARK: I can't and don't accept such a plan. While we are waiting the German troops are moving in. I want that order re-issued now. I'm not so sure that you aren't stalling just to help the Germans.

CLARK: Anyone who is going to be accepted by us must show concretely his willingness to march against the Germans. I asked you to do two simple things to prove you want to save France. First, I asked you to order the French fleet to North Africa. Second, I asked you to communicate with Admiral Esteva [Governor of Tunisia] to tell him that the Germans must be resisted. What have you done? There is no indication that the fleet is coming to North Africa. The French are not resisting moves into Tunisia.

DARLAN: I know that the fleet has received my message and I have received indications that it will be willing to come here if the Germans enter Toulon. I know the fleet is prepared to go to sea.

CLARK: The order to the commanders in Tunisia were revoked without any reference to me. That, to me, is almost treachery. Because of your promises I made certain military moves. These were made on the basis that both of you were acting in good faith.

Darlan and Juin began to talk and declared their hands are tied since Nogues is flying to Algiers, and Juin tells Clark, "The order has not been revoked. It has merely been suspended until we can confer with Nogues".

CLARK: And in the meantime, the Germans are coming into Tunisia. Where is your logic if you profess to want to protect French soil. We now have reports that the Germans plan to move into Constantine and Setif. The Germans may not be in Tunisia in force, but they are moving in and this is a matter of principle—you are doing nothing to block the Germans, nothing to protect your own colony.

JUIN: My attitude is unchanged. I want to fight the Germans! I will accept service with Giraud. [This is important because he is the first of this group to say that.]

CLARK: Alright then. I want your troops to resist at the Tunisian airdromes where Germans are moving in. I want them to resist where they are able to resist.

JUIN: No German troops arrived in Algeria last night.

CLARK: I demand that you issue orders to resist. If not, I am considering very gravely the establishment of a military government in French North Africa. I will put into custody everybody who will not come with us and help. I will set up a French official who can issue concrete orders and who has shown his willingness to march with us.

JUIN: I have expressed my desire. I want to march with you.

CLARK: You must prove it. You must issue the order to resist in Tunisia.

JUIN: The troops and officers are troubled by their consciences. I do not know whether they will obey the orders. You may have chaos on your hands. Please wait until Nogues arrives this afternoon.

CLARK: For your information our second convoy of troops arrived this morning. You have seen that there are now ships in the harbor. We have 40,000 more soldiers, fully armed, in here now. We have artillery. Before coming to this meeting I telephoned Oran. Another convoy has arrived there with 20,000 additional troops. I have the means to enforce what we want and I do not intend to tolerate this delay.

DARLAN: Yesterday you approved my request that Nogues come here. He is due in Oran at 1:30 this afternoon and he should be here by 2:30. Wait until Nogues confers with us before you do anything drastic.[4]

At this time Admiral Raymond Fenard, who spoke English, attempted to calm Clark down and whispered to him, "You are getting what you want if you will only be a little more patient and wait. Don't spoil everything. You almost have solution and a victory in hand."[5] To which Clark replied that he believed Darlan and Juin were just stalling for time. Fenard, again, attempted to cool the red-hot Clark, "That's not true. I swear it. You are blind, man, you are blind."[6] Jumping into the lull in the conversation, an excited Juin jumped and told Clark:

JUIN: I am with you.

CLARK: No. You're not!

JUIN: I am with you.

CLARK: Then prove it by issuing the orders to Tunisia immediately.

FENARD: Wait and you will have all the factions welded together!

CLARK: You are not moving fast enough to keep the Germans from coming into Tunisia. We will get a commander who will march with us. I am going to establish a military government.

CLARK TO MURPHY: Tell them that unless they decide to go along with us right now they are through and I'm prepared to place them under arrest.

JUIN: All we ask for is a suspension of the Tunis order until Nogues arrives.

CLARK: No! We don't recognize Petain's orders and we don't recognize Nogues unless he goes along with us.

JUIN: I think he will accept your terms.

DARLAN: I ask you to reconsider and wait until Nogues arrives. I think it will be worthwhile.

CLARK: No. Nogues' arrival is in no way connected with this. I have a lot of suspicions about a lot of people! [Darlan rips up his paper.

CLARK TO MURPHY: Tell them I am going to put them into custody.

DARLAN: Wait. You will be absolutely clear this afternoon after our meeting. Until then I can't assume my responsibility.

CLARK: I am not going to the meeting. I don't recognize Nogues. I will meet you [Darlan] afterward.

JUIN: If Nogues will not come with you I will put myself at your disposal.

CLARK: Giraud is going to be the military commander.

JUIN: Then I will go with him.

CLARK TO DARLAN: I have received no word about what action the French fleet will take.

DARLAN: My message was received about 10 last night at Toulon. Marseille was occupied by the Germans this morning and I have received no reply. Cabling is impossible now. I am waiting for a radio from the fleet.

CLARK: Do you understand that your position with us depends not only on your cooperation in the fight against the Germans but also in your ability to secure the fleet for us?

DARLAN: Yes. I understand very well. But I am no longer in command. It depends on the will of the leader of the squadron.

CLARK: We want results! Then do you think you will meet with Nogues?

DARLAN: About 4 o'clock.

CLARK: Will Giraud be there?

DARLAN: The first meeting will be held by the people in power. We will bring the results to you.

CLARK: Who is in power and who will be in power will be decided by the United States government.

DARLAN: I must consult with Nogues. I am not in power. My support is no good to you unless the people with the means come along.

JUIN: Time is wasting. I want to help.

CLARK: Then issue orders to resist the Germans.

FENARD TO CLARK: Wait. You have everybody with you. I swear it!

CLARK: If you will give me some indication, if you will issue the order to the troops, I won't accuse you of disloyalty. I just can't understand the attitude you take—saying you want to fight the Germans and then canceling an order that gave you the opportunity to fight them.

JUIN: Giraud has agreed to be your military advisor. I want to help him.

CLARK: I'll see Giraud. If he agrees to have you it is alright with me.

JUIN: I'm not being treated right.

FENARD TO CLARK: You are making a mistake. You will spoil everything."

DARLAN: Who is going to command?

CLARK: The supreme command will be American. I will settle the French commanders later.

JUIN: I suggest that Giraud be the military commander from Dakar to Bizerte. And that I command Algeria.

CLARK: Okay, if you will issue the order to the commanders in Tunisia to resist the Germans.

JUIN: Now or after the meeting?

CLARK: I mean now! I've told you I've had information that the Germans plan to land in Constantine and Setif. Your future with us depends on whether you do this or not!

JUIN: This puts me in a hell of a spot.

CLARK: I know it but I'm in a worse spot. The Germans are moving up.

JUIN: But the hell of it is that Nogues is my commander.

CLARK: Everything depends on whether you go to telephone now and tell your commanders to resist. I mean this from the bottom of my heart. I will send a plane to check on whether the order is phoned and whether it is being obeyed.

JUIN: Fine.[7]

Juin and Darlan talked outside. While Clark waited in the conference room Fenard told him, "You don't understand the internal situation. Everyone is behind Darlan. If you will wait you will have everyone with you. If not, you will upset the apple cart."[8]

CLARK: Yes, and if I wait, in addition to apples, I'll have Germans on top of us. They are building up resistance. Darlan, Juin and the rest of them want to throw Giraud out. I'm going to stick by Giraud. If Juin doesn't issue the orders now I will wait for them to confer with Nogues anyway. Still, I am not sure who are my friends.

FENARD: Then you are blind. You are making a mistake if you don't trust us. I am sure it is right!

CLARK TO MURPHY: Juin is weak. I know that the stand I am taking is right. I know that it is right![9]

Fenard told Clark that he was with him, and he would back Giraud "no matter what happens." Clark told him, "I can't afford to make any mistakes. The stakes are too high."[10] Quickly, Darlan and Juin rejoined the meeting:

JUIN: I have just checked. In Tunis, General Barre is covering the railroads. He says he got orders from Vichy yesterday not to resist the Germans. He thought I was a prisoner. I told him that if the Germans attack, he is to resist.

CLARK: Suppose the Germans come on the airports. What then?

JUIN: As you know, they are already on some airports. The French should have attacked but Barre had orders from Vichy.

CLARK: If the Germans come on to another airport are the French going to resist.

JUIN: Yes.[11]

NOTES

INTRODUCTION

1. George S. Patton, *The Patton Papers: 1940–1945*, ed. Martin Blumenson (Boston: Da Capo Press, 1974), 258.
2. Martin Blumenson, *Mark Clark* (London: Jonathen Cape, 1984), 1.
3. C.J.C. Molony, *The Mediterranean and Middle East*, vol, V, *The Campaign in Sicily 1943 and the Campaign in Italy, 3 September 1943 to 31st March 1944* (London: Her Majesty's Stationary Office, 1973), 192.
4. Martin Blumenson, *U.S. Army in World War Two, The Mediterranean Theater of Operations, Salerno to Cassino* (Washington DC: Center of Military History, 1993), 5.
5. Richard M. Leighton, "OVERLORD Versus the Mediterranean at the Cairo-Tehran Conferences," in *Command Decisions*, United States Army, Office of the Chief of Military History (Washington DC: Center of Military History, 1960), 259.
6. Blumenson, *U.S. Army in World War Two, The Mediterranean Theater of Operations, Salerno to Cassino*, 6.
7. Mark W. Clark, *Calculated Risk* (New York: Harper and Brothers Publishers, 1950), 1.
8. Carlo D'Este, *Fatal Decision: Anzio and the Battle for Rome* (New York: Harpers Collins, 1991), 58.
9. Ibid., 61.
10. Clark, *Calculated Risk*, 2.
11. Martin Blumenson, *Mark Clark*, 11.
12. Ibid., 13.
13. Ibid., 16.
14. Ibid., 17.
15. Ibid., 18.
16. Ibid., 19.
17. Ibid., 20.

18. Ibid., 21.
19. Ibid., 25.
20. Ibid., 31.
21. Ibid., 34.
22. Ibid., 34.
23. Ibid., 37.
24. Ibid., 40.
25. Ibid., 44.
26. Ibid., 46.
27. Ibid., 51.
28. Ibid., 52.
29. Ibid., 52.
30. Omar N. Bradley and Clay Blair, *A General's Life* (London: Sidgwick and Jackson, 1983), 204.
31. Ibid., 204.
32. Clark, *Calculated Risk*, 16
33. Martin Blumenson, *Mark Clark*, 54.

CHAPTER ONE: TWO MEN OF DESTINY

1. Winston S. Churchill, *The Second World War*, vol. V, *Closing the Ring* (Boston: Houghton Mifflin Co., 1951), 345.
2. Ibid., 472.
3. Mark W. Clark Papers, Diary, 5 July 1942, Box 64, Volume 1, 23 June 1942–24 September, The Citadel Archives and Museum, Charleston, South Carolina, 15.
4. Ibid., 1 July 1942, 12.
5. Ibid., 14 July 1942, 22.
6. Ibid., 14 July 1942, 23.
7. Ibid., 17 July 1942, 26.
8. Ibid., 17 July 1942, 28.
9. Ibid., 25 July 1942, 32.
10. Ibid., 25 July 1942, 35.
11. Ibid., 25 July 1942, 35.
12. Mark W. Clark, *Calculated Risk* (New York: Harper and Brothers Publishers, 1950), 38.
13. Mark W. Clark Papers, Diary, 6 August 1942, 52.
14. Ibid., 6 August 1942, 53.
15. Ibid., 10 August 1942, 56.
16. Ibid., 7 August 1942, 54.
17. Ibid., 11 August 1942, 58.
18. Ibid., 11 August 1942, 58.
19. Ibid., 4 September 1942, 121.

20. Ibid., 17 August 1942, 69.
21. Ibid., 23 August 1942, 82.
22. Ibid., 22 August 1942, 80.
23. Ibid., 25 August 1942, 84.
24. Ibid., 25 August 1942, 85.
25. Ibid., 25 August 1942, 87.
26. Ibid., 25 August 1942, 87.
27. Ibid., 31 August 1942, 104.
28. Ibid., 1 September 1942, 106.
29. Ibid., 3 September 1942, 113.
30. Ibid., 3 September 1942, 115.
31. Ibid., 4 September 1942, 121.
32. Ibid., 16 September 1942, 145.
33. Clark, *Calculated Risk*, 60.
34. Mark W. Clark Papers, Diary, 26 September 1942, Box 64, Volume 2, 25 September 1942–5 January 1943, 4.
35. Ibid., 11 October 1942, 27.
36. Clark, *Calculated Risk*, 58.
37. Mark W. Clark Papers, Diary, 14 October 1942, 34.
38. Clark, *Calculated Risk*, 66.
39. Rich Atkinson, *An Army At Dawn: The War in North Africa, 1942–1943* (New York: Henry Holt and Co., 2002), 65.
40. George Howe, *The U.S. Army in World War Two, The Mediterranean Theatre of Operations, Northwest Africa: Seizing the Initiative in the West* (Washington DC: Center of Military History, 1993), 79.
41. Robert Murphy, *Diplomat Among Warriors* (Garden City, NY: Doubleday and Co, Inc., 1964), 135.
42. Mark W. Clark Papers, Box 1, File 9, Seraph, Cables and Coded Messages, Oct–Nov 1942, Telegram from George C. Marshall to Dwight D. Eisenhower, 17 October 1942.
43. Ibid., 17 October 1942, 40.
44. Ibid., 18 October 1942, 43.
45. Mark W. Clark Papers, Box 64, File 8, Correspondence, Letter from Mark W. Clark to Maurine Clark, 18 October 1942.

CHAPTER TWO: ADVENTURE BELOW, POLITICS ABOVE

1. Mark W. Clark, *Calculated Risk* (New York: Harper and Brothers Publishers, 1950), 74.
2. Martin Blumenson, *Mark Clark* (London: Jonathan Cape, 1985), 80.
3. Norman Jewell, *Secret Mission Submarine* (Chicago: Ziff-Davis Publishing Co., 1944), 14.

4. Mark W. Clark Papers, Diary, 19 October 1942, Box 64, Volume 2, 25 September 1942–5 January 1943, The Citadel Archives and Museum, Charleston, South Carolina, 44.

5. Jewell, *Secret Mission Submarine*, 24.

6. Rich Atkinson, *An Army At Dawn: The War in North Africa, 1942–1943* (New York: Henry Holt and Co., 2002), 42.

7. Jewell, *Secret Mission Submarine*, 26.

8. Jewell, *Secret Mission Submarine*, 27.

9. Clark, *Calculated Risk*, 79.

10. Mark W. Clark Papers, Diary, 22 October 1942, 47.

11. Ibid., 22 October 1942, 47.

12. Blumenson, *Mark Clark*, 82.

13. Arthur Funk, *The Politics of TORCH: The Allied Landings and the Algiers Putsch* (Lawrence: The University Press of Kansas, 1974), 173.

14. Howe, *U.S. Army in World War Two, The Mediterranean Theatre of Operations, Northwest Africa: Seizing the Initiative in the West* (Washington DC: Center of Military History, 1993), 85.

15. Mark W. Clark Papers, Diary, 22 October 1942, 50.

16. Ibid., 22 October 1942, 51.

17. Clark, *Calculated Risk*, 83.

18. Mark W. Clark Papers, Diary, 22 October 1942, 51.

19. Ibid., 22 October 1942, 52.

20. Jewell, *Secret Mission Submarine*, 38.

21. Jewell, *Secret Mission Submarine*, 41.

22. Clark received his lost trousers from Murphy and tried to put them on, but the salt water had shrunk them to such an extent that the pants barely reached past his knees.

23. Clark, *Calculated Risk*, 87.

24. Mark W. Clark Papers, Box 1, File 9, Seraph, Cables and Coded Messages, October–November 1942, Cipher Telegram from Gibraltar, 24 October, 1942.

25. Blumenson, *Mark Clark*, 85.

26. Mark W. Clark Papers, Diary, 25 October 1942, 56.

27. Mark W. Clark Papers, Box 1, File 9, Seraph, Cables and Coded Messages, October–November 1942, Message from George C. Marshall to Dwight D. Eisenhower, 26 October 1942.

28. Mark W. Clark Papers, Box 1, File 8; Correspondence, October 1942, Cypher Telegram from Gibraltar 27 October 1942.

29. Mark W. Clark Papers, Diary, 28 October 1942, 60.

30. Ibid., 28 October 1942, 61.

31. Ibid., 29 October 1942, 62.

32. Mark W. Clark Papers, Box 2, Correspondence, November 1942–September

1943, File 1, November 1942–December 31, 1942, Louis Hollander to Maurine Clark.

33. Ibid., 29 October 1942, 62.
34. Ibid., 29 October 1942, 62.
35. Ibid., 29 October 1942, 63.
36. Mark W. Clark Papers, Box 1, File 9, Seraph, Cables and Coded Messages, Oct–Nov 1942, Draft cable Clark never sent, No date.
37. Mark W. Clark Papers, Diary, 6 November 1942, 75.
38. Mark W. Clark Papers, Diary, Foreword, 2.
39. Clark, *Calculated Risk*, 96.
40. Mark W. Clark Papers, Diary, 7 November 1942, 80.
41. Ibid., 7 November 1942, 81.
42. Ibid., 7 November 1942, 81.
43. Ibid., 8 November 1942, 90.
44. Ibid., 9 November 1942, 92.
45. Dwight Eisenhower, *At Ease: Stories I Tell to Friends* (Garden City, NY: Doubleday and Co, Inc., 1967), 256.
46. Mark W. Clark Papers, Diary, 10 November 1942, 93–96.
47. Mark W. Clark Papers, Diary, 10 November 1942, 93–96.
48. Mark W. Clark Papers, Diary, 10 November 1942, 95.
49. Ibid., 10 November 1942, 96–97.
50. Ibid., 10 November 1942, 98.
51. Howe, *The U.S. Army in World War Two, The Mediterranean Theatre of Operations, Northwest Africa*, 79.
52. Mark W. Clark Papers, Diary, 10 November 1942, 99.
53. Ibid., 11 November 1942, 102.
54. Ibid., 11 November 1942, 102.
55. Ibid., 11 November 1942, 102.
56. Ibid., 12 November 1942, 104.
57. Mark W. Clark Papers, Diary, 10 November 1942, 104–106.
58. Mark W. Clark Papers, Diary, 10 November 1942, 104.
59. Ibid., 12 November 1942, 106.
60. Ibid., 12 November 1942, 106.
61. Mark W. Clark Papers, Diary, 10 November 1942, 104–106.
62. Ibid., 12 November 1942, 109.
63. Ibid., 12 November 1942, 109.
64. Ibid., 12 November 1942, 109.
65. Ibid., 12 November 1942, 110.
66. Ibid., 12 November 1942, 110.
67. Ibid., 12 November 1942, 111.
68. Ibid., 12 November 1942, 111.

69. Ibid., 13 November 1942, 112.

70. Ibid., 13 November 1942, 114.

71. Ibid., 13 November 1942, 114.

72. Mark W. Clark Papers, Box 67, Personal Correspondence, File 6, Maurine Clark, 1942–1943, Letter from Mark W. Clark to Maurine Clark, 21 November 1942.

73. Mark W. Clark Papers, Diary, 15 November 1942, 117.

74. Ibid., 18 November 1942, 123.

75. Ibid., 21 November 1942, 132.

76. Ibid., 18 November 1942, 124.

77. Ibid., 22 November 1942, 135.

78. Blumenson, *Mark Clark*, 109.

79. Funk, *The Politics of TORCH*, 241.

80. Mark W. Clark Papers, Box 35, Darlan Episode November–December 1942, Subject Files, File 4.

81. Mark W. Clark Papers, Box 35, Darlan Episode November–December 1942, File 6, *Darlan Deal: Assessment 30 Years Later* by A.L. Funk in 1972.

82. Clark, *Calculated Risk*, 31.

83. Mark W. Clark Papers, Diary, 5 December 1942, 156.

84. Ibid., 4 December 1942, 155.

85. Ibid., 12 December 1942, 165.

86. Ibid., 20 December 1942, 175.

87. Ibid., 23 December 1942, 180.

88. Mark W. Clark Papers, Box 35, Darlan Episode November–December 1942, Subject Files, File 1, Political Data (Messages) November 1942–Janaury 1943, Cable from Mark W. Clark to Dwight D. Eisenhower, 24 December 1942.

89. Clark, *Calculated Risk*, 130.

90. Mark W. Clark Papers, Diary, 29 December 1942, 191.

91. Ibid., 31 December 1942, 194.

92. Ibid., 4 January 1943, 198.

93. *Fifth Army History, Activation to the Fall of Naples*, vol., 1 5 January–6 October 1943, 2. Records of the Adjunct General's Office Record Group 407; National Archives at College Park, College Park, Maryland.

94. Mark W. Clark Papers, Box 2, Correspondence, November 1942–September 1943, File 2, January 31–30 June, 1943, Letter from Mark W. Clark to Dwight D. Eisenhower, 5 January 1943.

95. Dwight Eisenhower, *Crusade in Europe* (New York: Doubleday and Co., Inc., 1948), 76.

96. Mark W. Clark Papers, Diary, 19 January 1943, Box 64, Volume 3, 6 January 1943–20 May 1943, 8.

97. Howe, *The Mediterranean Theatre of Operations, Northwest Africa*, 675.

98. Winston S. Churchill, *The Second World War*, vol. IV, *The Hinge of Fate* (Boston: Houghton Mifflin Co., 1950), 565.

CHAPTER THREE: THE BIRTH OF THE FIGHTIN' FIFTH

1. *Fifth Army History, Activation to the Fall of Naples*, vol. 1, 5 January–6 October 1943, 3. Records of the Adjunct General's Office, Record Group 407; National Archives at College Park, College Park, Maryland.
2. Mark W. Clark Papers, Diary, 8 January 1943, Box 64, Volume 3, 6 January 1943–20 May 1943, The Citadel Archives and Museum, Charleston, South Carolina, 3.
3. Ibid., 9 January 1943, 4.
4. Mark W. Clark Papers, Diary, 17 June 1943, Box 64, Volume 4, 7 June 1943–29 August 1943, 19.
5. Mark W. Clark Papers, Box 2, Correspondence, November 1942–September 1943, File 2, January 31–June 30, 1943, Mark W. Clark to his William Clark, 7 February 1943.
6. Mark W. Clark Papers, Box 3, Correspondence, October 1943–June 1944, File 4, January 1944, Mark W. Clark to Beckie Clark, 19 January 1943.
7. Mark W. Clark Papers, Box 67, Personal Correspondence, File 6, Renie Clark, 1942–1943, Mark W. Clark to Renie Clark, 16 May 1943.
8. Mark W. Clark Papers, Box 1, Clippings, Book 3, Philadelphia *Inquirer*, Louella O. Parsons, 17 November 1942.
9. Mark W. Clark Papers, Diary, Volume 3, 19 January 1943, 9.
10. Ibid., 21 January 1943, 13.
11. Ibid., 20 February 1943, 43.
12. Ibid., 2 April 1943, 97.
13. Ibid., 19 April 1943, 40.
14. Ibid., 20 April 1943, 126.
15. Mark W. Clark, *Calculated Risk* (New York: Harper and Brothers Publishers, 1950), 166.
16. Mark W. Clark Papers, Diary, 7 June 1943, Box 64, Volume 4, 7 June 1943–29 August 1943, 2.
17. *Fifth Army History, Activation to the Fall of Naples*, 16.
18. Mark W. Clark Papers, Diary, 17 July 1943, 57.
19. *Fifth Army History, Activation to the Fall of Naples*, 17.
20. Mark W. Clark Papers, Diary, 23 July 1943, 64.
21. *Fifth Army History, Activation to the Fall of Naples*, 17.
22. Mark W. Clark Papers, Diary, 26 July 1943, 66.
23. Ibid., 7 August, 81.
24. *Fifth Army History, Activation to the Fall of Naples*, 20.
25. Ibid., 20.
26. Ibid., 25.

27. Ibid., 25.

28. Mark W. Clark Papers, Diary, 16 August 1943, 91.

29. C.J.C. Molony, *The Mediterranean and Middle East*, vol. V, *The Campaign in Sicily 1943 and the Campaign in Italy, 3 September 1943 to 31ˢᵗ March 1944* (London: Her Majesty's Stationary Office, 1973), 186.

30. G.A. Shepperd, *The Italian Campaign, 1943–1945: A Political and Military Reassessment* (New York: Frederick A Praeger, 1968), 99.

31. Molony, *The Mediterranean and Middle East, The Campaign in Sicily*, 192.

32. Winston S. Churchill, *The Second World War*, vol. V, *Closing the Ring* (Boston: Houghton Mifflin Co., 1951), 435.

33. Molony, *The Mediterranean and Middle East, The Campaign in Sicily*, 207.

34. Ibid., 215.

35. Albert N. Garland, Howard McGaw Smyth and assisted by Martin Blumenson, *U.S. Army in World War Two, The Mediterranean Theater of Operations, Sicily and the Surrender of Italy* (Washington DC: Center of Military History, 1993), 50.

36. *Fifth Army History, Activation to the Fall of Naples*, 23.

37. Ibid., 24.

38. Mark W. Clark, *Calculated Risk* (New York: Harper and Brothers Publishers, 1950), 180.

39. Ibid., 181.

40. Garland, *U.S. Army in World War Two, The Mediterranean Theater of Operations, Sicily and the Surrender of Italy*, 552.

41. Alan Moorehead, *Eclipse* (New York: Harper and Row Publishers, 1945), 27.

42. Ralph S. Mavrogordato, "Hitler's Decision on the Defense of Italy," in *Command Decisions*, United States Army, Office of the Chief of Military History (Washington DC., 1960), 313 and 320.

43. Albert Kesselring, *The Memoirs of Field-Marshal Kesselring*, edited. translated by William Kimber (Novato, California: Presidio Press, 1989), 177.

44. Ibid., 176.

CHAPTER FOUR: DISASTER AVERTED

1. Mark W. Clark Papers, Diary, 30 August 1943, Box 64, Volume 5, 30 August 1943–31 December 1943, The Citadel Archives and Museum, Charleston, South Carolina, 3.

2. Martin Blumenson, *U.S. Army in World War Two, The Mediterranean Theater of Operations, Salerno to Cassino* (Washington DC: Center of Military History, 1993), 78.

3. Mark W. Clark Papers, Diary, 6 September 1943, 8.

4. C.J.C. Molony, *The Mediterranean and Middle East*, vol. V, *The Campaign in Sicily 1943 and the Campaign in Italy, 3 September 1943 to 31ˢᵗ March 1944* (London: Her Majesty's Stationary Office, 1973), 259.

5. *G-3 Operations Report*, September 1943, 2. Records of the Adjunct General's

Office, Record Group 407; National Archives at College Park, College Park, Maryland.

6. Blumenson, *U.S. Army in World War Two, The Mediterranean Theater of Operations, Salerno to Cassino*, 77.

7. *Fifth Army History, Activation to the Fall of Naples*, vol. I, 5 January–6 October 1943, 32. Records of the Adjunct General's Office, Record Group 407; National Archives at College Park, College Park, Maryland.

8. Eric Morris, *Salerno: A Military Fiasco* (London: Hutchinson and Co., 1983), 147.

9. *Fifth Army History, Activation to the Fall of Naples*, 34.

10. Mark W. Clark Papers, Diary, 9 September 1943, 20.

11. Blumenson, *U.S. Army in World War Two, The Mediterranean Theater of Operations, Salerno to Cassino*, 85.

12. Mark W. Clark Papers, Diary, 12 September 1943, 23.

13. Mark W. Clark Papers, Box 67, Personal Correspondence, File 6, Renie Clark, 1942–1943, Letter from Mark W. Clark to Renie, 12 September 1943, The Citadel Archives and Museum, Charleston, South Carolina.

14. *Fifth Army History, Activation to the Fall of Naples*, 37.

15. Mark W. Clark, *Calculated Risk* (New York: Harper and Brothers Publishers, 1950), 198.

16. Mark W. Clark Papers, Diary, 13 September 1943, 25.

17. Molony, *The Mediterranean and Middle East*, vol. V, *The Campaign in Sicily*, 299.

18. *G-3 Operations Report*, September 1943, 3.

19. Blumenson, *U.S. Army in World War Two, The Mediterranean Theater of Operations, Salerno to Cassino*, 112.

20. Ibid., 113.

21. Ibid., 123.

22. Mark W. Clark Papers, Diary, 13 September 1943, 24.

23. Mark W. Clark Papers, Diary, 13 September 1943, 25.

24. Blumenson, *U.S. Army in World War Two, The Mediterranean Theater of Operations, Salerno to Cassino*, 118.

25. Clark, *Calculated Risk*, 199.

26. *G-3 Operations Report*, September 1943, 4.

27. Mark W. Clark Papers, Diary, 14 September 1943, 28.

28. Ibid., 14 September, 30.

29. Mark W. Clark Papers, Box 2, Correspondence, November 1942–September 1943, File 3, July 1943–Sept 30, 1943, Letter from Bernard Montgomery to Mark W. Clark, 15 September 1943.

30. Mark W. Clark Papers, Box 2, Correspondence, November 1942–September 1943, File 3, July 1943–September 30, 1943, Letter from Mark W. Clark to Bernard Montgomery, 16 September 1943.

31. Mark W. Clark Papers, Diary, 15 September 1943, 32.

32. Ibid., 16 September, 33.

33. Mark W. Clark Papers, Box 2, Correspondence, November 1942–September 1943, File 3, July 1943–September 30, 1943, Letter from Bernard Montgomery to Mark W. Clark, 17 September 1943.

34. Mark W. Clark Papers, Diary, 20 September 1943, 43.

35. Mark W. Clark Papers, Box 2, Correspondence, November 1942–September 1943, File 3, July 1943–September 30, 1943, Letter from Mark W. Clark to Dwight D. Eisenhower, 16 September 1943.

36. Mark W. Clark Papers, Diary, 20 September 1943, 42.

37. Clark, *Calculated Risk*, 211.

38. Ibid., 211.

39. Ibid., 209.

40. Mark W. Clark Papers, Diary, 1 October 1943, 67.

41. Ibid., 28 September, 62.

42. Ibid., 5 October, 72.

43. Mark W. Clark Papers, Box 3, Correspondence, October 1943–June 1944, File 1, October, Mark W. Clark to Beckie Clark, 10 October 1943.

44. G.A. Shepperd, *The Italian Campaign, 1943–1945: A Political and Military Reassessment* (New York: Frederick A Praeger, 1968), 142.

45. *G-3 Operations Report*, September 1943, 6.

46. Clark, *Calculated Risk*, 223.

47. Mark W. Clark Papers, Box 3, Correspondence, October 1943–June 1944, File 1, October, Letter from Henry Morgenthau after touring with Mark W. Clark, 20 October 1943.

48. Mark W. Clark Papers, Diary, 15 October 1943, 85.

49. Clark, *Calculated Risk*, 229.

50. Mark W. Clark Papers, Diary, 25 October 1943, 100.

51. Blumenson, *U.S. Army in World War Two, The Mediterranean Theater of Operations, Salerno to Cassino*, 144.

52. Dwight D. Eisenhower, *Crusade in Europe* (Garden City, New York: Doubleday and Co., Inc., 1948), 187.

53. Mark W. Clark Papers, Box 3, Correspondence, October 1943–June 1944, File 1, October, Letter from Mark W. Clark to Beckie Clark, 6 October 1943.

54. Francis De Guinard, *Operation Victory* (London: Hodder and Stoughton Limited Publishers, 1947), 312.

55. Harold Alexander, *The Alexander Memoirs, 1940–1945*, edited by John North (New York: McGraw-Hill Book Co., Inc., 1961), 114.

56. Mark W. Clark Papers, Box 67, Personal Correspondence, File 6, Renie Clark, 1942–1943, Mark W. Clark to Renie Clark, 15 September 1943.

57. Winston S. Churchill, *The Second World War*, vol. V, *Closing the Ring* (Boston: Houghton Mifflin Co., 1951), 219.

58. George S. Patton Papers, Box 19, Folder 15, Letter from George S. Patton to Beatrice Patton, October 15, 1943, Library of Congress, Washington DC.

CHAPTER FIVE: STUCK IN THE MOUNTAINS

1. *Fifth Army History, The Winter Line*, vol. III, 16 November–14 January 1944, 2. Records of the Adjunct General's Office, Record Group 407; National Archives at College Park, College Park, Maryland.

2. Mark W. Clark, *Calculated Risk* (New York: Harper and Brothers Publishers, 1950), 233.

3. Mark W. Clark Papers, Diary, 4 August 1943, Box 64, Volume 5, 30 August 1943–31 December 1943, The Citadel Archives and Museum, Charleston, South Carolina, 115.

4. C.J.C. Molony, *The Mediterranean and Middle East*, vol. V, *The Campaign in Sicily 1943 and the Campaign in Italy, 3 September 1943 to 31st March 1944* (London: Her Majesty's Stationary Office, 1973), 377.

5. Ibid., 379.

6. *Fifth Army History, The Winter Line*, 7.

7. Ibid., 8.

8. Ibid., 8.

9. Ibid., 9.

10. Clark, *Calculated Risk*, 236.

11. *Fifth Army History, The Winter Line*, 10.

12. *Fifth Army History, Across the Volturno to the Winter Line*, vol. II, 7 October–15 November 1943, 57. Records of the Adjunct General's Office, Record Group 407; National Archives at College Park, College Park, Maryland.

13. Mark W. Clark Papers, Diary, 9 November 1943, 123.

14. Fifth Army History, The Winter Line, 14.

15. Mark W. Clark Papers, Box 67, Personal Correspondence, File 6, Renie Clark, 1942–1943, Letter from Mark W. Clark to Renie Clark, 7 November 1943.

16. Fred L. Walker, *From Texas to Rome: A General's Journal* (Dallas: Taylor Publishing Co., 1969), 290.

17. Mark W. Clark Papers, Diary, 8 November 1943, 121.

18. Clark, *Calculated Risk*, 239.

19. *Fifth Army History, The Winter Line*, 28.

20. Ibid., 35.

21. Ibid., 37.

22. Clark, *Calculated Risk*, 248.

23. Martin Blumenson, *U.S. Army in World War Two, The Mediterranean Theater of Operations, Salerno to Cassino* (Washington DC: Center of Military History, 1993), 285.

24. Mark W. Clark Papers, Box 3, Correspondence, October 1943–June 1944, File

3, December, Message from Mark W. Clark, 18 December 1943.

25. Clark, *Calculated Risk*, 242.

26. Mark W. Clark Papers, Box 3, Correspondence, October 1943–June 1944, File 3, December, 11 December 1943.

27. Mark W. Clark Papers, Box 3, Correspondence, October 1943–June 1944, File 3, December, Franklin D. Roosevelt to Mark W. Clark, 8 December 1943.

28. Mark W. Clark Papers, Box 3, Correspondence, October 1943–June 1944, File 3, December, Message from Harold Alexander to Mark W. Clark, 21 December 1943.

29. Mark W. Clark Papers, Box 34, Operation TORCH, Subject Files, File 2, Letters, January 3–December 28, 1943, 28 December 1943.

Chapter Six: Bloody River

1. Winston Churchill, *The Second World War*, vol. V, *Closing the Ring* (Boston: Houghton Mifflin Co, 1951), 432.

2. Mark Clark, *Calculated Risk* (New York: Harper and Brothers Publishers, 1950), 283.

3. Trumbull Higgins, *Soft Underbelly: The Anglo-American Controversy Over the Italian Campaign, 1939–1945* (New York: The Macmillan Co, 1968), 138.

4. *Fifth Army History, Cassino and Anzio*, vol. IV, 16 January–31 March 1944, 9. Records of the Adjunct General's Office, Record Group 407; National Archives at College Park, College Park, Maryland.

5. Carlo D'Este, *Fatal Decision: Anzio and the Battle for Rome* (New York: Harpers Collins, 1991), 74.

6. Martin Blumenson, *Anzio: The Gamble That Failed* (Philadelphia: J. B. Lippincott Co, 1963), 58.

7. Martin Blumenson, *U.S. Army in World War Two, The Mediterranean Theater of Operations, Salerno to Cassino* (Washington DC: Center of Military History, 1993), 158.

8. Lucian Truscott, *Command Missions: A Personal Story* (New York: E. P. Dutton and Co, 1954), 301.

9. D'Este, *Fatal Decision*, 95.

10. Another name for the Alban Hills

11. D'Este, *Fatal Decision*, 111.

12. Blumenson, *U.S. Army in World War Two, The Mediterranean Theater of Operations, Salerno to Cassino*, 313.

13. *Fifth Army History, Cassino and Anzio*, 10.

14. Blumenson, *U.S. Army in World War Two, The Mediterranean Theater of Operations, Salerno to Cassino*, 313.

15. Martin Blumenson, *Mark Clark* (London: Jonathan Cape, 1985), 171.

16. Truscott, *Command Missions*, 298.

17. Clark, *Calculated Risk*, 284.

18. *Fifth Army History, Cassino and Anzio*, 207.

19. Blumenson, *U.S. Army in World War Two, The Mediterranean Theater of Operations, Salerno to Cassino*, 356.

20. Peter Verney, *Anzio 1944: An Unexpected Fury* (London: B. T. Batsford Ltd, 1978), 27.

21. Mark W. Clark Papers, Diary, 19 January 1944, 29.

22. Blumenson, *U.S. Army in World War Two, The Mediterranean Theater of Operations, Salerno to Cassino*, 355.

23. Mark W. Clark Papers, Diary, 19 January 1944, 30.

24. Higgins, *Soft Underbelly*, 142.

25. Higgins, *Soft Underbelly*, 141.

26. Blumenson, *Anzio*, 65.

27. *Fifth Army History, Cassino and Anzio*, 27.

28. Clark mistakenly wrote "Liri River" in his diary. It was the Garigliano River that the 46th Division had attempted to cross. It was not uncommon for those in Italy to confuse the numerous rivers. The Rapido, Gari and Garigliano Rivers form a continuous line from Monte Santa Croce on the north to the Tyrrhenian Sea on the South, four miles south of Highway 6. The Cesa Martino Creek flows into the Rapido, thus becoming the Gari, then it flows southeast for about two and a half miles into the Liri River, combining to form the Garigliano until it hits the sea sixteen miles later.

29. Mark W. Clark Papers, Diary, 20 January 1944, 32.

30. Ibid., 20 January, 32.

31. Fred L. Walker, *From Texas to Rome: A General's Journal*, Diary, 20 January 1944 (Dallas: Publishing Co., 1969), 305.

32. Martin Blumenson, *Bloody River: The Real Tragedy of the Rapido* (Boston: Houghton Mifflin Co, 1970), 70.

33. Truscott, *Command Missions*, 295.

34. Walker, *From Texas to Rome*, Diary, 8 January 1944, 296.

35. Ibid., Diary, 16 January 1944, 299

36. Ibid., Diary, 17 January 1944, 301.

37. *Fifth Army History, Cassino and Anzio*, 41.

38. Ibid., 41.

39. Walker, *From Texas to Rome*, Diary, 20 January 1944, 305.

40. Ibid., Diary, 20 January 1944, 306.

41. *Fifth Army History, Cassino and Anzio*, 44.

42. Blumenson, *U.S. Army in World War Two, The Mediterranean Theater of Operations, Salerno to Cassino*, 333.

43. *Fifth Army History, Cassino and Anzio*, 44.

44. Ibid., 47.

45. Walker, *From Texas to Rome*, Diary, 21 January 1944, 310.

46. Mark W. Clark Papers, Diary, 21 January 1944, 35.

47. *Fifth Army History, Cassino and Anzio*, 47.

48. Mark W. Clark Papers, Diary, 23 January 1944, 41.

49. Walker, *From Texas to Rome*, Diary, 23 January 1944, 316.

50. Ibid., 25 January 1944, 320.

51. Ibid., 25 January 1944, 320.

52. Ibid., 28 January 1944, 321.

53. Blumenson, *Bloody River*, 129.

54. Ibid., 130.

55. Ibid., 130.

56. Mark W. Clark Papers, Box 39, Rapido River Controversy 1946, Subject Files, File 1, Correspondence 1946, 1946, Memo from Mark W. Clark to Dwight D. Eisenhower.

57. Mark W. Clark Papers, Box 39, Rapido River Controversy 1946, Subject Files, File 1, Correspondence 1946, Letter from Mark W. Clark to Al Gruenther, 7 January 1946.

58. Mark W. Clark Papers, Box 39, Rapido River Controversy 1946, Subject Files, File 1, Correspondence 1946, Letter from Mark W. Clark to Al Gruenther, 17 January 1946.

59. Mark W. Clark Papers, Box 39, Rapido River Controversy 1946, Subject Files, File 1, Correspondence 1946, Col. William A. Walker Memo for General North, Report of Interview with Major General Fred L. Walker, 4 February 1946.

60. Mark W. Clark Papers, Box 39, Rapido River Controversy 1946, Subject Files, File 1, Correspondence 1946, Col. William A. Walker Memo for General North, Report of Interview with Major General Fred L. Walker, 4 February 1946.

61. Mark W. Clark Papers, Box 39, Rapido River Controversy 1946, Subject Files, File 1, Correspondence 1946, Letter from Mark W. Clark to Beckie Clark, 2 April 1946.

62. Mark W. Clark Papers, Box 39, Rapido River Controversy 1946, Subject Files, File 1, Correspondence 1946, Letter from Mark W. Clark to Renie Clark, 24 March 1946.

63. Mark W. Clark Papers, Box 39, Rapido River Controversy 1946, Subject Files, File 1, Correspondence 1946, Quote from Randolph Churchill, 2 April 1946.

64. Clark, *Calculated Risk*, 279.

65. Ibid., 281.

66. Eric Sevareid, *Not So Wild A Dream* (New York: Atheneum, 1976), 366.

CHAPTER SEVEN: THE WILDCAT THAT BECAME A WHALE

1. Martin Blumenson, *Mark Clark* (London: Jonathan Cape, 1985), 172.

2. *Fifth Army History, Cassino and Anzio*, vol. IV, 16 January–31 March 1944, 61.

Records of the Adjunct General's Office, Record Group 407; National Archives at College Park, College Park, Maryland.

3. Ibid., 62.

4. Ibid., 20.

5. Ibid., 21.

6. Mark W. Clark Papers, Diary, 22 January 1944, Box 65, Volume 6, 1 January 1944–31 March 1944, The Citadel Archives and Museum, Charleston, South Carolina, 38.

7. *Fifth Army History, Cassino and Anzio*, 65.

8. Ibid., 67.

9. Mark W. Clark Papers, Diary, 23 January 1944, 42.

10. Ibid., 8 January 1944, 15.

11. Ibid., 26 January, 45.

12. Martin Blumenson, *Anzio: The Gamble That Failed* (Philadelphia: J. B. Lippincott Co, 1963), 88.

13. Ibid., 88.

14. Mark W. Clark Papers, Diary, 27 January 1944, 47.

15. Ibid., 27 January, 47.

16. Blumenson, *Anzio*, 76.

17. Peter Verney, *Anzio 1944: An Unexpected Fury* (London: B. T. Batsford Ltd, 1978), 86.

18. Carlo D'Este, *Fatal Decision: Anzio and the Battle for Rome* (New York: Harpers Collins, 1991), 5.

19. Albert Kesselring, *The Memoirs of Field-Marshal* Kesselring, edited. translated by William Kimber (Novato, California: Presidio Press, 1989), 194.

20. Martin Blumenson, *U.S. Army in World War Two, The Mediterranean Theater of Operations, Salerno to Cassino* (Washington DC: Center of Military History, 1993), 360.

21. Blumenson, *U.S. Army in World War Two, The Mediterranean Theater of Operations, Salerno to Cassino*, 360.

22. Ibid., 363.

23. Mark W. Clark Papers, Diary, 30 January 1944, 56.

24. *Fifth Army History, Cassino and Anzio*, 71.

25. Blumenson, *U.S. Army in World War Two, The Mediterranean Theater of Operations, Salerno to Cassino*, 390.

26. Ibid., 390.

27. *Fifth Army History, Cassino and Anzio*, 74.

28. Blumenson, *U.S. Army in World War Two, The Mediterranean Theater of Operations, Salerno to Cassino*, 391.

29. Ibid., 391.

30. Mark W. Clark Papers, Diary, 31 January 1944, 57.

31. D'Este, *Fatal Decision*, 2.
32. Gregory Blaxland, *Alexander's Generals: The Italian Campaign, 1944–1945* (London: William Kimber and Co, 1979), 46.
33. *Fifth Army History, Cassino and Anzio*, 108.
34. Ibid., 107.
35. Ibid., 107.
36. Mark W. Clark Papers, Diary, 7 February 1944, 67.
37. Ibid., 4 February, 65.
38. John Ellis, *Cassino: The Hollow Victory, The Battle for Rome, January–June 1944* (London: Andre Deutsch Limited, 1984), xiii.
39. Ibid., xiii.
40. Winston Churchill, *The Second World War*, vol. V, *Closing the Ring* (Boston: Houghton Mifflin Co, 1951), 449.
41. *Fifth Army History, Cassino and Anzio*, 93.
42. Ibid., 93.
43. Field Marshall Harold Alexander, Interview by Sidney Mathews, 10–15 January 1949 at Government House, Ottawa, Canada, 4. The Citadel Archives and Museum, Charleston, South Carolina.
44. *Fifth Army History, Cassino and Anzio*, 98.
45. *Report on Bombing of Abbey*, 1. Records of the Adjunct General's Office, Record Group 407; National Archives at College Park, College Park, Maryland.
46. Ibid., 1.
47. Ibid., 1.
48. Ibid., 1.
49. Ibid., 2.
50. Ibid., 2.
51. Ibid., 2.
52. Ibid., 2.
53. Ibid., 2.
54. Ibid., 2.
55. Ibid., 2.
56. Ibid., 2.
57. Mark W. Clark Papers, Diary, 13 February 1944, 81.
58. Blumenson, *U.S. Army in World War Two, The Mediterranean Theater of Operations, Salerno to Cassino*, 409.
59. Ibid., 409.
60. C.J.C. Molony, *The Mediterranean and Middle East*, vol. V, *The Campaign in Sicily 1943 and the Campaign in Italy, 3 September 1943 to 31st March 1944* (London: Her Majesty's Stationary Office, 1973), 713.
61. *Fifth Army History, Cassino and Anzio*, 99.
62. Mark W. Clark Papers, Diary, 15 February 1944, 83.

63. Blumenson, *U.S. Army in World War Two, The Mediterranean Theater of Operations, Salerno to Cassino*, 408.

64. D'Este, *Fatal Decision*, 259.

65. Harold Alexander, *The Alexander Memoirs, 1940–1945*, edited by John North (New York: McGraw-Hill Book Co., Inc., 1961), 119.

66. D'Este, *Fatal Decision*, 257.

67. Kesselring, *The Memoirs of Field-Marshal* Kesselring, 195.

68. Mark W. Clark, *Calculated Risk* (New York: Harper and Brothers Publishers, 1950), 312.

69. D'Este, *Fatal Decision*, 261.

70. Blumenson, *U.S. Army in World War Two, The Mediterranean Theater of Operations, Salerno to Cassino*, 419.

71. Blumenson, *U.S. Army in World War Two, The Mediterranean Theater of Operations, Salerno to Cassino*, 419.

72. *Fifth Army History, Cassino and Anzio*, 119.

73. *Special Reports-Diary of Anzio Operation*, 1 January–15 February 1944. Records of the Adjunct General's Office, Record Group 407; National Archives at College Park, College Park, Maryland.

74. *Fifth Army History, Cassino and Anzio*, 135.

75. Mark. W. Clark Papers, Box 3, Correspondence, October 1943–June 1944, File 5, February–March 1944, Letter from Dwight D. Eisenhower to Mark W. Clark, 18 February 1944.

76. Mark W. Clark Papers, Box 3, Correspondence, October 1943–June 1944, File 5, February–March 1944, Letter from Mark W. Clark to Dwight D. Eisenhower, 19 February 1944.

77. Blumenson, *U.S. Army in World War Two, The Mediterranean Theater of Operations, Salerno to Cassino*, 424.

78. Blumenson, *U.S. Army in World War Two, The Mediterranean Theater of Operations, Salerno to Cassino*, 424.

79. Alexander, *The Alexander Memoirs, 1940–1945*, 126.

80. Mark W. Clark Papers, Diary, 16 February 1944, 84.

81. Field Marshall Harold Alexander, Interview by Sidney Mathews, 10–15 January 1949 at Government House, Ottawa, Canada, 28.

82. Mark W. Clark Papers, Diary, 16 February 1944, 84.

83. Ibid., 18 February, 87.

84. Ibid., 24 February, 104.

85. Blumenson, *Anzio*, 122.

86. *Fifth Army History, Cassino and Anzio*, 146.

87. Ibid., 153.

88. Ibid., 155.

89. Ibid., 159.

90. Ibid., 160.

91. Alexander, *The Alexander Memoirs, 1940–1945*, 126.

92. Henry Wilson, *Eight Years Overseas, 1939–1947* (London: Hutchinson and Co, 1950), 194.

93. Lucian Truscott, *Command Missions: A Personal Story* (New York: E. P. Dutton and Co, 1954), 298.

94. Higgins, *Soft Underbelly*, 145.

95. Field Marshall Harold Alexander, Interview by Sidney Mathews, 10–15 January 1949 at Government House, Ottawa, Canada, 8.

96. Wilson, *Eight Years Overseas, 1939–1947*, 193.

97. Truscott, *Command Missions*, 311.

98. Mark W. Clark Papers, Box 67, Personal Correspondence, File 7, Renie Clark 1944, Letter from Mark W. Clark to Renie Clark, 27 February 1944.

99. Mark W. Clark, Interview by Sidney Mathews, 10–21 May 1948, 76. The Citadel Archives and Museum, Charleston, South Carolina.

100. Wilson, *Eight Years Overseas, 1939–1947*, 194.

101. Field Marshall Harold Alexander, Interview by Sidney Mathews, 10–15 January 1949 at Government House, Ottawa, Canada, 27.

102. Alexander, *The Alexander Memoirs, 1940–1945*, 124.

103. Dwight D. Eisenhower, *Crusade in Europe* (Garden City, New York: Doubleday and Co., Inc., 1948), 213.

104. Mark W. Clark Papers, Diary, 28 February 1944, 119.

105. D'Este, *Fatal Decision*, 406.

106. Ibid., 100.

107. Ibid., 103.

108. Mark W. Clark Papers, Diary, 29 February 1944, 120.

109. Ibid., 1 March, 122.

110. Ibid., 1 March, 122.

111. Ibid., 11 March, 142.

112. Ibid., 5 March, 133.

113. *Fifth Army History, Cassino and Anzio*, 177.

114. Mark W. Clark Papers, Diary, 16 March 1944, 149.

115. Ibid., 17 March, 152.

116. *Fifth Army History, Cassino and Anzio*, 181.

117. Mark W. Clark Papers, Diary, 26 February 1944, 112.

118. Ibid., 20 March, 161.

119. Ibid., 23 March, 168.

120. *Fifth Army History, Cassino and Anzio*, 188.

121. Mark W. Clark Papers, Diary, 22 March 1944, 165.

Chapter Eight: Rome

1. Maurine Clark, *Captain's Bridge, General's Lady: The Memoirs of Mrs. Mark W. Clark* (New York: McGraw-Hill Book Co., 1956), 114.

2. *Fifth Army History, The Drive to Rome*, vol. V, 1 April–4 June 1944, 2. Records of the Adjunct General's Office, Record Group 407; National Archives at College Park, College Park, Maryland.

3. Ernest F. Fisher, *U.S. Army in World War Two, The Mediterranean Theater of Operations, Cassino to the Alps* (Washington DC: Center of Military History, 1993), 22.

4. *Fifth Army History, The Drive to Rome*, 4.

5. Fisher, *U.S. Army in World War Two, The Mediterranean Theater of Operations, Cassino to the Alps*, 26.

6. *Fifth Army History, The Drive to Rome*, 11.

7. Ibid., 12.

8. Mark W. Clark, *Calculated Risk* (New York: Harper and Brothers Publishers, 1950), 336.

9. *Fifth Army History, The Drive to Rome*, 172.

10. *Fifth Army History, The Drive to Rome*, 173.

11. Mark W. Clark Papers, Diary, 5 May 1944, Box 65, Volume 7, 1 April 1944–30 June 1944, The Citadel Archives and Museum, Charleston, South Carolina, 41.

12. Clark, *Calculated Risk*, 341.

13. Ibid., 342.

14. *Fifth Army History, The Drive to Rome*, 106.

15. Lucian Truscott, *Command Missions: A Personal Story* (New York: E. P. Dutton and Co, 1954), 368.

16. Mark W. Clark Papers, Diary, handwritten note on page 51.

17. Ibid., 5 May 1944, 51.

18. Truscott, *Command Missions*, 369.

19. Mark W. Clark Papers, Diary, 7 May 1944, 55.

20. Ibid., 8 May 1944, 58.

21. Fisher, *U.S. Army in World War Two, The Mediterranean Theater of Operations, Cassino to the Alps*, 33.

22. *Fifth Army History, The Drive to Rome*, 25.

23. Mark W. Clark Papers, Box 3, Correspondence, October 1943–June 1944, File 6, April–May. Harold Alexander's message to the troops.

24. Mark W. Clark Papers, Box 3, Correspondence, October 1943–June 1944, File 6, April–May. Clark W. Clark's message to the troops.

25. *Fifth Army History, The Drive to Rome*, 33.

26. Chester G. Starr, ed., *From Salerno to the Alps: A History of the Fifth Army, 1943–1945* (Nashville: The Battery Press, 1986), 186.

27. Mark W. Clark Papers, Diary, 15 May 1944, 69.

28. Clark, *Calculated Risk*, 350.

29. Mark W. Clark Papers, Diary, 17 May 1944, 75.

30. Clark, *Calculated Risk*, 350.

31. Mark W. Clark Papers, Diary, 19 May 1944, 79.

32. Ibid., 19 May 1944, 79.

33. Ibid., 20 May 1944, 83.

34. Ibid., 20 May 1944, 84.

35. *Fifth Army History, The Drive to Rome*, 101.

36. Fisher, *U.S. Army in World War Two, The Mediterranean Theater of Operations, Cassino to the Alps*, 114.

37. Ibid., 136.

38. Ibid., 152.

39. Mark W. Clark Papers, Diary, 25 May 1944, 102.

40. Ibid., 24 May, 97.

41. Mark W. Clark Papers, Box 3, Correspondence, October 1943–June 1944, File 6, April–May, Mark W. Clark's message to the troops.

42. Mark W. Clark Papers, Diary, 24 May 1944, 100.

43. Carlo D'Este, *Fatal Decision: Anzio and the Battle for Rome* (New York: Harpers Collins, 1991), 363.

44. Mark W. Clark Papers, Box 67, Personal Correspondence, File 7, Renie Clark 1944, Letter from Mark W. Clark to Renie Clark, 26 May 1944.

45. Mark W. Clark Papers, Box 67, Personal Correspondence, File 7, Renie Clark 1944, Letter from Mark W. Clark to Renie Clark, 31 May 1944.

46. Fisher, *U.S. Army in World War Two, The Mediterranean Theater of Operations, Cassino to the Alps*, 165.

47. Ibid., 163.

48. Mark W. Clark Papers, Diary, 25 May 1944, 105.

49. Truscott, *Command Missions*, 375.

50. Ibid., 375.

51. Mark W. Clark Papers, Diary, 26 May 1944, 106.

52. Ibid., 27 May 1944, 111.

53. Ibid., 26 May 1944, 107.

54. Field Marshall Harold Alexander, Interview by Sidney Mathews, 10–15 January 1949 at Government House, Ottawa, Canada, 11. The Citadel Archives and Museum, Charleston, South Carolina.

55. Harold Alexander, *The Alexander Memoirs, 1940–1945*, edited by John North (New York: McGraw-Hill Book Co., Inc., 1961), 127.

56. Field Marshall Harold Alexander, Interview by Sidney Mathews, 10–15 January 1949 at Government House, Ottawa, Canada, 12.

57. Alexander, *The Alexander Memoirs, 1940–1945*, 127.

58. Mark W. Clark, Interview by Sidney Mathews, 10–21 May 1948, 50. The Citadel Archives and Museum, Charleston, South Carolina.

59. Clark, *Calculated Risk*, 352.

60. Mark W. Clark Papers, Diary, 22 May 1944, 93.

61. Ibid., 31 May 1944, 126.

62. Ibid., 30 May 1944, 123.

63. D'Este, *Fatal Decision*, 383.

64. *Ibid.*, 383.

65. Sidney T. Matthews, "General Clark's Decision to Drive on Rome," in *Command Decisions*, United States Army, Office of the Chief of Military History (Washington DC: Center of Military History, 1960), 356.

66. Mark W. Clark Papers, Diary, 30 May 1944, 122.

67. Ibid., 2 June 1944, 135.

68. Mark W. Clark Papers, Box 63, Messages 1943–1945, Subject Files, File 4, Important Messages, June–July 1944, Message from Clark to Al Gruenther, 3 June 1944.

69. Interview with Mark W. Clark by Dr. Sidney Mathews, May 10–21, 1948, 60.

70. Mark W. Clark Papers, Diary, 3 June 1944, 144.

71. Mark W. Clark Papers, Box 63, Messages 1943–1945, Subject Files, File 4, Important Messages, June–July 1944, Message from Al Gruenther to Mark W. Clark, 3 June 1944.

72. Fisher, *U.S. Army in World War Two, The Mediterranean Theater of Operations, Cassino to the Alps*, 205.

73. Ibid., 206.

74. *Fifth Army History, The Drive to Rome*, 156.

75. Eric Sevareid, *Not So Wild A Dream* (New York: Atheneum, 1976), 408.

76. *Fifth Army History, The Drive to Rome*, 157.

77. Clark could not remember the name of the priest.

78. Mark W. Clark Papers, Diary, 7 June 1944, 152.

79. Sevareid, *Not So Wild A Dream*, 414.

80. Mark W. Clark Papers, Box 67, Personal Correspondence, File 7, Renie Clark 1944, Letter from Mark W. Clark to Renie Clark, 8 June 1944.

81. Mark W. Clark Papers, Box 3, Correspondence, October 1943–June 1944, File 7, June, Letter from Dwight D. Eisenhower to Mark W. Clark, 6 June 1944.

82. Mark W. Clark Papers, Box 3, Correspondence, October 1943–June 1944, File 7, June, Congratulatory Message from Franklin D. Roosevelt, 20 June 1944.

83. Mark W. Clark Papers, Box 3, Correspondence, October 1943–June 1944, File 7, June, Letter from Winston S. Churchill to Mark W. Clark, No date.

84. Mark W. Clark Papers, Box 3, Correspondence, October 1943–June 1944, Box 1, file 10, undated song.

85. Clark, *Calculated Risk*, 374.

86. Mark W. Clark Papers, Diary, handwritten note between pages 149–150.

87. *G-3 Operations Report*, June 1944. Records of the Adjunct General's Office,

Record Group 407; National Archives at College Park, College Park, Maryland.

88. Mark W. Clark Papers, Diary, 12 June 1944, 160.

89. Ibid., 15 June 1944, 162.

90. Mark W. Clark Papers, Box 3, Correspondence, October 1943–June 1944, File 7, June, Letter from Mark W. Clark to Dwight D. Eisenhower, 26 June 1944.

91. *Fifth Army History, The Drive to Rome*, 166.

92. Alexander, *The Alexander Memoirs, 1940–1945*, 124.

93. Henry Wilson, *Eight Years Overseas, 1939–1947* (London: Hutchinson and Co, 1950), 199.

94. Wilson, *Eight Years Overseas, 1939–1947*, 199.

95. *The Advance on Rome*, 11 May–9 June 1944, 41. Records of the Adjunct General's Office, Record Group 407; National Archives at College Park, College Park, Maryland.

CHAPTER NINE: STARVING TIME

1. Albert Kesselring, *The Memoirs of Field-Marshal Kesselring*, edited. translated by William Kimber (Novato, California: Presidio Press, 1989), 207.

2. *Fifth Army History, Pursuit to the Arno*, vol. VI, 3. Records of the Adjunct General's Office, Record Group 407; National Archives at College Park, College Park, Maryland.

3. Ibid., 4.

4. Ibid., 4.

5. Ibid., 7.

6. Ernest F. Fisher, *U.S. Army in World War Two, The Mediterranean Theater of Operations, Cassino to the Alps* (Washington DC: Center of Military History, 1993), 269.

7. Mark W. Clark Papers, Diary, 8 July 1944, Box 65, Volume 8, 1 July 1944–31 December 1944, The Citadel Archives and Museum, Charleston, South Carolina, 6.

8. *Fifth Army History, Pursuit to the Arno*, 12.

9. Ibid., 12.

10. Mark W. Clark Papers, Box 4, Correspondence, July 1944–April 1945, File 1, July–August, Message from Mark W. Clark to Jacob Devers, 8 July 1944.

11. Mark W. Clark Papers, Diary, 26 July 1944, 25.

12. Ibid., 8 August 1944, 43.

13. Mark W. Clark Papers, Diary, handwritten note on page 71.

14. Mark W. Clark, Interview by Sidney Mathews, 10–21 May 1948, 49. The Citadel Archives and Museum, Charleston, South Carolina.

15. Mark W. Clark, *Calculated Risk* (New York: Harper and Brothers Publishers, 1950), 368.

16. Ibid., 369.

17. *Fifth Army History, Pursuit to the Arno*, 122.

18. Ibid., 8.
19. Ibid., 19.
20. Ibid., 20.
21. Mark W. Clark Papers, Diary, 10 August 1944, 46.
22. Ibid., 10 August 1944, 47.
23. Ibid., 10 August 1944, 47.
24. Ibid., 12 August 1944, 50.
25. *Fifth Army History, Pursuit to the Arno*, 18.
26. Ibid., 10.
27. Clark, *Calculated Risk*, 394.
28. *Fifth Army History, Pursuit to the Arno*, 91.
29. Mark W. Clark Papers, Diary, 6 October 1944, 106.
30. Ibid., 6 October 1944, 107.
31. Mark W. Clark Papers, Box 4, Correspondence, July 1944–April 1945, File 2, September–October, Letter from Mark W. Clark to Beckie Clark, 18 September 1944.
32. Mark W. Clark Papers, Diary, 9 October 1944, 110.
33. Ibid., 15 October 1944, 116.
34. Ibid., handwritten note between pages 134–135.
35. Ibid., 27 October 1944, 133.
36. Ibid., 10 November, 150.
37. *Fifth Army History, Pursuit to the Arno*, 186.
38. Ibid., 186.
39. Fisher, *U.S. Army in World War Two, The Mediterranean Theater of Operations, Cassino to the Alps*, 408.
40. Clark, *Calculated Risk*, 413.
41. Ibid., 413.
42. Mark W. Clark Papers, Diary, handwritten note between pages 37–38.
43. Clark, *Calculated Risk*, 403.
44. Fisher, *U.S. Army in World War Two, The Mediterranean Theater of Operations, Cassino to the Alps*, 399.
45. Mark W. Clark Papers, Diary, 23 November 1944, 164.
46. Mark W. Clark Papers, Box 33a, Speeches, 1944–1959, Farewell Speech to Fifth Army, 16 December 1944.

Chapter Ten: Victory at Last

1. Edwin P. Hoyt, *Backwater War: The Allied Campaign in Italy, 1943–1945* (Westport, Connecticut: Praeger Publishing, 2002), 190.
2. *15th Army Group History, 16 December 1944–2 May 1945* (Nashville: Battery Press, 1989), 45.
3. Mark W. Clark Papers, Diary, 12 February 1945, Box 65, Volume 9, 1 January

1945–1 July 1945, The Citadel Archives and Museum, Charleston, South Carolina, 33.

4. *Fifth Army History, The Second Winter*, vol. VIII, 5. Records of the Adjunct General's Office, Record Group 407; National Archives at College Park, College Park, Maryland.

5. Ibid., 6.

6. Ibid., 2.

7. Fisher, 450.

8. Ibid., 11.

9. Ibid., 7.

10. Ibid., 35.

11. Ibid., 42.

12. Mark W. Clark Papers, Box 4, Correspondence, July 1944–April 1945, File 5, January–February 24, 1945, Letter from Mark W. Clark to Beckie Clark, 9 February 1945.

13. Mark W. Clark Papers, Diary, 2 March 1945, 45.

14. Ibid., 15 March 1945, 51.

15. *Fifth Army History, The Second Winter*, 74.

16. Ibid., 78.

17. *Fifth Army History, The Second Winter*, 91.

18. Mark W. Clark Papers, Diary, 31 March 1945, 67.

19. *Fifth Army History, Race to the Alps*, vol. IX, 145. Records of the Adjunct General's Office, Record Group 407; National Archives at College Park, College Park, Maryland.

20. *Fifth Army History, Race to the Alps*, 10.

21. Mark W. Clark Papers, Diary, 9 April 1945, 77.

22. Ibid., 13 April 1945, 80.

23. *Fifth Army History, Race to the Alps*, 52.

24. Ernest F. Fisher, *U.S. Army in World War Two, The Mediterranean Theater of Operations, Cassino to the Alps* (Washington DC: Center of Military History, 1993), 484.

25. *15th Army Group History*, 119.

26. Mark W. Clark Papers, Diary, 21 April 1945, 84.

27. *Fifth Army History, Race to the Alps*, 89.

28. Fisher, *U.S. Army in World War Two, The Mediterranean Theater of Operations, Cassino to the Alps*, 495.

29. Mark W. Clark Papers, Diary, handwritten note between pages 85–86.

30. Mark W. Clark Papers, Box 67, Personal Correspondence, File 8, Renie Clark 1945, Letter from Mark W. Clark to Renie Clark, 24 April 1945.

31. *Fifth Army History, Race to the Alps*, 119.

32. *15th Army Group History*, 134.

33. Ibid., 143.

34. Fisher, *U.S. Army in World War Two, The Mediterranean Theater of Operations, Cassino to the Alps*, 513.

35. Ibid., 528.

36. *Fifth Army History, Race to the Alps*, 166.

37. Mark W. Clark, *Calculated Risk* (New York: Harper and Brothers Publishers, 1950), 440.

38. Mark W. Clark Papers, Diary, 1 May 1945, 91.

39. Mark W. Clark Papers, Box 5, Correspondence, May–December 1945, File 1, May 1–May 31, Letter from Dwight D. Eisenhower to Mark W. Clark, 5 May 1945.

40. Mark W. Clark Papers, Diary, 2 May 1945, 98.

41. Ibid., 9 May 1945, 116.

42. *Fifth Army History, Race to the Alps*, 137.

43. Ibid., 173.

44. Ibid., 173.

45. Fisher, *U.S. Army in World War Two, The Mediterranean Theater of Operations, Cassino to the Alps*, 545.

46. Clark, *Calculated Risk*, 493.

CONCLUSION:

1. *Fifth Army History, Race to the Alps*, vol. IX, 136. Records of the Adjunct General's Office, Record Group 407; National Archives at College Park, College Park, Maryland.

2. Mark W. Clark, *Calculated Risk* (New York: Harper and Brothers Publishers, 1950), 450.

3. Ernest F. Fisher, *U.S. Army in World War Two, The Mediterranean Theater of Operations, Cassino to the Alps* (Washington DC: Center of Military History, 1993), 544.

4. Winston Churchill, *The Second World War*, vol. V, *Closing the Ring* (Boston: Houghton Mifflin Co, 1951), 225.

5. Fisher, *U.S. Army in World War Two, The Mediterranean Theater of Operations, Cassino to the Alps*, 535.

6. Lucian Truscott, *Command Missions: A Personal Story* (New York: E. P. Dutton and Co, 1954), 553.

7. Albert Kesselring, *The Memoirs of Field-Marshal Kesselring*, edited. translated by William Kimber (Novato, California: Presidio Press, 1989), 222.

8. Ibid., 222.

9. Chester G. Starr, ed., *From Salerno to the Alps: A History of the Fifth Army, 1943–1945* (Nashville: The Battery Press, 1986), 449.

10. Martin Blumenson, *Mark Clark* (London: Jonathan Cape, 1985), 261.

11. Ibid., 262.

12. Ibid., 269.

13. Ibid., 275.

14. Ibid., 276.

15. Ibid., 286.

16. Martin Blumenson, Interview by author, 14 February 2004 in Washington DC.

17. Truscott, *Command Missions*, 547.

18. Field Marshall Harold Alexander, Interview by Sidney Mathews, 10–15 January 1949 at Government House, Ottawa, Canada, 11.

19. Bob Greene, *Duty: A Father, His Son, and the Man Who Won the War* (New York: Harper Large Print, 2000), 194.

Appendix A:

1. Mark W. Clark Papers, Diary, 10 November 1942, 93–96.

2. Ibid., 10 November 1942, 96–97.

3. Ibid., 12 November 1942, 104.

4. Ibid., 12 November 1942, 104–106.

5. Ibid., 12 November 1942, 106.

6. Ibid., 12 November 1942, 106.

7. Ibid., 12 November 1942, 106–108.

8. Ibid., 12 November 1942, 109.

9. Ibid., 12 November 1942, 109.

10. Ibid., 12 November 1942, 109.

11. Ibid., 12 November 1942, 109.

WORKS CITED

ARCHIVES:
The Citadel Archives and Museum, Charleston, South Carolina:
Mark W. Clark Papers
Sidney T. Mathews Papers:
Interview with Mark W. Clark
Interview with Harold Alexander
Library of Congress, Washington, DC:
George S. Patton Papers
National Archives:
Fifth Army G-2 Periodic Reports
Fifth Army G-3 Operation Reports
Report on Monte Cassino Abbey Bombing
The Advance on Rome
Fifth Army History, Vols. 1–9

PRIMARY:
Alexander, Sir Harold. *The Alexander Memoirs, 1940–1945*. Edited by John North. New York: McGraw-Hill Book Co., Inc., 1961.
Blumenson, Martin. Interview by Jon Mikolashek, 14 July 2004. Washington, D.C.
Bradley, Omar. *A General's Life: An Autobiography by General of the Army Omar N.Bradley*. London: Sidgwick and Jackson, 1983.
Churchill, Winston S. *The Second World War*, vol. 4, *The Hinge of Fate*. Boston: Houghton Mifflin Co., 1950.
———*The Second World War*, vol. 5, *Closing the Ring*. Boston: Houghton Mifflin Co., 1951.
———*The Second World War*, vol. 6, *Triumph and Tragedy*. Boston: Houghton Mifflin Co., 1953
Clark, Mark W. *Calculated Risk*. New York: Harper and Brothers Publishers, 1950.

Clark, Maurine. *Captain's Bridge, General's Lady: The Memoirs of Mrs. Mark W. Clark.* New York: McGraw-Hill Book Co., 1956.

De Guinard, Sir Francis. *Operation Victory.* London: Hodder and Stoughton Limited Publishers, 1947.

Eisenhower, Dwight, ed. Alfred D. Chandler. *The Papers of Dwight D. Eisenhower, The War Years: II.* Baltimore: John Hopkins Press, 1970.

———ed. Robert H. Ferrell. *The Eisenhower Diaries.* New York: W.W. Norton and Co., 1981.

———*At Ease: Stories I Tell to Friends.* Garden City, NY: Doubleday and Co, Inc., 1967.

———*Crusade in Europe.* New York: Doubleday and Company, Inc., 1948.

Jewell, Norman. *Secret Mission Submarine.* Chicago: Ziff-Davis Publishing Co., 1944.

Kesselring, Albert. *The Memoirs of Field Marshal Kesselring,* translated by William Kimber. Novato, California: Presido Press, 1953.

Montgomery, Bernard Law. *The Memoirs of Field-Marshal the Viscount Montgomery of Alamein.* Cleveland: The World Publishing Co., 1958.

Moorehead, Alan. *Eclipse.* New York: Harper and Row Publishers, 1945.

Murphy, Robert. *Diplomat Among Warriors.* Garden City, NY: Doubleday and Co, Inc., 1964.

Patton, George S. *The Patton Papers: 1940–1945.* Edited by Martin Blumenson. Boston: Da Capo Press, 1974.

Sevareid, Eric. *Not So Wild a Dream.* New York: Atheneum, 1976.

Truscott, Lucian K. *Command Missions: A Personal Story.* New York: E. P. Dutton and Co, 1954.

Walker, Fred L. *From Texas to Rome: A General's Journal.* Dallas: Taylor Publishing Co., 1969.

Wilson, Henry M. *Eight Years Overseas, 1939–1947.* London: Hutchinson and Co, 1950.

Secondary Sources:

15th Army Group History, 16 December 1944–2 May 1945. Nashville: The Battery Press, 1989.

Atkinson, Rick. *An Army at Dawn: The War in North Africa, 1942–1943.* New York: Henry Holt and Co., 2002.

Blaxland, Gregory. *Alexander's Generals: The Italian Campaign, 1944–1945.* London: William Kimber and Co, 1979.

Blumenson, Martin. *Bloody River: The Real Tragedy of the Rapido.* Boston: Houghton Mifflin Co., 1970.

——— *Anzio: The Gamble That Failed.* Philadelphia: J. B. Lippincott Co., 1963.

——— *Mark Clark.* London: Jonathan Cape., 1985.

——— *U.S. Army in World War Two, The Mediterranean Theater of Operations: Salerno to Cassino*. Washington, D.C.:U.S. Government Printing, 1969.

D'Este, Carlo. *Eisenhower: A Soldier's Life*. New York: Henry Holt and Co., 2002.

———*Fatal Decision: Anzio and the Battle for Rome*. New York: Harper Collins, 1991.

Ellis, John. *Cassino: The Hollow Victory, the Battle for Rome, January–June 1944*. London: Andre Deutsch Limited, 1984.

Fisher, Ernest F. *U.S. Army in World War Two, The Mediterranean Theater of Operations: Cassino to the Alps*. Washington, D.C.: Center of Military History, 1993.

Funk, Arthur. *The Politics of TORCH: The Allied Landings and the Algiers Putsch, 1942*. Lawrence, Kansas: The University Press of Kansas, 1974.

Garland, Albert, and Howard McGaw Smyth. *U.S. Army in World War Two, The Mediterranean Theater of Operations: Sicily and the Surrender of Italy*. Assisted by Martin Blumenson. Washington, D.C.: Center of Military History, 1993.

Greene, Bob. *Duty: A Father, His Son, and the Man Who Won the War*. New York: Harper Large Print, 2000.

Higgins, Trumbull. *Soft Underbelly: The Anglo-American Controversy Over the Italian Campaign, 1939–1945*. New York: The Macmillan Co, 1968.

Howe, George. *U.S. Army in World War Two, The Mediterranean Theatre of Operations, Northwest Africa: Seizing the Initiative in the West*. Washington, D.C.: Center of Military History, 1993.

Hoyt, Edwin P. *Backwater War: The Allied Campaign in Italy, 1943–1945*. Westport, Connecticut: Praeger Publishing, 2002.

Jackson, W.G.F. *Alexander of Tunis: As Military Commander*. London: B.T. Batsford, L.T.D., 1971.

Kelly, Orr. *Meeting the Fox: The Allied Invasion of Africa, from Operation Torch to Kasserine Pass to Victory in Tunisia*. New York: John Wiley and Sons, Inc., 2002.

Leighton, Richard M. "OVERLORD Versus the Mediterranean at the Cairo-Tehran Conferences." In *Command Decisions*, United States Army, Office of the Chief of Military History, 255–285. Washington D.C.: Center of Military History, 1960.

Mathews, Sidney T. "General Clark's Decision to Drive on Rome." In *Command Decisions*, United States Army, Office of the Chief of Military History, 351–365. Washington D.C., Center of Military History, 1960.

Mavrogordato, Ralph S. "Hitler's Decision on the Defense of Italy." In *Command Decisions*, United States Army, Office of the Chief of Military History, 303–332. Washington D.C., Center of Military History, 1960.

Molony, C.J.C. *The Mediterranean and Middle East: The Campaign in Sicily 1943 and the Campaign in Italy, 3 September 1943–31 March 1944*. Vol. V. London: Her Majesty's Stationary Office, 1973.

Molony, C.J.C. *The Mediterranean and Middle East: Victory in the Mediterranean, 1 April to 4 June 1944*. Vol. VI, Part 1. London: Her Majesty's Stationary Office, 1986.

Morris, Eric. *Salerno: A Military Fiasco*. London: Hutchinson and Co., 1983.

Playfair, S. O., and C. J. C. Molony. *The Mediterranean and Middle East: The Destruction of the Axis Forces in Africa*. Vol. IV. London: Her Majesty's Stationery Office, 1966.

Shepperd, G. A. *The Italian Campaign, 1943–1945: A Political and Military Re-Assessment*. New York: Frederick A. Praeger, 1968.

Starr, Chester, ed. *From Salerno to the Alps: A History of the Fifth Army, 1943–1945*. Nashville: The Battery Press, 1986.

Verney, Peter. *Anzio 1944: An Unexpected Fury*. London: B. T. Batsford, 1978.

INDEX

References to illustrations appear in italics

ACKNOWLEDGMENTS

The idea for this book started in 2002 as an undergraduate student at Longwood College. Initial research led me to the doorstep of Martin Blumenson. Over the next few years we met monthly for lunch and a Gimlet (with gin only!). Dr. Blumenson convinced me to continue on with my studies and to write my dissertation on Mark W. Clark. He believed a more critical look into Clark's career was needed and wanted me to be the one to write it. I hope that Dr. Blumenson would be proud of this study.

There are numerous people that helped me along the way. My wife, Colleen, was there from the beginning of this project and has moved across the United States a few times now as I've progressed in my career. I could not have finished this book without her love and support. I hope one day Alexander and Jacob will read their Dad's "old book."

I could not have ended up where I am today without my family. Especially my father, who also became Mr. Mom after my mother passed away in 1989. I also learned a lot of history from my uncle, who was always ready and able to edit my early writings—and my aunt was always there to make sure I stayed on the right path. I must also thank my parents-in-law, Kris and Bill Ganley. There was always a spare bedroom for me, and Mamie Kris was always willing to feed me!

I also need to thank my department and Team 29 colleagues at CGSC. They allowed me ample time to complete revisions and finish up research, and I am eternally grateful for their flexibility. I also would not have completed school and this book without my mentors David "Scoop" Coles and Jim Jones. Along with Martin Blumenson, they are the two greatest historians I have ever known. Last but not least, my small group of friends, Scott, Fox, Fertick, Vin, and Wags were always there to help me move, read my rough drafts, and to make jokes at my expense.